JAY SCHABACKER'S
WINNING IN
MUTUAL FUNDS

Advance praise for *Jay Schabacker's Winning in Mutual Funds*

"Jay gives investors an easy-to-understand commonsense system for developing mutual fund strategies best suited to their needs."
—Paul Merriman, President of Merriman Mutual Funds and author of *Investing for a Lifetime*

"A clear-headed, savvy view of the world of mutual funds. If you want to build your wealth through mutual funds, your first investment should be *Jay Schabacker's Winning in Mutual Funds*. Follow Jay's advice and you are guaranteed an outstanding result."
—John P. Dessauer, Editor, *Investors World*

"If you invest in mutual funds, you simply can't afford to be without Jay Schabacker's new book."
—James U. Blanchard III, President, Jefferson Financial

"The concepts of investing can often seem complicated and intimidating. They don't have to be. Jay Schabacker has written a financial book that is both easy and informative to read. It's a must for all mutual fund investors."
—Frank Holmes, President & CEO, United Services Funds

JAY SCHABACKER'S
WINNING IN MUTUAL FUNDS

Practical advice
from the editor of
Mutual Fund Investing
—the newsletter that's
helped hundreds of
thousands of Americans

Jay Schabacker
with Marjory Ross

American Management Association

New York • Atlanta • Boston • Chicago • Kansas City • San Francisco • Washington, D.C.
Brussels • Mexico City • Tokyo • Toronto

This publication is designed to provide accurate and authoritative information in regard to the subject matter covered. It is sold with the
understanding that the publisher is not engaged in rendering legal,
accounting, or other professional service. If legal advice or other expert
assistance is required, the services of a competent professional person
should be sought.

Library of Congress Cataloging-in-Publication Data

Schabacker, Jay.
    Jay Schabacker's winning in mutual funds / Jay Schabacker with
Marjory Ross.
        p.   cm.
    Includes index.
    ISBN 0-8144-0216-X
    1. Mutual funds.   I. Ross, Marjory.   II. Title.   III. Title:
Winning in mutual funds.
HG4530.S374   1994
332.63'27—dc20   94-1665
                                                              CIP

Printing number

10   9   8   7   6   5   4   3   2   1

This book is dedicated to my parents, **Elizabeth** and **Richard,** and to **God,** the giver of all wisdom and wealth.

Contents

Acknowledgments

I am deeply grateful to my key assistant in the completion of this book, Marji Ross, for it was she who took my investment information and turned it all into readable style.

To the hardworking staff at Schabacker Investment Management, Inc., especially Barbara Doane, Brian Barbazette, and Ron Rough, goes my thanks for their help with research and the editorial details that are so necessary to bring a large book to completion.

This book probably would not be on the bookshelves now except for the encouragement and professional advice given to me by Richard Crawford, Ted Mathews, and MacRae Ross, for which I am extremely grateful.

For the painstakingly prepared set of graphics, which are so important to the delivery of the advice in this book, we all are thankful to L. Diane Johnson of Southwind Studios, who is truly a professional.

My respect and applause go to Tony Vlamis of AMACOM Books for his guidance in the production of this book through the millions of details only a book publisher is fully aware of.

Lastly, but foremost, I thank my wife, Nancy Schabacker, who saw this book through with me from idea to completion, and always was there with encouragement, marketing ideas, and just plain good advice.

Introduction

You may wonder why anyone could possibly need another book on investing in mutual funds. There are scores of books on investing, and an increasing number are devoted exclusively to mutual funds. The funny thing is, though, that almost every book you can find explains what mutual funds are and how they work. But it's almost impossible to find a book with practical, real-life advice on how to use funds to make money safely, easily, and reliably.

Which is precisely why I wrote this book. My name is Jay Schabacker, and I've been a mutual fund advisor and money manager for the past 18 years. I manage approximately $130 million in assets invested in mutual funds for private clients. I've worked with several hundred thousand individual and institutional investors, showing them how to become wealthy—or build their already substantial wealth.

And I'd like you to join me—and the hundreds of thousands of folks who've subscribed over the last 15 years to my monthly mutual fund investing newsletter—in reaping the many benefits that mutual funds have to offer. I want you to know precisely how to invest wisely, to be more comfortable with your investment program, to design a strategy that meets your needs and abilities, to spend as little time and effort as possible, to sleep well at night, and to grow your nest egg safely and steadily through the years.

In this book, I'll describe, as clearly and fully as I can, the system I've successfully used in my mutual fund advisory and money management firm—an approach that's yielded an average annual return of over 14% per year for the past 18 years. As you may know, that performance exceeds the S&P 500 for the same time period. What you probably don't know, however, is that I achieved those results with far less risk (and worry) than the market as a whole presents.

So how will this book really help you? If you are planning and saving for retirement (whether that retirement is 3 years away or 30 years away), I can help you set up a plan that's easy, comfortable, and certain to build your nest egg substantially. Whether you're looking for current income from your portfolio, or sizeable long-term gains, I can help you increase your return without increasing your risk.

Of course, your long-range goals needn't be retirement. You may have a child's college education, a daughter's wedding, even a trip around the world, on the distant horizon. Setting up a safe and proven system for building wealth *now* will help ensure you're able to meet your goals (and dreams) later on.

No matter what your goals, you'll need a program that keeps you ahead of inflation and taxes. After all, the costs of a nicer home, a trip to Europe, (to say nothing of a college education) are all rising year by year. Your investments must be able to keep pace with these costs in order to ensure your financial security. Frankly, that's the problem with most "safe" investments, like CDs or savings bonds. Yes, they guarantee that you'll get your money back, but how much will that money buy in 10 or 20 years? A prudent investment program will give you a positive return *after* inflation and taxes have been taken into account.

And if you are saving and investing for your future retirement, you have the added concern about relying on Social Security and your pension. Will the money be there when you retire? Will the payments have kept up with inflation? Chances are high that we will have to count increasingly on our own savings, rather than on government (or even employer-funded) programs.

Plainly put, it's getting tougher to meet your financial goals. The good news is, successful mutual fund investing can help you meet these challenges. My goal in this book is to help you use mutual funds, with their built-in advantages, to ensure your future financial security. Those built-in advantages include safety through diversification, professional full-time money management, low minimum investments, and flexibility and choices to meet every goal and personal style.

But I must warn you that mutual funds can be used to build wealth reliably and consistently—or they can drown you in paper work, overwhelm you with choices, and permit you to indulge your worst impulses as an investor. The secret to doing it right lies in designing a system that fits you and your needs—and then following it. I urge you to read this book carefully, and to use my advice to help you set up a personal system for success. This book will help you know yourself, understand how the markets work, choose the very best funds, and trade them wisely. I hope you find some of my guidance and strategies useful. But whatever you do, don't put off planning, and don't second-guess your system once you've set it up. Your family's financial security depends on it. I'll do my best to help you meet your goals and your dreams.

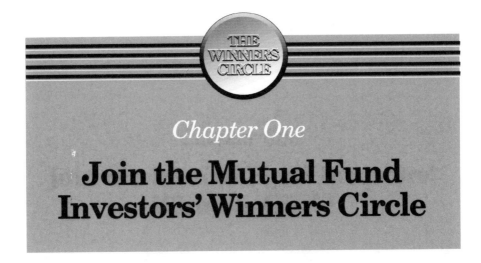

Chapter One

Join the Mutual Fund Investors' Winners Circle

Successful mutual fund investors know that success depends on more than just picking a good fund. It involves more than timing the market's peaks and valleys. And it requires more than smart switching and prudent asset allocation. All of these are important elements of making money in mutual funds. But no single factor will do the trick.

The fact is, successful mutual fund investing is made up of four key ingredients: knowing yourself, staying on the right side of the economy, choosing the best funds, and buying and selling smart. Omit one or more of these four, and you water down your investment returns. Put them all together, and you earn yourself a place in what I call the Mutual Fund Winners Circle (see Figure 1-1).

The good news is: Mastering the Winners Circle is really quite simple. It involves merely a little advance planning, a better understanding of what makes the markets tick, and a good dose of common sense. Every investor I've ever met is capable of joining that Winners Circle if someone just shows him or her what it takes.

The Benefits of Safety-First Investing

You know, there are dozens of so-called experts giving mutual fund investment advice. Many of these advisors capitalize on the "telephone switching" feature of mutual funds, which allows you to switch from one fund to another with a simple phone call. But

Figure 1-1

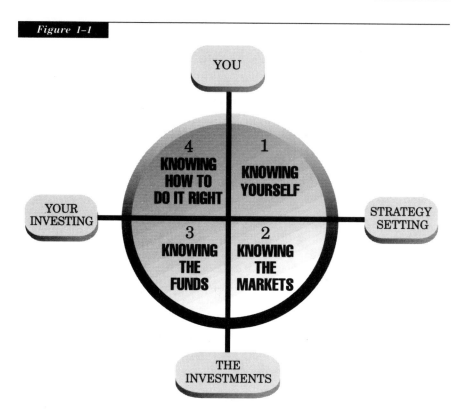

the niche I've carved out in the mutual fund industry is **safety-first investing.**

Safety-first investing means never taking a risk unless you have to; it means constantly searching for the most conservative way to make money; it means investing in a way that makes you comfortable as well as wealthy. Over the years, I have learned (and relearned) that reducing your risks does *not* mean reducing your returns. You can, indeed, pursue a safety-first approach and still join that Mutual Fund Winners Circle. In fact, the fewer risks you take, the more likely you are to succeed.

That's true for two reasons. First is the difficulty of gaining back a loss. It's twice as hard to recoup as it is to make money in the first place (see Figure 1-2). Look at it this way. If you start with $100 and lose $50, your investment has gone down by 50%. But a 50% gain won't make up your loss. You now have to double your money, go from $50 to $100—a 100% gain—just to get back to

Figure 1–2

A Loss Is Hard to Regain

*If you start with a dollar and take a loss,
what do you need to break even?*

10% loss:	First a	10% loss: $1.00 − .10 = $ .90
	Need an	11% gain: $ .90 + .10 = $1.00
30% loss:	First a	30% loss: $1.00 − .30 = $ .70
	Need a	43% gain: $ .70 + .30 = $1.00
50% loss:	First a	50% loss: $1.00 − .50 = $ .50
	Need a	100% gain: $ .50 + .50 = $1.00
80% loss:	First a	80% loss: $1.00 − .80 = $ .20
	Need a	400% gain: $ .20 + .80 = $1.00

400%

Possible reward
should equal
this amount

100%

You must gain
this amount
...just to
break even

43%

11%

10%

If you lose
this amount

30%

50%

80%

If you take this
amount of risk

ground zero. If you think it's hard to lose 50% (and I'm sorry to say it's not), you'd better believe it's harder to double your money. The real solution is to avoid big losers in the first place.

The second reason that fewer risks translate into better success is human nature. Unfortunately, the more risky your investments, the harder they are on the nerves. Even if super-high-risk funds eventually reward investors handsomely, the vast majority of investors bail out after bad news has forced the market down. My experience shows that the more risks you take, the less likely you are to stick with a program. And you certainly won't join the Winners Circle by throwing in the towel!

My First Loser Was a Doozy

Perhaps I'm particularly sensitive to risks because of my first losing investment, back when I was 25 years old and just out of engineering school. I'd had some success in stocks, following in the footsteps of my father, Richard W. Schabacker. My dad was a famous investment technician, one of the early financial editors of *Forbes* magazine, a man insiders called "the pioneer of sophisticated technical research." He died when I was very young, but I had always wanted to build on the research he'd started and principles he'd formulated.

So, even as an engineering student at Cornell University in the 1950s, I dabbled in stocks. And I thought I was pretty good. Then I heard about this great opportunity, a chance to participate in a supposed huge rent explosion in commercial real estate. I acted on that hunch. I took a big portion of my eggs, as they say. Then I sat back and waited for the money to pile up at my door.

Of course, I didn't really sit back; I was too excited. I watched the paper every day. And I saw my shares go from $10 to $8 to $5 to $4 to $2. . . . Nine months after I'd invested at $10 per share, I sold all my shares at $1.27 per share.

That experience had a profound effect on my life as an investor. I vowed that *safety* would be my first priority. It didn't matter how many times I'd been right before, that one risky investment seemed to wipe out every smart move I'd ever made. I was never going to let that happen again.

Mutual Funds: The Natural Choice for Safety-First Investors

Which brings us back to safety-first investing with mutual funds. My early investing career was not in mutual funds, but I learned the hard way that safety comes from careful research, from expert management, and from diversification—all of which make mutual funds the single best investment vehicle in the world for most people.

First, you get the expert, professional, full-time management of an investment pro, who guides and grows each fund you own. When you buy a fund, you are hiring a professional—the mutual fund portfolio manager—to watch over your assets and make them grow. That's a privilege that used to be reserved for very wealthy individuals only.

You also get the safety of diversification. Your investment, no matter how small, is spread out over dozens, maybe even hundreds, of stocks and/or bonds. An unexpected drop or problem in any single holding, such as a single real estate stock, won't have a big impact on your overall results. Again, this kind of safety through diversification was once available only to the very rich, who could afford to buy hundreds of shares of dozens of stocks on their own.

A third advantage of mutual funds is the ease with which you can buy and sell them. You can buy a new fund by filling out an application and sending in a check. It gets even easier after that, because in most cases you can sell that fund and/or switch to another fund with a single phone call. Furthermore, with the funds I recommend, you never need deal with a broker or salesperson again, so there is no pressure and no guilt. You make your own buy/sell decisions and simply instruct the fund to execute your trade.

Of course, as with many things in life, mutual funds are a good thing that can be used well or poorly. In this book, I want to show you how to get the *most* out of your funds, how to be in the right place at the right time, and how to make safety-first investing extremely profitable.

The Four Parts of the Winners Circle

As I said, my safety-first approach to mutual fund investing consists of four parts. Again, they are: knowing yourself, staying on the right side of the economy, choosing the best funds, and buying and selling smart. Of these four steps, the first two really refer to your investment *strategy*, while the second two refer to the *execution* of your strategy.

Part 1: Knowing Yourself

To construct a successful investment strategy, the first thing you need to do is understand your own **Personal Investor Profile.** This means taking a good look at how much money you currently have, how many years you can allow your investments to grow before you need to withdraw money, what your current income needs are, and how comfortable you are with volatility. All of these factors should be taken into account when you are developing your investment strategy.

I have designed an easy-to-use questionnaire, which you'll find in Chapter Two, to help guide you through these areas and establish your Investor Profile. The Profile will help direct you toward keeping the proper balance of stock funds, bond funds, and cash in your portfolio at any given time. (By the way, when I say *cash*, I mean money market funds. They're liquid, they're ultra-safe, and they usually pay higher interest rates than your bank—even your bank's money market account.)

Knowing yourself also involves admitting how much you like (or don't like) actively monitoring and interpreting economic indicators, market indexes, and stock statistics. There's nothing wrong with saying you just don't want to spend time looking up numbers in *The Wall Street Journal;* you may be uncomfortable with numbers and calculations or simply don't have the time. By recognizing your own **Investor Activity Profile,** you can choose a method of investing you're comfortable with.

So, I've developed a second quick questionnaire to help you determine what *style* of investing is best for you. This material on knowing yourself—part 1 of our Mutual Fund Winners Circle—is explained fully in Chapter Two.

Part 2: Staying on the Right Side of the Economy

Once you've determined your Investor Profile, your next step on the road to mutual fund success is to understand how the economy affects the stock market—and your own investments. In Chapters Three and Four, I discuss various economic and technical indicators—such as P/E ratios, inflation, interest rates, investor sentiment, recession—and I'll show you what they mean for you as an investor. I also explain how to position yourself during the different stages of the economic cycle so that you can seize opportunities to make money *and* minimize your risks.

I believe you need to know the markets, but I don't think you need to be a professional economist! In fact, there's such a thing as knowing too much; you might trip yourself up second-guessing the basic common sense that has made you a success elsewhere in your life. You simply need to know why investments do what they do and how to take advantage of most situations. So in these two chapters, I'll tell you what I have learned over the years about what makes the markets and your investments tick, and what you should do as a result to prosper.

Part 3: Choosing the Best Funds

The first two quadrants of our Winners Circle help you design an investment strategy that will suit both you and the economic climate around you. They are your blueprint for mutual fund success. Now you're ready to put your plan into action. Part 3 of our Winners Circle involves choosing the very best mutual funds in existence. Based on several key variables, including past performance, portfolio manager expertise, fees, size, useful investor services, and (of course) risk, you can pick out the top-quality funds from the vast universe of mutual fund choices. I explain this selection process and these criteria fully in Chapter Five, along with giving you an insider's look at some of my own favorites.

I find a lot of people making mistakes in this quadrant of the Winners Circle. They buy high-load funds when they could buy commission-free funds, or they buy something they read about in a magazine without really understanding the risks. Do this step right, however, and you can multiply your wealth much faster than can the average investor.

Part 4: Buying and Selling Smart

By the time you've reached the fourth and final quadrant of our Winners Circle, you are light-years ahead of almost every other mutual fund investor today. Your strategy is in tune with your personal needs and desires and with the economic environment, and you're using the number one funds in the country to make your money work for you. Now, to really supercharge your returns—and your peace of mind in the process—you want to execute your strategy in the smartest way possible. Most investors fall short in this area, either because they don't know the intricacies and mechanics of investing or because they rush into an investment decision. Buying and selling smart, on the other hand, can bring many rewards.

Smart means simple as well as shrewd, so I've collected for you (in Chapters Six, Seven, and Eight) my wealth of knowledge and experience in cutting costs, wiping out risks, slashing the time and effort involved in investing, filling out forms, reading the prospectus, keeping taxes low, and planning for retirement. These dozens of tips and techniques will help make your mutual fund investing more successful and more enjoyable.

Also in this part of the book, I'll review some common mistakes people make when buying and selling. That can save you hundreds of wasted hours and thousands of lost dollars.

By the end of the book, you'll have come full circle, from knowing yourself and your needs, to understanding what makes the markets go up and down (and how to profit accordingly), to choosing the very best funds, to understanding the secrets of making your funds work harder for you. You will be fully equipped to become—if you're not already—a confident, comfortable, successful, and safety-first investor. And you most certainly will be ready to take your place in the Mutual Fund Winners Circle (see Figure 1-3).

Summary of Chapter One

- My approach to investing puts safety first. That means never taking a risk you don't have to. It produces an investment strategy that makes you comfortable as well as wealthy.

- A loss is doubly hard to regain, which is why you must avoid losses so scrupulously.

- Mutual funds are the natural choice for safety-first investors because they offer expert management, diversification, and ease of buying and selling.

- Being a successful investor requires mastering four disciplines: knowing yourself, knowing the markets and economy, choosing the best funds, and buying and selling smart. The first two help determine your *strategy;* the second two help dictate your *actions.*

- Knowing yourself (part 1 of the Winners Circle) means knowing your own goals, risk tolerance, interest in investing, and willingness and ability to devote time and attention to managing your portfolio.

- Knowing the markets/economy (part 2) means understanding what makes the economy expand and contract, what makes the stock market go up and down, and what role interest rates and inflation play in your investment.

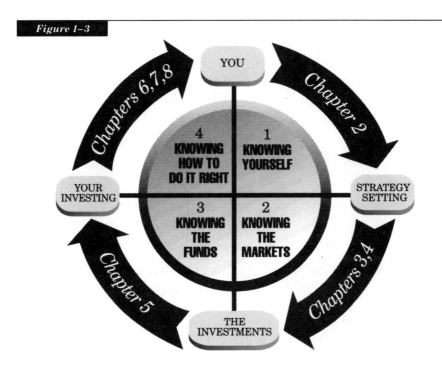

Figure 1–3

- Choosing the best funds (part 3) involves understanding the various categories of funds, as well as how to interpret fees, risks, and track records, and how to read a prospectus.
- Buying and selling smart (part 4) involves techniques and practices for cutting costs, wiping out risks, minimizing time and effort, and avoiding mistakes in execution.
- By mastering all four parts, you'll certainly join the Winners Circle.

Chapter Two

Knowing Yourself

Over the past 18 years, I've seen and heard of just about every investing "system" imaginable. I've listened to the debates on market timing, buy-and-hold, commodities trading, staggered maturities, you name it.

But one thing almost every system forgets to include is *you.* The system might work fine—*if* you or I didn't have to implement and manage it, *if* life didn't sometimes interrupt the computer program to require a grandchild's college tuition or a daughter's wedding, *if* the white-knuckle volatility and the hair-trigger switching didn't make you miserable and convince you not to buy when the signals all said "now!"

So before talking about mutual funds that suit certain market conditions or economic trends, let's talk for a moment about what suits you!

Three Personal Considerations

I have found that different investors are comfortable with different levels of volatility. Some can withstand a fairly bumpy ride—with up months and down months—along the road to building their nest egg. Other investors are "Nervous Nellies" and just hate the peaks and valleys that sometimes accompany investing in the stock market. They prefer a smooth, steady, if somewhat slower, pace. This **volatility** or **risk tolerance** plays a large role in deciding which strategy is right for you.

Yes, everyone wants to make money; that's why we invest. But what trade-offs are you willing to make along the way? For instance, how long can you afford to let your money grow (this affects your risk tolerance) before you'll need to tap it? These are questions you need to answer for yourself *before* you start investing. I *also* advise my clients and newsletter subscribers to check their volatility tolerance every year or so to make sure their investments are still in step with their comfort level.

How do you determine your volatility tolerance? It really comes down to three basic considerations:

1. Your time frame for investing
2. Your current financial situation
3. Your feelings

Your feelings? Yes, indeed. If you try to follow a program of investing that doesn't *feel* right, one that makes you uncomfortable, nervous, anxious, or downright depressed, it probably won't work for long. Why not? Because at some critical moment, your emotions will override the system and you'll zig when you should zag. Trust me. I've seen it happen many, *many* times. People almost always second-guess the system at precisely the wrong time: when the system says one thing and their feelings tell them to do something else.

When Doing the Right Thing Feels Right

The good news is that I can show you how to construct a strategy for making money in mutual funds that feels right, that won't keep you up at night, that won't constantly pit you against yourself, and that works.

As I said, your volatility tolerance also depends on how much money you have, how much time you have, and what you want from your investments—both now and in the future.

In Chapter Four, I'll show you how to factor in the market and economic conditions too, like inflation, interest rates, recession, yields, the value of the dollar, price-to-earnings ratios, even 39-week moving averages. I'll help you put all these considerations together into a strategy that works, both for you and for the market environment. But first, let's determine what kind of investing suits *you.*

When I talk about *you*, I'm referring to your feelings and attitudes toward (1) the risk you can take in your investing and (2) the process that you should use. By *risk,* I really mean volatility—how much you can withstand up and down swings, and therefore how aggressive you should be in your wealthbuilding. And by *process,* I mean how active you should be in your method of investing, what type of analysis process is best for you, and how and how often you should adjust your portfolio.

You Have All the Answers

To get to the bottom of the *you* in investing, I have devised a series of ten simple questions that address your risk tolerance, and another series of ten simple questions that address the process of investing that might be best for you. The answers to these 20 questions are the key to evaluating your Investor Profile. Answer them as honestly and candidly as you can. Remember, your financial future depends on devising a strategy that's right for you. And from the answers to these 20 questions, we can design a strategy tailor-made for your life.

First, fill out the Investor Risk Profile Questionnaire that begins on page 17 and tally up your answers on the scoresheet on page 21. We'll talk about what your score means for your investing. Second, fill out your Activity Profile Questionnaire on pages 22–25 and tally up your answers on the scoresheet that follows. Once you've answered these 20 questions, you will know more about yourself—both in the amount of risk you can take and in the process that is best for you as an investor.

Your Investor Risk Profile

Your score gives you an idea of what level of investment risk-taking suits your needs and temperament. If you came out as a Conservative investor, you don't like volatility at all and you're willing to advance a bit more slowly in the interest of safety. You may be close to retirement or you may be starting with a small amount of investment capital—but no matter what your age, you prefer to avoid risks above all else. As you can see from Figure 2-1, you won't want to have more than 50% of your money invested in the stock market at any given time.

If you scored in the Moderate range, you want a blend of safety and growth and you're willing to take some moderate risks to achieve better returns. You don't need your investment money right away, but you also don't want to see big swings in the value of your portfolio. For you, a range between 30% and 70% invested will be comfortable, depending on the economic climate and market outlook (see Figure 2-1).

If you are an Aggressive investor, you want big, long-term gains and you're willing to ride out some storms to accomplish this goal. You probably have more than five years before you need to tap your nest egg—which means you may be a younger investor or an older investor of substantial means. Your comfort zone will be between 50% and 90% invested, as illustrated in Figure 2-1.

From time to time, I'll refer to Mr. Conservative, Mr. Moderate, and Mr. Aggressive to show you how each of our three typical investors should act and react in different economic climates.

Now let's discuss our second questionnaire.

Your Investment Activity Profile

By Investment Activity Profile, I'm referring to your attitude toward the *process* of investing, your desire to be involved in the process, and your interest in the technicalities of the investment world. Your Investor Risk Profile helped us see what types of short-term results you'll be most comfortable with. What we'll arrive at with your Investment Activity Profile is the *process* of investing that makes you most comfortable.

Again, you'll answer a few simple questions on pages 22–25. Just circle the number of points that corresponds to your answer for each of these ten questions. Then we'll add them up at the end and see where it leads.

What Your Activity Profile Score Means for Your Investing

If your scores for both A and B are each below 8, you are probably best suited to a **Buy and Hold** investing approach.

Figure 2–1

Investment Ranges Per Your Risk Tolerance

Type of Funds Used	CONSERVATIVE Investor	MODERATE Risk Investor	AGGRESSIVE Investor
Stock Funds	10–50%	30–70%	50–90%
Bond Funds	20–65%	10–45%	10–30%
Cash (Money Market Funds)	10–60%	5–45%	0–40%

If at least one of your two scores is 8 or higher, and your A total is higher than B, you are best suited for a periodic analysis of stock market risks and to my **Asset Allocation** approach.

If your B total is higher than your A, you are best suited for more involved fundamental economic analysis and to my **Market Timing** investment approach.

If your scores for A and B are both high (above 11), then investing is in your blood and you may try combining both technical and fundamental analysis.

See Figure 2-2 on page 27, which uses a graph to help you interpret your questionnaire scores.

Your Next Step

You've now taken a giant step toward *successful* mutual fund investing. You know what your personal Investor Risk Profile is—Conservative, Moderate, or Aggressive. And you know what your Investment Activity Profile is—Buy and Hold, Asset Allocation, or Market Timing.

In the next two chapters, I show you how to combine your Investor Profile with your Activity Profile. As you'll see, the Buy and Hold investor will stay with a fixed ratio of stocks-bonds-cash throughout all economic conditions. The Asset Allocation investor will vary his or her mix of stocks-bonds-cash depending on the general market risk or forecast. To help you understand and be a winner at some technical asset allocation, I have devised for you what I call my **Back of the Envelope** technical stock market forecaster (more about that in Chapter Three). And the Market Timing investor will vary both the mix of stocks-bonds-cash and the types of stock funds and bond funds, depending on the outlook for the various markets based on a reading of the business cycle (see Chapter Four).

Of course, the best investment strategy is as much a function of the economy as of personal goals and preferences. So, also in the next two chapters, I take you beyond yourself to help you understand how the outside world affects your investments. I'll show you how to take advantage of the opportunities the market presents while protecting yourself from the risks around you. I'll show you exactly how to set up your portfolio, whether you want to "set it and forget it," buy and hold, allocate based on a Back of the Envelope market forecast, or actively time the market to the business cycle.

Ready for part two of our Winners Circle? OK, let's go!

Summary of Chapter Two

- To be a successful investor, you must design a plan that fits your needs and comfort level. That means evaluating your time frame for investing, your current financial situation, and your feelings.

- My Investor Risk Profile Questionnaire (pages 17–21) will tell you how much short-term volatility you can weather in your investing. This information will help you determine whether you should follow advice for a Conservative, Moderate, or Aggressive investor.

- My Investment Activity Profile Questionnaire (pages 22–26) will tell you how much time, attention, and expertise you can devote to managing your mutual fund program. You'll consider how comfortable you are with the technical and fundamental areas of analysis, such as monitoring investor sentiment and relative yields, or judging the direction of inflation and economic growth. This information will help you determine whether you should pursue a Buy and Hold, an Asset Allocation (technical), or a Market Timing per the business cycle (fundamental) approach.

YOUR INVESTOR RISK PROFILE QUESTIONNAIRE

Please answer the following 10 questions as candidly as you can. Circle your score for each question in the column on the right.

For example, Question #1, asks how many years you can let your money grow. If you expect to wait four years, circle 2 points in the right–hand column.

1. TIME FRAME

Take a look at how many years you can let your money grow before you'll need to tap your nest egg. (This is important because it indicates your financial ability to ride out down-cycles.)

If the working time frame for your investment portfolio is...

GIVE YOURSELF:

1–2 years	1 point
3–5 years	2 points
6–10 years	3 points
More than 10 years	4 points

2. YEARS TO RETIREMENT

Where are you in relation to retirement? The farther you are from retirement, the more risk you can take in your investing.

If the number of years between now and your retirement is...

GIVE YOURSELF:

Retired now	0 points
1–5 years	1 point
6–9 years	2 points
10–15 years	3 points
More than 15 years	4 points

3. FINANCIAL CUSHION

Take a look at your total financial position and the cushion you have set aside (outside of your investment portfolio for emergencies). This will help you decide how much risk you should prudently take in your investing.

If you have...

GIVE YOURSELF:

Little outside savings set aside, hence
preservation of principal is very important .... 1 point

Reasonable savings set aside, and are willing
to take moderate risk for moderate returns .... 2 points

Ample savings set aside (mortgage is paid off,
own CD's, insurance, etc.) hence you feel
comfortable taking larger risks for
maximum return potential .... 3 points

4. CASH FLOW

What is your planned cash flow into and out of your investment portfolio over the next 3–5 years? Do you plan to contribute regularly to your investment portfolio, or do you intend to take out more than you put in? Negative cash flow (withdrawing principal) would suggest a low risk tolerance, while positive cash flow, (adding money on a regular basis) would tend to allow for some short–term volatility in the pursuit of higher returns.

If your plans are to...

GIVE YOURSELF:

Withdraw money on a continuing basis .... 1 point
Neither add nor withdraw money .... 2 points
Add new money on a continuing basis .... 3 points

5. SPECIAL CIRCUMSTANCES

Although it's difficult to plan for the unexpected, are there any special circumstances you can envision (college tuition, home purchase, retirement, extended travel, medical, etc.) outside your usual contributions and withdrawals, that might necessitate the immediate liquidation of a major portion of your portfolio over the next 3–5 years?

If you can envision...

GIVE YOURSELF:

Full portfolio could be liquidated .... 1 point
Major liquidations .... 2 points

Some small liquidations..3 points
No liquidations..4 points

6. NEED FOR INCOME

How important is current income to you in the near term?
Do you depend on income from your investment portfolio
for living expenses?

If current income is...

GIVE YOURSELF:

Critical...1 point
Needed to a large degree..2 points
Needed to a minor extent...3 points
Not important..4 points

7. INVESTING ATTITUDES

Your current attitude toward investing over the next
decade will help dictate what type of strategy you should
adopt, and how much risk your investments should entail.

If your current attitude is...

GIVE YOURSELF:

I cannot afford any significant loss of
capital regardless of potential return..1 point

If I can get high yields from bonds,
it's not worth suffering through the
ups and downs of the stock market...2 points

I believe in the power of compounding
income and the potential for gain from
equities and want a combination of the two................................3 points

Higher risk investors will earn higher
returns, and I want higher returns
no matter how they're achieved..4 points

8. LONG-RANGE ATTITUDE

Are you this type of investor: "My investment is for the
long range and volatility is not a problem."

*If your attitude toward the
above statement is...*

GIVE YOURSELF:

Totally disagree with this statement...0 points

Willing to tolerate some variability of
return, but rarely any loss of capital..1 point

Willing to endure a reasonable amount
of annual fluctuation in total annual return.................................2 points

(continues)

Willing to accept an occasional year of negative
return in the interest of building capital .... 3 points

Agree completely with this statement .... 4 points

9. PRIMARY OBJECTIVE

Lastly, two specific questions on your perceptions and
wishes. First, think about your personal goals as an
investor.

If you would generally categorize
your primary objective in investing as...

GIVE YOURSELF:

Capital preservation — emphasis on maximizing
principal stability; future growth of income and
principal are of minor importance; short investment
time horizon and low tolerance for big fluctuations
in current income .... 1 point

Current income — emphasis on providing a high
and stable level of current income; future growth
of income and principal are secondary objectives .... 2 points

Balanced — approximately equal emphasis
on current income and the potential for
future appreciation and income growth .... 3 points

Long–term growth — emphasis on future
appreciation, not current income; year–to–year
principal stability is not important; long–term horizon .... 4 points

10. FEELING TOWARD RISK

Finally, give your personal feeling about investment
losses, and how willing you are to tolerate losses
emotionally, by rating your risk tolerance.

If your characterize yourself as...

GIVE YOURSELF:

Low risk .... 0 points
Below average risk .... 1 point
Average risk .... 2 points
Above average risk .... 3 points
High risk .... 4 points

THAT'S IT! Now please tally your score on the next page.

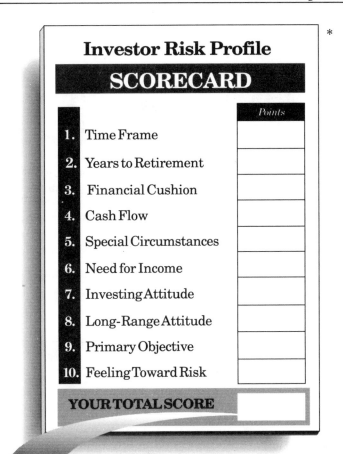

*

Investor Risk Profile

SCORECARD

		Points
1.	Time Frame	
2.	Years to Retirement	
3.	Financial Cushion	
4.	Cash Flow	
5.	Special Circumstances	
6.	Need for Income	
7.	Investing Attitude	
8.	Long-Range Attitude	
9.	Primary Objective	
10.	Feeling Toward Risk	

YOUR TOTAL SCORE

What Your Score Means		
If your total score is:	This is the amount of risk you should take:	And this is the type of investment plan you should follow:
7–15	Low Risk	CONSERVATIVE
16–30	Medium Risk	MODERATE
31–38	High Risk	AGGRESSIVE

see "Appendix 3: Worksheets" for additional copies of Scorecard

YOUR INVESTMENT ACTIVITY PROFILE QUESTIONNAIRE

Please answer the following ten questions as candidly as you can. Circle your score for each question in the column on the right.

For example, Question #1, asks about your interest in the "technicals" of the stock market. If you have a moderate amount of interest, circle "2 points" in the right–hand column.

1. INTEREST IN TECHNICALS

What is your interest in technical stock market data and analysis, such as stock market direction, bullish sentiment, stock market valuation, etc?

If your interest is...

GIVE YOURSELF:

Nonexistent...0 points
Low interest...1 point
Moderate interest..2 points
High interest..3 points

2. UNDERSTANDING STOCK MARKET INDICATORS

What is your understanding and degree of capability in dealing with various measurements and indicators, such as CPI, Federal funds rate, P/E ratio, price-to-book ratio, bullish sentiment, dividend yield, etc?

If your understanding
and capability is...

GIVE YOURSELF:

Non–existent..0 points
Low..1 point
Moderate..2 points
High...3 points

3. ABILITY WITH NUMBERS

What is your interest and ability in using numbers, mathematics, formulas and graphs?

If your interest with numbers is...

GIVE YOURSELF:

No good with numbers...0 points

Can handle simple calculations..1 point

Can handle complex calculations...2 points

Enjoy complex calculations and formulas,
enjoy reading graphs...3 points

4. AMOUNT OF READING AND STUDY PERFORMED

How much study and analysis are you willing to perform in the course of managing your investments, and how much research reading in publications like the Wall Street Journal and Barron's are you willing to do?

If you are willing to spend...

GIVE YOURSELF:

No time at all..0 points

Just a small amount of time per quarter....................................1 point

A little time each month..2 points

A little time each week.. 3 points

5. FEELING TOWARD SHIFTING YOUR INVESTMENT PORTFOLIO HOLDINGS

What is your comfort level toward changing the percentage of your investment money that is in stock funds, bond funds and money market funds?

If you...

GIVE YOURSELF:

Don't like repositioning at all...0 points

Don't mind making changes from time to time..........................1 point

Are comfortable making frequent changes...............................2 points

Enjoy making frequent trades and feel prudent shifting
is paramount to good portfolio performance..............................3 points

6. INTEREST IN FUNDAMENTAL ECONOMIC TRENDS

What is your interest in major, fundamental economic trends, such as economic growth and inflation, and in determining how the market reacts to changes in economic growth and the inflation rate?

(continues)

If your interest is...

GIVE YOURSELF:

Non-existent..0 points
Low interest...1 point
Moderate interest..2 points
High interest..3 points

7. UNDERSTANDING OF ECONOMIC GROWTH AND INFLATION RATES

What is your understanding and degree of capability in monitoring and measuring economic trends such as the Gross Domestic Product and inflation rates such as the Consumer Price Index?

If your understanding and capability are...

GIVE YOURSELF:

Non–existent...0 points
Low...1 point
Moderate...2 points
High..3 points

8. AMOUNT OF STUDY GIVEN TO HOLDINGS

How much thought and study are you willing to give to the individual holdings of your portfolio and the factors that make them move up or down?

If you are willing to give...

GIVE YOURSELF:

Little or no thought and study...0 points

Some thought and study..1 point

A moderate amount of thought and study ....2 points

I give my holdings a lot of study now, and
plan to continue or expand my activities....................................3 points

9. TIME SPENT ON UNDERSTANDING MUTUAL FUND APPROACHES

How much time and energy are you ready and willing to spend in researching and selecting stock funds among the various investment approaches, such as small cap growth, large cap growth, small cap value and large cap value?

If you are willing to spend...

GIVE YOURSELF:

No time at all...0 points
Just a small amount of time per quarter....................................1 point
A little time each month...2 points
A little time each week...3 points

10. FEELING TOWARD CHANGING FROM ONE FUND TO ANOTHER

Finally, what is your comfort level toward actively trading in and out of different types of stock funds when you feel that the investment climate is changing?

If you...

GIVE YOURSELF:

Like to buy a good fund and hold it long-term............................0 points

Don't mind trading a little...1 point

Don't get attached to your funds, and feel
"OK" with buying and selling regularly.....................................2 points

Enjoy making frequent trades and feel prudent
shifting is paramount to good portfolio performance................3 points

THAT'S IT! Now please turn the page and tally your score.

(continues)

Your Activity Profile

SCORECARD

Add up your score for questions 1–5:

Question	1	
Question	2	
Question	3	
Question	4	
Question	5	

TOTAL A
for questions 1–5

Now add up your score for questions 6–10:

Question	6	
Question	7	
Question	8	
Question	9	
Question	10	

TOTAL B
for questions 6–10

What Your Score Means for Your Investing

IF your scores for both A and B are each below 8, you are probably best suited to a BUY AND HOLD investing approach. See Chapter 3.

IF at least one of your two scores is 8 or higher, and your "A" total is higher than "B," you are best suited for a "Back of the Envelope" periodic analysis of stock market risks, and to my ASSET ALLOCATION approach. See Chapter 3.

IF at least one of your two scores is 8 or higher, and your "B" total is higher than your "A," you are best suited for more involved fundamental economic analysis and to my MARKET TIMING per the business cycle investment approach. See Chapter 4.

IF your scores for A and B are both high (above 11), then investing is in your blood and you may try combining both asset allocation and market-timing strategies. Use both Chapters 3 and 4.

see "Appendix 3: Worksheets" for additional copies of Scorecard

Figure 2–2

How to Interpret Your Investment Activity Profile
Questionnaire Scores

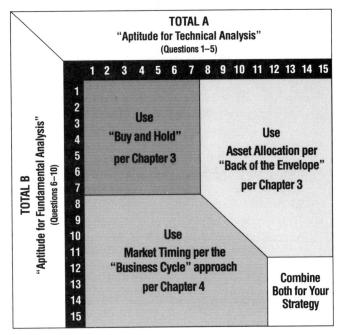

Chapter Three

Asset Allocation for Buy and Hold and Back of the Envelope Investors

In part 2 of our Winners Circle, we factor external events into the picture as we add structure to your investment plan. How those external events are factored in depends on what type of investor you are, that is, the process that is most applicable to you. Let's start with the inactive Buy and Hold investor.

Safe Growth for Buy and Hold Investors

If you scored as a Buy and Hold investor, your job is really quite easy! You don't want to do mutual fund trading, and you are willing to ride out temporary market setbacks as you take a longer-term perspective. So you won't be jumping in and out of the market. You'll set your course and keep your eye on the horizon.

I have advised thousands of Buy and Hold mutual fund investors over the past 18 years. Like you, they wanted to enjoy the long-term growth of the stock market, but they also wanted a plan they could live with, a plan that did not demand constant attention or frequent tweaking. So I devised a program that has proved enormously successful and popular. Figure 3-1 is your ticket to balance in your investing and to the Winners Circle.

As you can see, you will divide up your money among stock funds, bond funds, and money market funds. In Chapter Five, I'll give you some guidance on picking the very best funds, and I'll name my personal favorites. And in Appendix 2, I'll give you some

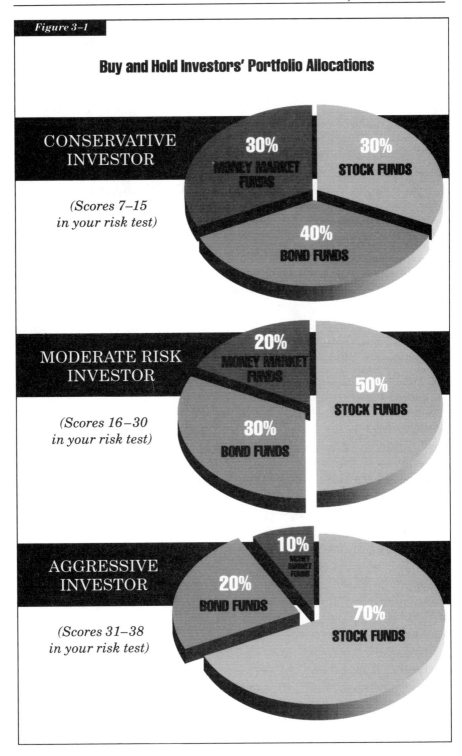

Figure 3–1

Buy and Hold Investors' Portfolio Allocations

CONSERVATIVE INVESTOR

(Scores 7–15 in your risk test)

30% MONEY MARKET FUNDS

30% STOCK FUNDS

40% BOND FUNDS

MODERATE RISK INVESTOR

(Scores 16–30 in your risk test)

20% MONEY MARKET FUNDS

50% STOCK FUNDS

30% BOND FUNDS

AGGRESSIVE INVESTOR

(Scores 31–38 in your risk test)

10% MONEY MARKET FUNDS

20% BOND FUNDS

70% STOCK FUNDS

real life examples of model portfolios for you, using my favorite funds.

You'll invest your money . . . and then go about your professional and family life without worrying about your investments. They will take care of themselves.

It's very important for you to choose "all weather" stock funds with solid, long-term track records of double-digit growth. For simplicity's sake (remember, you don't want your investments to be complicated and time-consuming), choose high-quality bond funds from the same mutual fund companies managing the stock funds you buy. If your Investment Activity score classified you as a Buy and Hold investor, turn now to Chapter Five for help with part 3 of our Winner's Circle.

Seizing Opportunities With My Asset Allocation Approach

If, however, you scored higher in the Investment Activity Questionnaire, you're not content to "set it and forget it." You want a mix of funds that responds to the changing investment climate. At the same time, you don't want to devote a major portion of your time and attention to managing your investments. So you will pick strong, diversified stock and bond funds that you can live with over the long term, but your allocation among stocks, bonds, and cash funds will fluctuate. When the market looks low-risk and hence potentially strong, you'll want to have the majority of your investment account in stock funds. But when the stock market looks vulnerable, you will want to sock away a large portion of your portfolio in bonds and cash, where you can ride out the storm in a safe harbor.

Let's take a closer look at how your investment mix will vary according to market conditions—and according to your profile as a Conservative, Moderate, or Aggressive investor.

As Figure 3-2 shows, Mr. Conservative will hold anywhere from 10% to 50% of his money in stocks, depending upon the risk or outlook for the stock market. Mr. Moderate will hold somewhere between 30% and 70% in stock funds, again depending upon the market outlook. And Mr. Aggressive will hold from 50% (when the market looks weak) to 90% (in a roaring bull market) in stock funds.

Figure 3–2

Ranges of Allocations in Stock Funds

Market Outlook	CONSERVATIVE	MODERATE	AGGRESSIVE
Bull Market	50%	70%	90%
	40%	60%	80%
	30%	50%	70%
	20%	40%	60%
Bear Market	10%	30%	50%

Actually, you will operate within prudent bands or ranges for each of the three major investments—stock funds, bond funds, and cash—as Figure 3-3 indicates (see Appendix 2 for model portfolios using specific funds).

But how do you know how much money to have in stock funds at any given time? How do you calculate the strength or weakness of the market in order to reach the proper allocation in stocks? This is where my technical Back of the Envelope Forecaster comes into play.

Be Your Own Market Forecaster

Accurately predicting where the stock market is heading may sound virtually impossible. That's what professional analysts get paid six-figure salaries to do, and half the time *they* get it wrong! What chance do you have of outfoxing the experts?

Actually, it's easier than you might think. With a little research and a few simple calculations, you can become a pretty good market forecaster yourself. In fact, I have developed a simplified model to help predict major market moves, a model you can build literally on the back of an envelope.

Now, this Back of the Envelope Forecaster won't predict every dip and blip of the stock market, but it can help you enjoy a share of the spoils when the market is in a bullish phase, and protect your hard-earned money when a bear market takes hold.

Figure 3–3

Ranges of Investment for Asset Allocation Investors

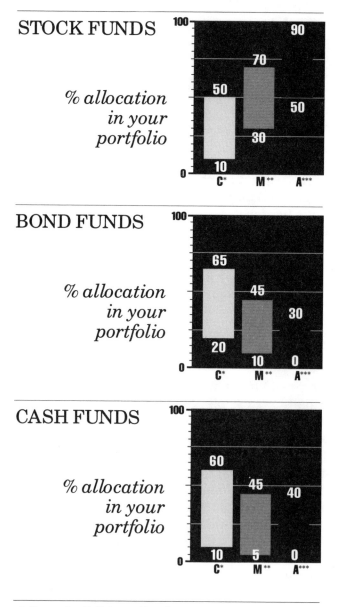

STOCK FUNDS

% allocation in your portfolio

BOND FUNDS

% allocation in your portfolio

CASH FUNDS

% allocation in your portfolio

* **Conservative**   7–15   in your risk profile
** **Moderate**   16–30   in your risk profile
*** **Aggressive**   31–38   in your risk profile

One of the secrets to this, and *any*, system is consistency. You must use the same sources, the same indicators, and the same rationale every time you run your Forecaster. You should calculate your Forecaster at regular intervals, and you should *never* introduce any personal discounting mechanism or exceptions to the rules. That takes discipline, but it's not really all that hard to do.

Under the next six headings, I'll show you the ten key indicators (see Figure 3-4) that you can use to construct your Back of the Envelope Forecaster, and tell you where to find these important indicators and how to interpret them. Follow my guidelines, and you'll always be able to keep your investments on track.

Here is what makes the markets move—and makes my Back of the Envelope Forecaster such a help to your portfolio.

- Inflation rate
- Relative yields
- Investor sentiment
- Valuation of the stock market
- Market extremes
- Market momentum

The Inflation Rate

The rate of price inflation is probably the single biggest determinant of stock market action. When price inflation is high, companies have a higher earnings growth rate hurdle to jump in order to impress investors. When inflation is low, modest earnings growth looks quite respectable, and they can keep a company very profitable. Thus, a high inflation reading, especially an upward trend in the rate of inflation, is generally a bad sign for the future direction of stocks, whereas a low rate or downtrend in inflation is bullish for stocks.

The level, as well as the direction, of inflation is important for the future of stock prices. A slow increase in prices will not usually set off a market sell-off or decline by itself. But a steep and abrupt increase is very ominous. However, please remember that my total forecaster has ten different indicators, and it is the combination of all ten that determines the forecast for the market. No single indicator, no matter how negative, will be able to pull the market into a sustained dive if all the other indicators are positive. Thus, the

Figure 3–4

Your Forecaster Really Can Fit on the Back of an Envelope
Technical Forecaster

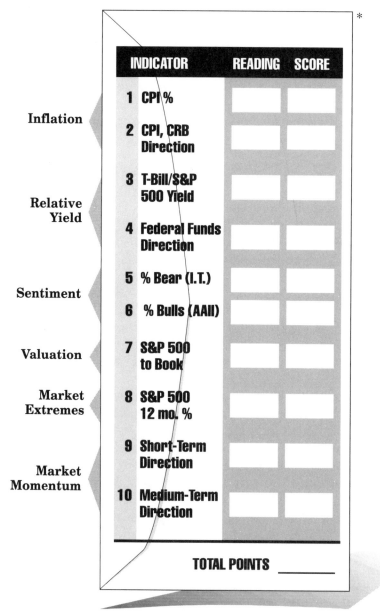

	INDICATOR	READING	SCORE
Inflation	1 CPI %		
	2 CPI, CRB Direction		
Relative Yield	3 T-Bill/S&P 500 Yield		
	4 Federal Funds Direction		
Sentiment	5 % Bear (I.T.)		
	6 % Bulls (AAII)		
Valuation	7 S&P 500 to Book		
Market Extremes	8 S&P 500 12 mo. %		
Market Momentum	9 Short-Term Direction		
	10 Medium-Term Direction		
		TOTAL POINTS	

*see "Appendix 3: Worksheets" for additional copies of Technical Forecaster worse the other indicators are, the more likely a small uptick in inflation will push the market over the edge.

Inflation is important not only because of its relevance to corporate earnings but because of its implications for interest rates. Specifically, a rising inflation rate usually triggers higher interest rates. The Federal Reserve's best weapon against inflation is its ability to manipulate interest rates, so when inflation starts to heat up, the Fed will try to apply the brakes by raising them. Unfortunately, higher interest rates tend to make bonds and cash look attractive to investors, and often steal money away from the stock market. Investors who might have bought stocks when bonds and cash were yielding a paltry 3% may opt for bonds and cash (money makets) instead when interest rates go up to 5% or 6%. Thus, just when higher inflation is making corporate earnings look less impressive, higher interest rates are making bonds increasingly attractive—producing a double whammy for stocks.

Since inflation is so important in predicting the direction of stocks, I include two inflation indicators in my Back of the Envelope model: the **Consumer Price Index (CPI)** (see Figure 3-5) and the **Commodities Research Bureau (CRB) Futures Index** (see Figure 3-6). The government announces the CPI each month around the 16th of the month, and you can find it in *The Wall Street Journal*, Section C, or *Investor's Business Daily*. You want to look at the year-to-year percentage change each month, as well as the trend for the past three to six months. The CRB Futures Index is listed daily in the Markets Diary section of *The Wall Street Journal*. You want to look at the direction of the Index for the past week and for the past three months.

In general, an inflation rate of 3% or lower is good for stocks, a rate of 3% to 6% is neutral, and a rate of over 6% is worrisome. As for the CRB Index, the key indicator is the short-term (past week) and medium-term (past three months) trend—whether up (which is bad for stocks), down (which is good for stocks), or sideways (which is neutral).

The worksheet shown in Figure 3-7 shows you how to calculate inflation, as well as all of our other indicators, into an overall forecast.

Relative Yields

Our next two indicators look at interest rates as they relate to stocks. Investors are always comparing yields and trying to deter-

Figure 3-5

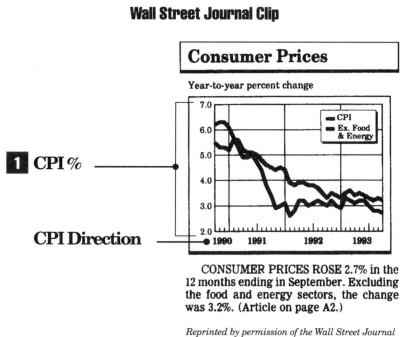

Wall Street Journal Clip

Consumer Prices

Year-to-year percent change

CONSUMER PRICES ROSE 2.7% in the
12 months ending in September. Excluding
the food and energy sectors, the change
was 3.2%. (Article on page A2.)

mine where they can get the best reward for the least risk. Since
bonds are generally considered income investments, investors are
usually willing to accept lower stock yields than bond yields in
return for the potential capital appreciation that stocks offer. But
when the yield on stocks goes too low, investors will return to
bonds.

Thus, a low stock market yield is a negative indicator for the
future of the market. Remember, stock market yield goes up when
stock prices go down.

How can you tell when stock yields are too low? It's all relative,
so you want to compare the **T-bill yield to the S&P 500 yield** to
find the answer. A normal relationship is indicated when the T-bill
yield is double the S&P 500 yield. For example, if T-bills are yielding 6%, a normal or acceptable S&P 500 yield would be 3%. When
the T-bill is considerably less than double the S&P 500 yield, the

Figure 3–6

Wall Street Journal Clip

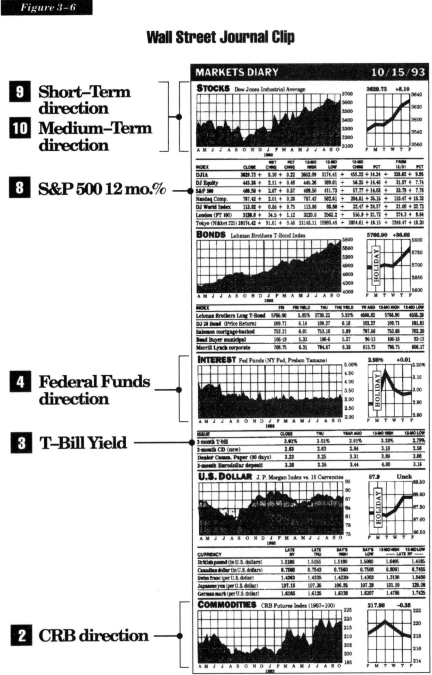

9 **Short–Term direction**

10 **Medium–Term direction**

8 **S&P 500 12 mo.%**

4 **Federal Funds direction**

3 **T–Bill Yield**

2 **CRB direction**

Figure 3-7

How to Calculate Your
Back of the Envelope Forecaster

Ten Major Indicators of Stock Market Risk	VERY BULLISH	SLIGHTLY BULLISH	NEUTRAL	SLIGHTLY BEARISH	VERY BEARISH
	5	4	3	2	1
INFLATION RATE					
1 Consumer Prices (CPI) Year–to–year % change	2%–4%	4%–6%	6%–8%	8%–10%	10%–12%
2 Direction of CPI and /or Commodities CRB index	↓	↘	→	↗	↑
RELATIVE YIELDS					
3 T–Bill yield dividend by S&P 500 dividend yield	0.75–1.25	1.25–1.75	1.75–2.25	1.35–2.75	2.75–3.25
4 Direction of Federal Funds Interest Rate	↓	↘	→	↗	↑
INVESTOR SENTIMENT					
5 % Bears, Investors Intelligence	50–55	45–50	35–45	30–35	25–30
6 % Bulls, AAII Index	10–20	20–30	30–40	40–50	50–60
STOCK MARKET					
7 Valuation: S&P 500 Price–to–Book value ratio	0.8–1.2	1.2–1.6	1.6–2.0	2.0–2.4	2.4–2.8
8 Overbought/Oversold: S&P 500; last 12 mo. % change	–15% to –30%	0% to –15%	0% to +15%	+15% to +30%	+30% to +45%
9 Direction of Stock Markets, Short Term	↑	↗	→	↘	↓
10 Direction of Stock Market, Medium Term	↑	↗	→	↘	↓

market is probably underpriced and likely to rise. In extreme cases, when the S&P 500 yield is equal to or even greater than the T-bill yield, our yield indicator is very bullish. On the other hand, when T-bill yields are more than double the S&P 500 yield, stock prices could be vulnerable to a fall.

You can find the T-bill yield in the Markets Diary section of *The Wall Street Journal* every day, and the S&P 500 dividend yield in the Indexes' P/Es and Yields section of *Barron's* each week (see Figures 3-6 and 3-8). Simply divide the T-bill yield by the S&P 500 yield to find your ratio.

Our fourth indicator also looks at interest rates, this time through the direction of the **Federal Funds Rate,** shown daily in the Interest section of *The Wall Street Journal*'s Markets Diary. Look at the graph for the direction of the Fed Funds rate for both the past week and for the past three to four months.

Figure 3-8

Barron's Clip

10/4/93

Indexes' P/Es & Yields			
	Last Week	Prev. Week	Year Ago Week
DJ Ind.-P/E	43.3	42.8	55.5
Earns Yield, %	2.31	2.34	1.80
Earns, $	82.78	82.78	57.69
Divs Yield, %	2.85	2.88	3.24
Divs, $	101.92	101.92	103.81
Mkt to Book, %	312.48	309.16	245.95
Book Value, $	1146.03	1146.03	1301.31
DJ Tran.-P/E	Nil	Nil	Nil
Earns Yield, %	Nil	Nil	Nil
Earns, $	(d14.39)	(d14.39)	(d49.25)
Divs Yield, %	1.18	1.18	1.61
Divs, $	19.37	19.37	20.09
Mkt to Book, %	330.72	330.25	185.32
Book Value, $	495.53	495.53	672.75
DJ Util.-P/E	14.6	14.6	14.7
Earns Yield, %	6.82	6.85	6.78
Earns, $	17.02	17.02	14.77
Divs Yield, %	5.30	5.32	6.27
Divs, $	13.21	13.21	13.64
Mkt to Book, %	180.80	180.08	159.96
Book Value, $	137.95	137.95	136.10
S&P 500-P/E	23.86	23.67	24.07
Earns Yield, %	4.19	4.22	4.15
Earns, $	19.33	19.33	17.05
Divs Yield, %	2.72	2.75	3.08
Divs, $	12.55	12.58	12.64
Mkt to Book, %	317.28	314.76	254.82
Book Value, $	145.39	145.39	161.08
S&P Ind.-P/E	27.84	27.66	26.86
Earns Yield, %	3.59	3.61	3.72
Earns, $	18.66	18.66	17.90
Divs Yield, %	2.48	2.49	2.75
Divs, $	12.88	12.85	13.22
Mkt to Book, %	371.51	369.08	305.88
Book Value, $	139.85	139.85	157.20

DJ latest 52-week earnings and dividends weekly file adjusted by the Dow Divisors in effect at Friday's close. S&P June 30 12-month earnings and indicated dividends based on Friday close. DJ and S&P book values latest available for FY December 1992 and 1991.

3 **S&P 500 Yield**

7 **S&P 500 to Book**
(Divide the 317% by 100)

caster is that the market usually does the opposite of what most people expect. How do you avoid getting caught up with the crowd? Our forecaster uses sentiment as a negative indicator. That means when people are optimistic, our indicator scores a negative reading, and when most people are pessimistic, our indicator is positive.

Why are investors' hopes and fears so often misplaced—or backwards? Frankly, it couldn't be any other way. You see, when most people are optimistic, they are generally fully invested; whereas when most people are worried and scared, they have a lot of money on the sidelines. Not surprisingly, when investors' carts are fully loaded with stocks or stock funds, their most likely next move is to sell—usually in the wake of sudden or surprising bad news. But when most investors have a lot of cash on the sidelines, stocks have nowhere to go but up. Simply put, high bullish sentiment is a bad sign for the stock market's future, high bearish sentiment is good news for stocks.

My two favorite sentiment indicators can easily be found in *Barron's* under the heading Investor Sentiment Readings (see Figure 3-9). They are the % **Bears** from the weekly *Investors Intelligence Newsletter*'s poll of investment advisors and the % **Bulls** from the American Association of Individual Investors (AAII) weekly percent bullish poll. Remember, high bullish % is bad; high bearish % is good.

The Valuation of the Stock Market

Another important indicator for the future direction of stock prices is the valuation of stocks. This refers to whether stock prices accurately reflect the underlying value of the companies they represent. First, let me tell you what *not* to look at. You've probably heard about the P/E, or price-to-earnings, ratio. This ratio is determined by comparing a stock's price to the company's earnings. Most investors use P/E as the basic measurement of value, but I don't like it. I have found that P/E's are not reliable statistical tools. One problem with P/E ratios is that people define the "E" part in many different ways. The question is, Which earnings are you looking at? Last year's? This month's? Predictions for next year? It's so easy to wind up comparing apples to oranges when it comes to P/E that I do not include this ratio in my forecaster.

Figure 3–9

Barron's Clip

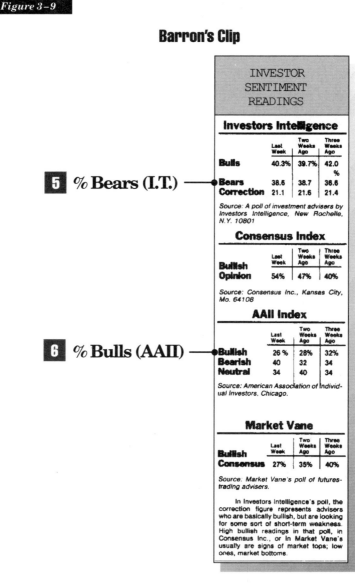

5 **% Bears (I.T.)**

6 **% Bulls (AAII)**

INVESTOR SENTIMENT READINGS		

Investors Intelligence

	Last Week	Two Weeks Ago	Three Weeks Ago
Bulls	40.3%	39.7%	42.0%
Bears	38.6	38.7	36.6
Correction	21.1	21.6	21.4

Source: A poll of investment advisers by Investors Intelligence, New Rochelle, N.Y. 10801

Consensus Index

	Last Week	Two Weeks Ago	Three Weeks Ago
Bullish Opinion	54%	47%	40%

Source: Consensus Inc., Kansas City, Mo. 64108

AAII Index

	Last Week	Two Weeks Ago	Three Weeks Ago
Bullish	26%	28%	32%
Bearish	40	32	34
Neutral	34	40	34

Source: American Association of Individual Investors, Chicago.

Market Vane

	Last Week	Two Weeks Ago	Three Weeks Ago
Bullish Consensus	27%	35%	40%

Source: Market Vane's poll of futures-trading advisers.

In Investors Intelligence's poll, the correction figure represents advisers who are basically bullish, but are looking for some sort of short-term weakness. High bullish readings in that poll, in Consensus Inc., or in Market Vane's usually are signs of market tops; low ones, market bottoms.

Instead, I like to look at **price-to-book-value (P/B)** ratios when I gauge market valuation. It's much harder to fudge book value—it's right there, on the books, for all to see. The P/B ratio compares a stock's price to the company's net assets. And, if you look at the average price-to-book for the market as a whole, you get a very good indication of whether or not the market is overvalued (and ripe for a fall). An average P/B ratio of about 1.5, meaning share prices are about one-and-a-half times book value, is normal (and neutral for our forecaster). A P/B ratio of 2.5 or more suggests that the market is overpriced (a negative indicator in our forecaster). And a price-to-book of less than one (when share prices are actually below net assets per share) is very bullish for stocks.

To find the S&P 500's price-to-book (or market-to-book) ratio, look in *Barron's* under Indexes' P/Es and Yield statistics (see Figure 3-8).

When the Market Moves to an Extreme

Stocks move in phases—like politics, sometimes moving to the left and sometimes to the right—sometimes moving up too far, sometimes down too far. Often it takes an extreme condition to spark a change. Thus, it's instructive to be alert to extreme conditions in the stock market, namely, overbought and oversold markets.

One of the more difficult ways to spot an extreme in the market is to calculate the percentage of stocks trading above their price moving average. The simplest form of moving average consists of the average of the sum of the closing price of the stock for a certain period—for example, 10 days, 20 days, and so forth. If a high percentage of stocks are trading at unusually high prices or above their moving averages, the market is usually vulnerable to a sell-off. Conversely, if very few stocks are trading above their moving average, this is often a sign that the market is oversold, and will soon be rising again.

An easier way to spot overbought and oversold conditions is to track the short-term gains (last 12 months) in the stock market. Past experience has shown that when the market has rocketed to a gain of 30% or more in 12 months, danger lies ahead. On the other hand, a 15% loss in 12 months usually means the market is ready for an upturn.

The Markets Diary of *The Wall Street Journal* shows the last 12 months' percentage change for all major market averages, in the column 12-MO. CHNG, PCT (see Figure 3-6).

What you're looking for is an extreme. A rising market is not necessarily bad, nor is a falling market always good. But a steep and dramatic increase usually cannot be sustained and is a warning sign that a correction could lie ahead. I use the **last 12 months change in the S&P 500** as my Back of the Envelope indicator.

Recent Stock Market Momentum

Despite the warning signs flashed when a market has seen extreme movement, general momentum in the market tends to be maintained. It could be likened to the law of inertia—that objects in motion tend to stay in motion. Just so for stocks: A rising stock market tends to keep rising (barring extreme conditions), and a falling market tends to keep falling. Obviously, a market won't rise or fall forever, but when it's on a roll, it just doesn't make sense to stand in its way.

The trick here is to distinguish between momentum and some of the contrary indicators discussed earlier. In my experience, the most reliable measurement of sustainable momentum is the combination of **short-term** (the past week) and **medium-term** (the past six months) **stock market direction.** If *both* the short term and the medium term are pointing in the same direction, you can reasonably expect the trend to continue. Thus, short-term and medium-term stock price advances tend to signal continued advances for the next 6–12 months. Contradictory short-term and medium-term advances are generally neutral for our Forecaster. But when both trends are down, expect continued declines on share prices.

Again, look in the Markets Diary section of *The Wall Street Journal* under Stocks, and factor into your Forecaster the direction of the graph of the Dow Jones Industrial for the week (short term) and for the past 6–12 months (medium term), as shown in Figure 3-6.

Putting the Back of the Envelope Together

Each one of these various indicators makes sense and has a track record of reliability, but like just about everything else, individually they don't work perfectly all the time. The important thing is that they tend to be useful and, when taken all together, are very likely to keep you in the game when stocks are going to make you more money—and out of trouble when the market is headed for a crash.

As I show in Figure 3-7, you'll want to assign a number to each of our ten indicators each time you calculate your Forecaster. Points range from 1 to 5, depending on how bullish the indicator is.

Indicator Reading	*Points Assigned*
Very bullish	5
Slightly bullish	4
Neutral	3
Slightly bearish	2
Very bearish	1

As I've noted, no single indicator on its own is fully reliable in predicting the future direction of the market. But when taken together, the ten indicators will give you a reading of anywhere from 50 (very bullish) to 10 (very bearish), on which you can then base your investment strategy. (see Figure 3-10). Note that a total forecaster of 30 is neutral—neither bullish nor bearish.

Avoiding a Crash

You can see now that with a little homework, you can easily put together your own forecasting model to help you enjoy opportunities at certain times and avoid risks at others. When the forecaster reading is bullish (35 or higher), you'll want to have a heavy allocation toward stock funds. When the forecaster reading is bearish (below 25), it's time to head for safer, dry land.

Does it work? Let's take a look at Figure 3-11 to see how the Forecaster tallies for September 30, 1987, a little more than two weeks before the October '87 stock market crash, when the Dow Jones Industrials Average fell by 500 points.

The Forecaster Reading for September 30, 1987

1. *Consumer prices (CPI) year-to-year % change.* Inflation as measured by the annual CPI was fairly well-behaved at an annual increase of 4.4%, giving a slightly bullish score of 4.

Figure 3–10

Total Points Score for Forecaster

(Sum of all Ten Indicators)

Total Points	Market Risk	Stock Market Viewpoint
40–50	Lowest Risk	Very Bullish
35–39	Low Risk	Bullish
30–35	Below Average	Slightly Bullish
25–29	Above Average	Slightly Bearish
20–24	High Risk	Bearish
10–19	Highest Risk	Very Bearish

2. *Direction of "CPI" and/or "Commodities CRB Index."* The direction of inflation, however, was on the increase, since the CPI was creeping up a little each month. The increases were not dramatic, so we gave a slightly bearish score of 2.
3. *T-bill yield dividend by S&P 500 dividend yield.* When you divided the T-bill yield by the low S&P 500 common stock dividend yield, you got a relatively high reading of 2.3. Remember, the normal ratio is about 2.0, so this gave us a slightly bearish score of 2.
4. *Direction of Federal Funds Interest Rate.* The direction of the Federal Funds Rate was trending up, probably because the Fed was worried about inflation returning, giving us another slightly bearish score of 2.
5. *Percent bears, "Investors Intelligence."* Investors Intelligence reported a very low percentage of bears (26.2%) in September 1987, translating into a very bearish score of 1.
6. *Percent bulls, "AAII Index."* Similarly, the AAII Index of bullish sentiment showed a high percentage (46%) of bulls, providing a slightly bearish score of 2.
7. *Valuation: S&P 500 price-to-book value ratio.* The price-to-book

Figure 3–11

Example of the Back of the Envelope
Forecaster Method
Technical Forecaster

September 30, 1987

INDICATOR	READING	SCORE
1 CPI %	4.40%	4
2 CPI, CRB Direction	↗	2
3 T-bill/S&P 500 Yield	2.30%	2
4 Federal Funds Direction	↗	2
5 % Bear (I.T.)	26.6%	1
6 % Bulls (AAII)	46%	2
7 S&P 500 Price-to Book	2.41%	1
8 S&P 500 12 mo. %	43.4%	1
9 Short-term Direction	→	3
10 Medium-term Direction	↗	4
TOTAL POINTS		22

HIGH RISK/BEARISH

ratio of the S&P 500 at that time was an expensive 2.41 reading. We saw that anything above 1.5 puts the market in "expensive" territory, and 2.41 gave us a very bearish reading of 1.

8. *Overbought/oversold: S&P 500; last 12 mo. % change.* As of September 30, 1987, the S&P 500 had jumped up 43.4% in the preceding 12 months (9/30/86–9/30/87), a very worrisome sign of an extreme market, rating a bearish 1 in our forecaster.

9. *Direction of stock market, short-term.* The short-term direction of the market was flat, giving us a neutral score of 3.

10. *Direction of stock market, medium-term.* The medium-term trend was up, giving our forecaster a bullish score of 4.

Putting together all ten of our indicators, the Back of the Envelope forecast for September 30, 1987, was an extremely negative 22. Indeed, October 1 would have been an excellent time to move out of stocks and stock mutual funds—or at least cut back on portfolio risk.

Part 2 of Our Winners Circle

My Back of the Envelope Forecaster won't call every move the market makes. No system that is humanly possible can do that. But you can use it along with your Investor Risk Profile, to help you allocate your assets into the smartest funds allocation at any given time. In Figure 3-12, I show you how to combine your Back of the Envelope reading with your Investor Risk Profile.

Let's walk through a few examples to see how this approach might work in practice. As you can see, Mr. Conservative will be anywhere from 10% to 50% invested in stock funds, depending on the outlook for the market. If the future looks particularly rosy, he will have 50% of his portfolio invested in stock funds, with 40% in bond funds as a safety counterweight and the remaining 10% in cash, or money market funds. As the storm clouds gather, Mr. Conservative will shift gradually from stock funds to money market funds, keeping a constant 40% in bonds. By the time we reach a bear market, Mr. Conservative will have only 10% invested in stock

Figure 3–12

Asset Allocation Using Back of the Envelope
Stock Market Forecaster

Stock Forecaster Reading	CONSERVATIVE	MODERATE	AGGRESSIVE
LOWEST RISK MARKET **40 – 50** "Bull Market"	50% Stock Funds 40% Bond Funds 10% Cash	70% Stock Funds 30% Bond Funds 0% Cash	90% Stock Funds 10% Bond Funds 0% Cash
LOW RISK MARKET **35 – 39**	45% Stock Funds 40% Bond Funds 15% Cash	65% Stock Funds 30% Bond Funds 5% Cash	85% Stock Funds 15% Bond Funds 0% Cash
BELOW AVERAGE RISK MARKET **30 – 35**	35% Stock Funds 40% Bond Funds 25% Cash	55% Stock Funds 30% Bond Funds 15% Cash	75% Stock Funds 20% Bond Funds 5% Cash
ABOVE AVERAGE RISK MARKET **25 – 29**	25% Stock Funds 40% Bond Funds 35% Cash	45% Stock Funds 30% Bond Funds 25% Cash	65% Stock Funds 20% Bond Funds 15% Cash
HIGH RISK MARKET **20 – 24**	15% Stock Funds 40% Bond Funds 45% Cash	35% Stock Funds 30% Bond Funds 35% Cash	55% Stock Funds 20% Bond Funds 25% Cash
HIGHEST RISK MARKET **10 – 19** "Bear Market"	10% Stock Funds 40% Bond Funds 50% Cash	30% Stock Funds 30% Bond Funds 40% Cash	50% Stock Funds 20% Bond Funds 30% Cash

funds and a full 50% in cash, again with 40% in bonds. See Appendix 2 for model portfolios using actual funds.)

Mr. Moderate will take the middle ground, keeping anywhere from 30% to 70% in stock funds, based on market strength. Again, when the market is strongly bullish, he will hold 70% of his investment money in stock funds, with 30% in bonds and no money market position. Mr. Moderate will only reduce his stock fund position when danger signs start to appear. As the risks in the market grow, Mr. Moderate will move money from his stock funds into his money market funds, keeping 30% in bond funds. When the market risks look most grave, Mr. Moderate will have just 30% in stock funds, 30% in bond funds, and 40% in cash.

Naturally, Mr. Aggressive will have the heaviest concentration of stock funds, but even he will not reach 100% in stock funds—and he can have as much as 50% on the sidelines—in cash or equivalents when times look tough. When the market is healthy and the outlook is bright, Mr. Aggressive will have 90% of his money in stock funds and 10% in bond funds. He will be watching for risks, however, and when they start to appear, he will begin shifting out of stock funds and into bond funds. Notice that unlike Mr. Conservative and Mr. Moderate, Mr. Aggressive will not be moving into cash right away. First, he will move just 5% from stocks into bonds (putting his bond allocation at 15%). As the warning bells get louder, Mr. Aggressive will next move 10% more out of stocks, putting 5% more into bond funds (to reach 20%) and 5% into money market funds. When the market risks go well above average, Mr. Aggressive will continue adding to his cash position and whittling down his stock position to reach a bear market balance of 50% in stock funds, 30% in money market funds, and 20% in bond funds.

This mainly technical approach will suit you well if you watch just a handful of market indicators and put pen to paper once a month to make the required calculations. Less than an hour of time spent with your worksheet, *The Wall Street Journal*, and *Barron's* is all you need to keep you on the right side of the markets.

Testing the Back of the Envelope Forecaster

In back-testing my Back of the Envelope Forecaster, I measured its hypothetical performance from March 1978 to June 1993. In the back-test, with quarterly forecaster readings, the allocations in stock funds, bond funds, and cash funds were varied each quarter. The average annual test return for the Conservative Investor Profile was 12.7%/year, for the Moderate Investor Profile, 14.2%/year, and for the Aggressive Investor Profile, 15.1%/year. These performances exceeded a Buy and Hold portfolio for each of the three profiles. As an added note, my Back of the Envelope Forecaster is designed to be *most* valuable in protecting you from bear-market losses. My back-test showed that not only does this method outperform Buy and Hold investing in a bull market (such as most of the past ten years have been) but protects you in any rough weather still to come.

Summary of Chapter Three

- We're ready to combine what you've learned about yourself with what's happening in the outside world.

- If you are a Buy and Hold investor, your balance of stock funds, bond funds, and money market funds will be fixed, regardless of external conditions. If you are an investor who wants to "set it and forget it," but you still want to minimize risks and maximize returns, you will hold my "all-weather" funds.

- If you are a Conservative Buy and Hold investor, you'll set up your portfolio with 30% in stock funds, 40% in bond funds, and 30% in money market funds.

- If you are a Moderate Buy and Hold investor, you'll set up your portfolio with 50% in stock funds, 30% in bond funds, and 20% in money market funds.

- If you are an Aggressive Buy and Hold investor, you'll set up your portfolio with 70% in stock funds, 20% in bond funds, and 10% in money market funds.

- If your Investment Activity Profile scored you as an Asset Allocation investor, you'll want to modulate your balance of stocks-bonds-cash according to the outlook for the stock market. At any given time, a Conservative investor will hold 10–50% in stock funds; a Moderate investor will hold 30–70% in stock funds, and an Aggressive investor will hold 50–90% in stock funds.

- To help determine the future strength of the market and how much you want to emphasize stock funds, you can use your own forecasting models or guru, or you can use my handy Back of the Envelope Forecaster.

- My Forecaster factors in inflation, yields, investor sentiment, valuations, market extremes, and market momentum to arrive at ten indicators that measure the likely direction of the stock market.

Chapter Four

Market Timing per the Business Cycle

If you are a Market Timer, you will want to vary the *types* of stock and bond funds you hold, depending on what stage of the business cycle we are in. Your portfolio could be a dynamic blend of small cap value, small cap growth, large cap value, and large cap growth funds—as well as short-term bonds, long-term bonds and cash—a blend that shifts with the external environment.

Economic Growth and Inflation as Weather Vanes

That blend will depend on two key economic trends: economic growth (as measured by gross domestic product—GDP) and inflation (as measured by the consumer price index—CPI).

You'll hear a lot of talk about leading indicators, unemployment, national debt, and so on, but when it comes right down to it, you really only need pay attention to these two trends. They encompass a lot of the other, smaller indicators and show the broad direction of the economy.

What does this have to do with your investments? A lot! In general, the stock market does best in an expanding economy with falling inflation, and worse in a contracting economy with rising inflation.

Let me explain how the direction of inflation and economic growth affect stocks, bonds, and money markets. Then I'll show you which types of equities are best for each scenario.

Effects of Inflation

When the rate of inflation is falling, bonds and common stocks do best.
That's because falling inflation means falling interest rates. Falling
interest rates help bond owners because, as yields fall, the bonds
they own pay higher yields than the new bonds being issued. After
all, if you have a five-year bond paying 7%, you're not going to pay
full price for a 5-year bond paying 5%. The higher-yielding bond
is worth more. At the same time, falling inflation and interest rates
are good for most common stocks, because the goods and materials
they buy are not skyrocketing in price and because new bonds are
not stealing away would-be stock investors. In other words, if an
investor is choosing between stocks and bonds, the low interest
rates on new bonds make stocks relatively more attractive.

However, when inflation is rising, cash and natural resources do best.
Inflation often results from a shortage of commodities (due to such
factors as high consumer demand, floods, drought, and political
unrest). And the basic rule of supply and demand states that when
supply shrinks and demand remains constant, prices rise. Thus,
gold, oil, copper, corn, and all kinds of other natural resources go
up in price. Meanwhile, money market funds do well because their
yields rise with inflation. Unlike bonds, where investors are stuck
with their yields until maturity, money market funds are not hurt
by rising interest rates. Rather, money market funds have a fixed
price of $1 per share, and investors receive higher dividends when
rates go up. Also, since rising inflation and rising interest rates
usually hurt stocks and bonds, money markets look like an attractive, safe harbor for many investors when rates start to rise.

Effects of Economic Growth

What about the effect of economic growth on various investments?
It depends on two factors.

1. *When the economy is speeding up and expanding, common stocks,
gold, and natural resources do best.* Investors expect economic growth
to translate into higher demand for raw materials and commodities, and into higher corporate profits for most businesses. On the
other hand, bonds often respond negatively to economic expan-

sion, because economic expansion usually leads to higher interest rates, which hurt bonds and bond funds.

2. *When the economy slows down, however, cash and bonds do best.* Since these two areas don't rely on corporate earnings, an economic slowdown doesn't hurt them. In fact, slow (or no) economic growth sends investors searching for safe havens, which often means investments that pay reliable dividends, such as money markets and bonds. At the same time, investors downplay stocks when the economy slows down (or is in a recession), because a sluggish economy usually entails lower sales—and profits—for corporate America.

Putting the two factors together, you can see (in Figure 4-1) that

Figure 4–1

Effects of Inflation and the Economy

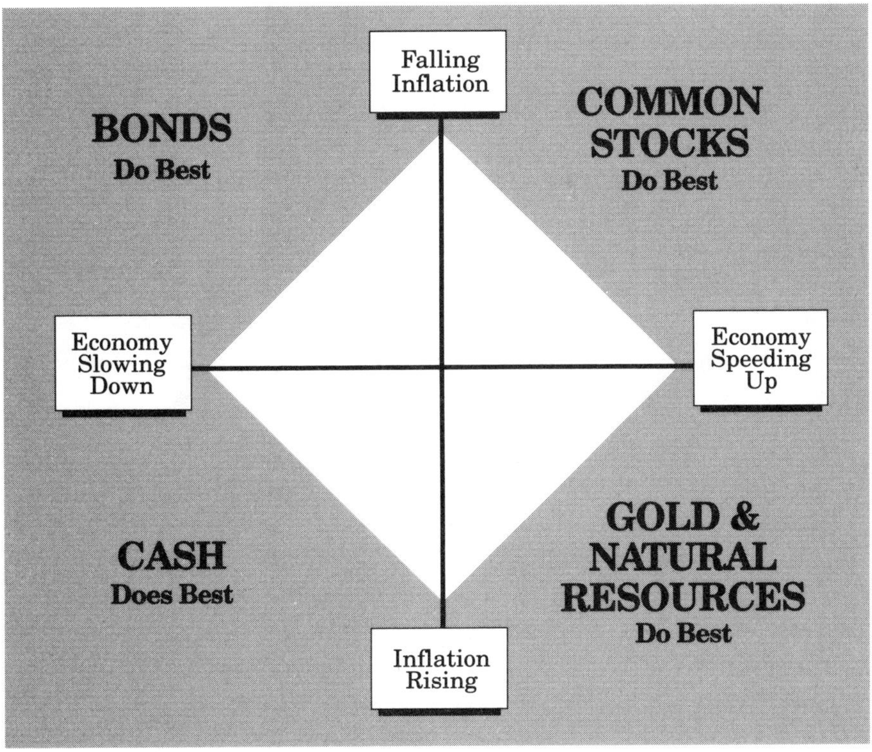

(1) when inflation is falling (or low) and the economy is speeding up, common stocks do best; (2) when inflation starts rising and the economy is still expanding, gold and natural resources do best; (3) when inflation is rising (or high) but the economy starts to slow down, cash or money markets do best; and (4) when inflation begins to fall and the economy is slowing down or in recession, bonds do best.

As you can see from Figure 4-2, these four scenarios take us through a normal business cycle, from early recovery (phase I), to late recovery (phase II), to stagflation (phase III), to recession (phase IV), and back to early recovery. The cycle doesn't always work perfectly—

Figure 4-2

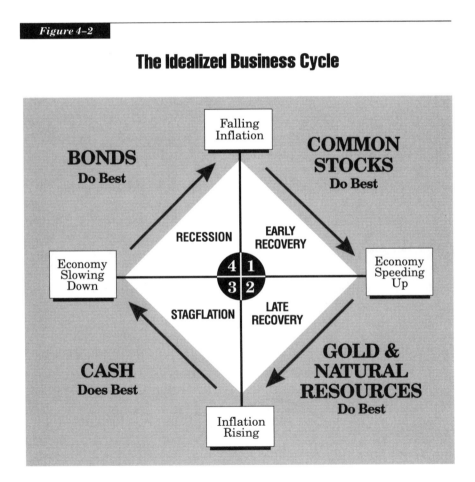

The Idealized Business Cycle

sometimes the economy falls back or skips ahead—but that is the general progression.

But remember, safety-first investing means diversification. You don't want to keep all your eggs in one basket, moving 100% into common stocks in phase I, 100% into gold in phase II, and so on. You want balance and prudence. Still, you can *emphasize* certain types of stock and bond funds in each phase to maximize profits while minimizing risks. So let me explain how these two factors, inflation and economic growth, affect different types of stock funds and bond funds, and which type is best in each of the four phases of the business cycle.

How These Fundamental Trends Affect the Markets— And Your Investments

The rate of economic growth determines whether you want to invest in *large* or *small* companies (see Figure 4-3); the rate of inflation dictates whether you should focus on *growth* or *value* companies (see Figure 4-4). Let me explain:

Effect of the Economic Direction

1. *When the economy is speeding up.* An expanding or accelerating economy is usually very good for the stock market. It usually means that production is advancing, sales are advancing, and profits are increasing (or will be soon). Demand for goods and services is probably picking up. Eventually, a speeding-up economy, which means higher corporate earnings, also leads to rising prices (inflation) for goods and services and a rising demand for money, which in turn pushes up interest rates.

Which areas do best in a speeding-up economy? *Small companies* usually do best. The small companies are better able to increase production, to hire employees, and to take quick advantage of economic recovery. With low numbers of employees and less bureaucracy, these companies can usually react quickly and spurt ahead. Therefore, small companies usually have the best gains, not only in earnings but in stock market price increases as well, when the economic growth is accelerating. Natural resources and commodities companies—such as oil, natural gas, steel, and aluminum—also do well in the later stages of an economic recovery, because demand for these materials increases as economic activity heats up.

Now, how do we define a "small" company? I call a company small if it has a capitalization of $1 billion or less. That means that the value of all its outstanding shares does not exceed $1 billion. **Small cap** companies are often young, start-up companies, and they usually experience greater volatility in earnings and sales than their **large cap** counterparts. Many trade on the NASDAQ over-the-counter (OTC) market.

The stocks that tend to lag behind in an expanding economy are the large companies. You can expect to see profit taking (selling) in these stocks after the economy speeds up.

2. *When the economy is slowing down.* When the economy slows down, however, corporate America's sales and profits usually fall—or are expected to fall. You often see bankruptcies and corporate restructuring, as well as layoffs. The Federal Reserve usually lowers interest rates to try to spark a recovery, and prices (inflation) eventually fall as companies struggle to keep business activity going.

Large established companies fare best in an economic downturn, because they have reliable, diversified sales outlets and the financial reserves to weather that downturn. These large-cap companies have over $5 billion stock market capitalization (value of shares outstanding), and they tend to diversify a bit more in the marketplace, which further reduces their risk when the economy slows down. Many refer to these large-company stocks as **blue chips** because they are large and stable enough to protect their shareholders. Blue chips generally include electric and telephone utility stocks, as well as big corporate giants like GE, Procter & Gamble, Coca-Cola and Disney.

The areas that tend to be hit hard by an economic downturn include the more volatile small cap companies, which depend on an active economy. You will also see profit taking in natural resource and commodity companies, whose products are in less demand as the economy slows down. For a comparison of large and small cap companies, see Figure 4-3.

Effect of the Level of Inflation

1. *When inflation is rising.* First, what's inflation? Inflation is simply rising prices. **Consumer inflation** is the rise in prices of con-

Figure 4-3

Large Cap vs. Small Cap

	Best Stocks for Economy Slowing Down	Best Stocks for Economy Speeding Up
	LARGE CAP	**SMALL CAP**
Focus	Emphasis on large companies well established.	Emphasis on small emerging start-up companies.
Company Characteristics	▪ Reliable sales and dividends ▪ Size of $5 billion and above	▪ Sales and earnings fluctuate ▪ Dividends are minor ▪ Size of $1 billion or less
Risk	▪ Usually diversified so risk is low.	▪ Undiversified so volatility of earnings and risk is high.
Return	▪ Moderate returns that include dividends.	▪ No dividends but potential high or low capital appreciation.
Performance Periods	▪ Tends to perform better on a relative basis when economy is slowing down.	▪ Tends to perform better on a relative basis when economy is speeding up.
Sample Companies	▪ IBM ▪ Merck ▪ GM	▪ Office Depot ▪ Banner Aerospace ▪ Charles Schwab
Other Names	▪ Blue Chip ▪ Large Company ▪ Dow Stocks	▪ Emerging Companies ▪ Small Company ▪ OTC Stocks

sumer goods and services, including everything from cars to candy. **Producer inflation** is the rise in prices of the raw materials used by big corporations, such as steel, lumber, and paper. Rising inflation is usually accompanied by rising interest rates, because higher prices lead to more borrowing in order to pay those higher prices.

Which investments are best when inflation is on the rise? **Value companies** tend to do best. These are companies that offer higher-than-average dividends and lower-than-average P/E ratios. These are also the companies that can raise their prices during inflation, such as steel companies, auto companies, and forest products companies. Certain types of value companies are referred to as **cyclical,** because they tend to do well when the economic cycle points toward recovery. These include automobile companies, forest products companies, and oil and gas companies. When the price of crude oil goes up, for example, the companies that sell gasoline usually do well. See Figure 4-4.

Bonds and other "interest rate sensitive" investments usually suffer when inflation is rising. Such investments include corporate and government bonds—particularly long-term bonds—as well as utility stocks.

The longer-term the investment, the more it will be harmed by rising interest rates. For example, a bond that matures in one year and yields 10% will lose 0.9% of its value if interest rates rise by 1%. But a 30-year bond yielding 10% will lose 8.7% of its value if rates rise by 1%. Why does this happen? Because when interest rates go up, a new bond with this new higher yield will be more attractive than the old bond at the old, lower yield. For example, if you own a 7% bond and rates go up 1%, then I can go buy a new bond yielding 8%. It stands to reason, then, that I won't be willing to pay as much for your 7% bond as for the new 8% bond. So the *value* of your bond has gone down.

2. *When inflation is falling.* Falling inflation is usually good for the economy, because it frees up money to spend on everything from basic necessities to technical innovations and even to stocks. But you often see inflation falling when the economy is in a recession and both government and business are lowering prices to try to encourage us to spend money.

The companies that benefit most from falling inflation are those that benefit from consumer spending and nondurables. Often referred to as **growth companies,** these firms are characterized by rapid growth in sales and profits but typically low or no dividends paid to shareholders. They include companies in communications, technology, biotechnology, health care, pharmaceuticals, and spe-

Figure 4–4

Growth vs. Value

	Best Stocks for Falling Inflation **GROWTH INVESTING**	*Best Stocks for Rising Inflation* **VALUE INVESTING**
Focus	Emphasis on companies and industries in stage of rapid and expanding growth with earnings momentum.	Emphasis on companies and industries whose market values are low relative to share value measures based on earnings, dividends or assets.
Company Characteristics	▪ Rapid and increasing growth in sales and earnings. ▪ Low or no dividends. ▪ Typically high price–to–value measures such as price–to–book, price–to–earnings, etc.	▪ Often unglamorous or out–of–favor businesses. ▪ Low price–to–value measures such as price–to–earnings, price–to–book, etc. ▪ High dividend yields.
Risk	▪ Tend to be more volatile, higher beta stocks. ▪ Prices can move up or down substantially with small changes in expectations or actual earnings performance relative to expected performance.	▪ Tend to be less volatile, lower beta stocks. ▪ It may take considerable time for the market to recognize value. ▪ Upturns in company performance may not occur.
Return	▪ High capital appreciation. ▪ Little or no dividend income.	▪ Capital appreciation. ▪ High dividend income.
Performance Periods	▪ Tend to perform better on a relative basis when the economy is slightly down.	▪ Tend to perform better on a relative basis during middle to late stages of an economic recovery.
Sample Companies	▪ Healthcare ▪ Communications ▪ Biotechnology ▪ Pharmaceuticals ▪ Technology ▪ Specialty retailing	▪ Transportation ▪ Automotive ▪ Machinery ▪ Forest products ▪ Insurance ▪ Oil and gas
Other Names	▪ Glamour ▪ Emerging company/market	▪ Contrarian ▪ Out–of–favor ▪ Neglected

cialty retail. On the other hand, natural resource and cyclical companies generally do poorly when inflation is falling.

Falling inflation usually means falling interest rates as well. And when interest rates fall, the value of bonds goes up. So in a falling inflation environment, you want to own some bond funds, as you can see in Figures 4-1 and 4-2.

Riding the Business Cycles

How do you put inflation and economic growth together? And how do the two combine to direct you to the right investments? It's quite simple, really: When you put economic growth and inflation together, you get the **business cycle.** And a normal business cycle takes us through four different combinations of economic growth and inflation (see Figure 4-5).

In phase I, the economy is in **early recovery** from recession. Economic growth is picking up, but inflation is still falling or low because of that previous recession.

As the economy continues to expand, prices start to rise and we enter phase II, where the economy is speeding up and inflation is rising. I call this the **late recovery phase.** Phase III is sometimes called **stagflation,** where consumers and the economy both start to lose steam but prices are still rising or are high. Thus, you have a slowing-down economy but rising inflation. Finally, in phase IV, slowdown turns to **recession.** Prices begin to fall as economic activity continues to decline, which means the economy is slowing down with inflation falling.

Figure 4–5

How Economic Environment & Inflation Environment Dictate the Best Fund Categories

	Phase I	Phase II	Phase III	Phase IV
ECONOMIC ENVIRONMENT	Economy Recovering *(Small Cap Funds)*	Economy Recovering *(Small Cap Funds)*	Economy Slowing *(Large Cap Funds)*	Economy Slowing *(Large Cap Funds)*
INFLATION ENVIRONMENT	Inflation Falling *(Growth Funds)*	Inflation Rising *(Value Funds)*	Inflation Rising *(Value Funds)*	Inflation Falling *(Growth Funds)*
BEST FUND CATEGORIES	Small Cap Growth	Small Cap Value *Also Natural Resource Funds*	Large Cap Value *Also Money Market Funds*	Large Cap Growth *Also Bond Funds*

That's what you can expect to see in a typical economic cycle: early recovery, late recovery, stagflation, recession, and back to recovery.

Putting our inflation and economic growth story together, then, let's look at what the economic cycle tells us about how we should invest.

Phase I: Early Recovery

We know that small companies do best when the economy is growing, and we know that growth companies do best in falling inflation. So small cap growth companies are the ideal choice for phase I of the economic cycle, when the economy is expanding but inflation is not yet a problem. That means stocks like Office Depot, Charles Schwab, and Medco Containment. Small cap growth mutual funds like Twentieth Century Ultra, Columbia Special, Kaufmann Fund, and Strong Discovery do best.

An early recovery usually sees falling or low inflation—also good news for bond fund investors. Eventually, however, economic recovery will lead to rising inflation and rising interest rates. So you want to choose bond funds in the short-term area, such as Vanguard Fixed-Income Short-Term Federal, Vanguard Fixed-Income Short-Term Corporate, Fidelity Short-Term Bond, Dreyfus Short-Intermediate Government, T. Rowe Price U.S. Treasury-Intermediate, and Twentieth Century U.S. Government. (More about these particular stock and bond mutual funds in Chapter Five, which discusses how to choose the best funds.)

Phase II: Late Recovery

While small companies are still well-suited to the economic growth of a recovery, we want to switch from small growth companies to small value companies as inflation starts to heat up. That means stocks in the cyclical and natural resource area, such as Santa Fe Energy Resources, Banner Aerospace, Cleveland Cliffs, and United Insurance. Mutual funds that fit the bill include the small cap value funds such as Pennsylvania Mutual, T. Rowe Price Small Cap Value, Fidelity Value, Lindner Fund, Mutual Beacon and Oakmark. (Again, more on these in Chapter Five.) We also want to sell our bond funds, which will suffer as interest rates rise.

Phase III: Stagflation

At this point in the cycle, with the economy slowing yet inflation picking up, cyclical and natural resource (value) companies are still good, but we want to focus on the larger, more stable companies in these industries. That means stocks such as John Deere, Westinghouse Electric, Ford Motor Co., and Texaco. Mutual funds that fare best in this environment are the large cap value funds including T. Rowe Price Equity Income, Neuberger Berman Guardian Mutual, Scudder Growth & Income, Vanguard Windsor II, and Vanguard Equity Income (details in Chapter Five).

Phase IV: Recession

Lastly, during a recession, when the economy is slowing and inflation is falling, we want to focus on large companies that stress growth. These generally include companies that depend not on business conditions but on consumer spending on items that are still bought during recessions. That means large cap growth stocks like Merck, Apple Computer, and PepsiCo, and mutual funds like Vanguard U.S. Growth, Janus Fund, Twentieth Century Growth, and Twentieth Century Select—all of which invest in large cap growth companies.

You also want to buy some long-term bond funds in phase IV, as interest rates start to fall from their phase III peaks, as the economy weakens, and as inflation starts to fall. You'll be able to grab some nice high yields—and probably some sizeable capital gains as well, for as interest rates fall, bond prices rise. My favorite long-term bond funds include Vanguard Fixed-Income Treasury Long-Term and Vanguard Muni Bond Long-Term (see Chapter Five for details). Figure 4-6 outlines the four phases and how to invest during each.

You may ask, How do I measure when inflation is rising, falling, or somewhere in the middle? And how do I measure when the economy is expanding, contracting, or somewhere in the middle? Well, as for inflation, I have seen that the long-term average inflation rate is about 5%, so I feel that when investors see 6% inflation or more, they react as if inflation is on the rise. With the rate at 4% or below, I call inflation on the downtrend. A range of between 4%

Figure 4-6

Investing per the Business Cycle

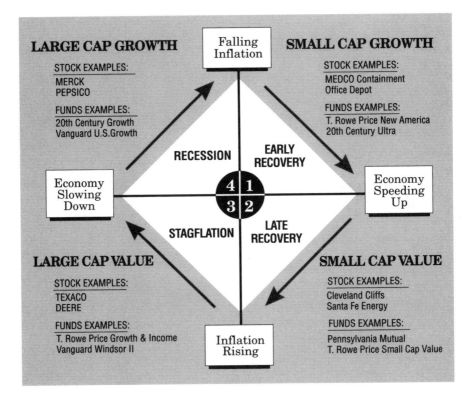

and 6% is neutral, and in this case the *direction* of the move is what is important.

When we look at the economic growth, a gross domestic product (GDP) advance of about 3% per year net, or after inflation, is about normal. I feel that when investors see 4% annual GDP growth or more, they react as if the economy is on the rise. When the economic growth rate comes in at 2% or below, the economy is growing more slowly than normal, so I call the economic direction as down. In the range of between 2% and 4%, economic growth is neutral. In such cases, the *direction* of the change is what is most important (see Figure 4-7).

So there you have it. By watching just these two fundamental

Figure 4–7

Business Cycle & The Asset Allocation Decision

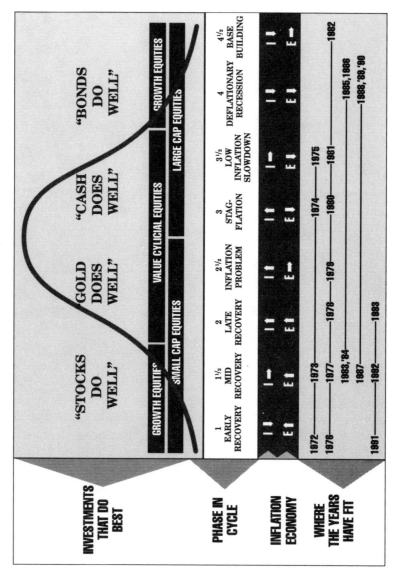

trends of the economy—growth and inflation—you can ride through the entire business cycle. Economic growth will dictate whether you want to invest in large or small companies; inflation will determine whether growth or value companies are best (see Figure 4-5).

A Winning Strategy for the Business Cycle Market Timer

Which brings us to the very important subject of "putting it all together." You now understand a little bit about the four stages of the economic cycle, including which investments thrive in each phase, as well as how to tell when the cycle is moving from one phase to the next. Put it all together, and you have a blueprint for successful market timing in all climates.

How do you turn this blueprint into a working plan for *your* investing? By combining my business cycle approach with your own Investor Risk Profile as determined in Chapter Two. Whether you're Conservative, Moderate, or Aggressive, you can use the business cycle to keep your mutual fund investing simple, safe, and successful.

My strategy for successfully staying calm, cool, and on the right side of the major economic trends is quite simple. The entire story is captured in Figure 4-8, which I'll explain step-by-step for you once you've had a chance to look at where you fall on the matrix.

As you can see, this figure takes each of our three typical investors through the entire business cycle. The columns to the far right show which type of stock (or **equity**) funds and bond funds you should emphasize for each stage of the business cycle, while the other three columns show the percentages of stock funds, bond funds, and money market funds investors should use to balance their portfolios during each of the four phases.

In Chapter Five, I show you which specific mutual funds I like best, and I tell you exactly how to buy and sell funds with the least amount of time, effort, and expense. And in Appendix 2, I show you some model portfolios, with specific funds for the Business Cycle Market Timer. First, though, let's get our action plans straight. Figure 4-8 may look a bit daunting at first, but I think

Figure 4-8

Portfolio Allocation for Each Stage of the Cycle

YOUR INVESTOR RISK PROFILE

PHASE IN BUSINESS CYCLE	CONSERVATIVE	MODERATE	AGGRESSIVE	BEST TYPE OF STOCK FUND	BEST TYPE OF BOND FUND
Phase I **EARLY RECOVERY** Economy Expanding Inflation Falling or Low	50% Stock Funds 40% Bonds 10% Cash	70% Stock Funds 25% Bonds 5% Cash	90% Stock Funds 10% Bonds 0% Cash	Small Cap Growth	Intermediate
Phase II **LATE RECOVERY** Economy Growing Inflation Rising or High	30% Stock Funds 20% Bonds 50% Cash	50% Stock Funds 10% Bonds 40% Cash	70% Stock Funds 30% Cash	Small Cap Value Natural Resources	Short-Term
Phase III **STAGFLATION** Economy Slowing Inflation Rising or High	10% Stock Funds 30% Bonds 60% Cash	30% Stock Funds 25% Bonds 45% Cash	50% Stock Funds 10% Bonds 40% Cash	Large Cap Value	Short-Term
Phase IV **RECESSION** Economy Slowing Inflation Falling	15% Stock Funds 65% Bonds 20% Cash	40% Stock Funds 45% Bonds 15% Cash	60% Stock Funds 30% Bonds 10% Cash	Large Cap Growth	Long-Term

you'll find it quite easy to use once I walk you through a couple of examples.

Market Timing in Action

Walking Mr. Conservative Through the Business Cycle

Let's start with Mr. Conservative. As you can see, Mr. C. starts the business cycle with 50% invested in small cap growth stock funds. Here, in phase I (early recovery), the risks are lowest because the economy is expanding and inflation is not a problem. Mr. C. also holds 40% of his money in short- to intermediate-term bond funds and 10% of his money in cash. Since inflation has been falling for some time (it started falling in phase IV of the previous cycle), he keeps his bond funds in the short to medium range, and the 10% cash is a nice safety cushion.

Once we enter phase II (late recovery), Mr. C. reduces his stock fund holdings, because the threat of inflation is making stock investing a bit more risky. At this point, Mr. C. holds just 30% of his mutual fund money in stock funds, and within that 30%, he concentrates on small cap value and natural resource funds. The other 70% of Mr. C.'s money should be in cash and short-term bonds, since longer-term bond funds will get hurt in phase II.

By phase III (stagflation), with the economy slowing but inflation still rising or high, Mr. C. is almost completely out of the stock market. Since inflation is still a problem, he doesn't want to have his money invested in longer-term bond funds either (which get hurt when interest rates are rising), so in phase III, he is 10% in stock funds (large cap value), 30% in short-term bond funds, and 60% in cash, safe and secure on the sidelines, waiting for his opportunities to open up in phase IV.

Once inflation starts to fall, we've entered phase IV (recession), and Mr. C. gets back into stocks and bonds. He invests 15% in large cap growth funds and 65% in long-term bond funds (which should do very nicely as inflation and interest rates fall). When recovery begins, Mr. C. gets even further into the market, and the cycle starts all over again.

Our Low-Risk, High-Return Action Plan for Mr. Moderate

Mr. Moderate starts the business cycle in phase I (early recovery) with 70% of his money invested in small cap growth equity funds, balanced with a nice 25% position in short-and intermediate-term bonds (remember, with inflation likely to start rising soon, we don't want long-term bonds now, they're just too risky). A 5% cash cushion keeps things even smoother.

As we move into phase II (late recovery), Mr. M. decreases his stock fund exposure somewhat, moving part of his stock funds and part of his bond funds to cash, for a cozy total of 40% in cash. With the remaining 10% in bond funds and 50% in stock funds, he shifts into some small cap value funds and natural resource funds, which should do best in a rising inflation/expanding economy environment.

When we reach phase III (stagflation), Mr. M. moves even further to the sidelines by transferring some of his stock funds to short-term bonds and cash (raising his cash position now to a defensive 45%) and keeping just 25% in bond funds and 30% in the stock market. This 30% is invested in large cap value funds (the most protective).

And finally, in phase IV (recession), as inflation starts to fall, Mr. M. ventures back into the market, placing 40% of his mutual fund money in large cap growth funds and keeping 60% on the sidelines. But he puts that sidelines money to work by placing most of it (45%) in long-term bonds, which, as interest rates fall, should sport some nice high yields—and capital gains as well. The remaining 15% is placed in cash for added stability.

Seizing Business Cycle Opportunities With Mr. Aggressive

Mr. Aggressive, you'll remember from Chapter One, seeks high growth with little concern for current income. So he's more likely to be heavily invested in the stock market. But which funds he buys and how he balances these funds out with bonds and cash can have a very big effect on his peace of mind and his bottom line. In phase I (early recovery), Mr. A. is 90% invested in stock funds. The risks are low, because the economy is recovering and inflation has not yet reared its ugly head. Which stock funds are best? As we learned earlier in this chapter, small cap growth stock funds are best for phase I.

When we enter phase II (late recovery), Mr. A. protects himself from rising inflation in two ways. First, he moves more than one-quarter of his mutual fund money (30%) to cash. Second, he moves the remaining 70% from small cap growth to small cap value and natural resource funds.

In phase III (stagflation), the slowing-down economy joins our worry list along with high inflation, and Mr. A. moves a full 40% of his money to cash and 10% to short-term bonds. At this point, the other 50% is invested in large cap value funds, the safest stock funds there are.

Once we enter phase IV (recession), however, Mr. A. puts his shopping hat back on and places 60% of his mutual fund money in the stock market, specifically in large cap growth funds. This will also be the point in the business cycle when he should own some bond funds (30%). Mr. A. buys these not so much for current income (in fact, he'll reinvest his dividends) as for the capital appreciation these funds will bring as interest rates decline. A small 10% remains in cash.

My research has proved that staying on the right side of the business cycle will work for you, even if you don't market-time your moves perfectly. In various back-tests that I have run for the 19-year time period from 1973 to 1992, an investment method that changed allocation among stocks, bonds, gold, and cash has proven very useful. The back-tests show average investment results between 12.1% and 17.6% per year. In 19 years, the power of compounding of returns proved powerful, and at 17.6% per year total return (untaxed), $100,000 initial investment grew to a healthy $2,195,000.

When I tested the reallocation of a portfolio among small cap growth, small cap value, large cap value, and large cap growth, the back-test results were even more impressive. Between 1973 and 1992, average results of between 17.6% per year and 19.1% per year were obtainable. Here again the power of compounding of investment results proved impressive. At an average untaxed annual return of 19.1%, $100,000 grew to $2,700,000 in 19 years!

Good Portfolio Management

Of course, you'll want to follow some basic guidelines for good portfolio management. You won't want to own too few funds—

remember, diversification and balance are key to my safety-first approach. You never want to have all your eggs in one basket, because you then have just one chance to be right. Instead, choose a handful of excellent funds in three or four key areas or management styles to increase the arrows in your quiver. You won't hit the bull's eye every time, so give yourself a few shots (see Appendix 2 for some examples).

At the same time, don't hold too many funds. Not only is it too much work, but overdiversification will dilute your returns. I generally recommend three funds for investors with $15,000 or less; four to six funds for investors with $15,000–$50,000; six to eight funds for investors with $50,000–$100,000; and no more than ten funds for investors with over $100,000.

Putting Your Action Plan to Work

We're halfway through our Winners Circle now. We've established an asset allocation strategy, for Buy and Hold and Back of the Envelope investors, and a market-timing program for Business Cycle investors, both of which incorporate your personal risk tolerance, desired process for investing, and amount of trading just right for you. Now we're ready to put your plan into action!

For my Hall of Fame All Star Mutual Funds, turn now to Chapter Five.

Summary of Chapter Four

- If your Investment Activity Profile identified you as a Business Cycle Market Timer, you will want to adjust both the balance of stocks, bonds, and cash and the type of funds in your portfolio, based on the economy and inflation trends.

- For balance, in stock funds you'll have 10–50% if you're a Conservative investor, 30–70% if you're a Moderate investor, and 50–90% if you're an Aggressive investor.

- Which funds you emphasize in your portfolio will depend on where we are among the four typical phases of the business cycle.

- In phase I, when the economy is expanding and inflation is falling or low, you'll emphasize small cap growth funds.

- In phase II, when the economy is expanding and inflation is rising, you'll emphasize small cap value funds.

- In phase III, when the economy is slowing down but inflation is still rising, you'll emphasize large cap value funds.

- And in phase IV, when the economy is contracting and inflation is falling, you'll emphasize large cap growth funds.

Chapter Five

Knowing the Funds

We're now in the third segment of the Mutual Fund Winners Circle. We've discussed how to devise a strategy that you are comfortable with, that meets your needs, and that suits your lifestyle. We've also talked about how to blend your own needs and desires with the risks and opportunities in the marketplace.

That's the strategy side of our Winners Circle. But how do you put your strategy into action?

In this chapter, I discuss what I look for in any fund I buy or recommend to my clients. I'll talk about how to evaluate fees, services, risks, and rewards, as well as how to interpret a fund's track record. I'll explain the role of a portfolio manager, how to compare a fund to others in the same category, and how to read a prospectus so that you know what you're buying. And after I show you what to look for, I'll give you an inside peek at the funds I myself like to buy, funds I call my **Hall of Fame All Star Mutual Funds.** And I'll list for you my **Schabacker 100 funds,** which are best for your own particular need or occasion.

A Lot More Than 57 Varieties

Back in the early 1940s, choosing a mutual fund was relatively easy. There were only 68 funds in existence, and only $500 million were invested in mutual funds at all. Most funds were either stock or bond funds; there were no money market funds, never mind asset allocation funds, international equity funds, global bond funds, or sector funds.

There are now about 3,800 mutual funds in existence, representing $1.5 *trillion* in total invested assets (see Figure 5-1). "Why," you ask, "are there so many mutual funds?" The answer is about the same as would be the answer to the question, "Why are there so many different types of shoes in the shoe store?" Because different shoes are made for different purposes and different tastes, and so are mutual funds. The major fund categories are shown in Figure 5-2.

As you can see from Figure 5-1, there was an explosion of mutual funds in the 1980s, from 564 at the start of the decade to 3,124 at the end of the 1980s. Today, with more than 3,800 mutual funds—more than all the common stocks on the New York Stock Exchange—investors' money is really spread around in a very broad way. Only 40% is in stock funds. Bond funds and money market funds account for 30% each. Figure 5-3 shows the distribution of funds in each category.

Figure 5–1

Growth of the Mutual Fund Industry

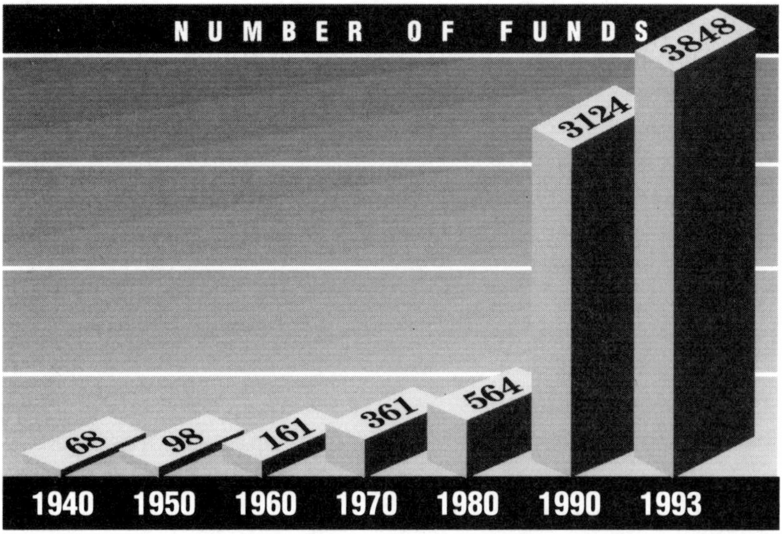

Source: *Investment Company Institute*

Figure 5-2

Four Main Categories of Mutual Funds

Major Fund Categories	# of Funds	Assets $ Bil	Average Risk	Average Annual Return Last 20 yrs.
Stock Funds *Invest in common stocks.*	781	$422	4 "Above Average"	13.8%
Hybrid Funds *Invest in mixture of stocks, bonds and cash.*	118	$82	3 "Average"	12.4%
Bond Funds *Invest in bonds.*	574	$381	2 "Below Average"	9.5%
Cash Funds *Invest in short term money instruments.*	794	$403	0 "Nil"	8.3%
GRAND TOTAL	2,267	$1,288		

Note: These funds are available to the general public and are more than one year old; therefore, the totals are less than those available from the Investment Company Institute.

Glance again at Figure 5-2 as I walk you through the shoe store of mutual funds and tell you about all the different categories. As a reminder, the largest single category of funds is stock funds, second is the bond fund category, third is the money market funds that give daily dividends with basically no risk. In addition, **hybrid funds** have been devised as smart, all-weather mixtures of all three—stocks, bonds, and cash. Let's take a look at these four main categories now.

Understanding Investment Objectives and Categories

"Now wait a minute, Jay," you say. "Can't I just tell the category from the name of the fund?" When you approach a fund like Fidelity Short-Term Bond, you know what it is, right? Well, yes, you know it is a fund made up of short-term bonds. But how short is short? And what kinds of bonds are we talking about here? Trea-

Figure 5-3

Number of Funds in Each Category

CATEGORY	NUMBER OF FUNDS
Aggressive Growth	233
Long–Term Growth	429
Growth and Income	345
Flexible Income	138
International Stock	138
Global Stock	98
Precious Metals	32
Balanced	99
Income	262
Global Bonds	87
Government Bonds	257
Ginnie Mae	77
Corporate Bonds	71
High Yield Bonds	89
Long–Term Municipals	216
Single–State Municipals	413
Tax Exempt–Money Market Funds	279
Money Market Funds	585
TOTAL NUMBER OF FUNDS	**3848**

Source: Investment Company Institute

suries? Mortgage-backed securities? Junk bonds? Investment grade corporates? The situation is far more confusing when you confront a fund with a name like Vanguard Windsor II. What is this? A stock fund? A bond fund? An international fund? A balanced fund?

How can you sort through this confusion *and* be sure you're buying what you want to be buying? The answers are in the prospectus and the annual report, and the secret is in knowing what to look for. Figure 5-4 provides a rundown of the categories of bonds and their relationship to the four cyclical phases.

Stock Funds

A stock, or equity, fund invests primarily in common stocks. I give the stock funds a risk rating of 4 (or above-average in risk), because they involve more volatility than bond or money market funds. But the return of stock funds has been rather good over the last 20 years—about 13% in average annual gain (this includes dividend reinvestment).

As you can see from Figure 5-5, in their best year over the last 20 years, growth stock funds gained a 44% return; but in their worst year, they suffered a troubling 35% loss. Even though the performance of stock funds is tops, you don't want to be holding a lot of them in the down years unless you are a very patient long-term investor unconcerned about short-term swings.

Within the broad universe of stock funds, there are many specific categories, with different goals and uses for different types of investors. Major categories include aggressive growth (AGGRO), long-term growth (GRO), growth & income (G&I), gold (Gold), sector (SECTR), global stock (GLSTK), international stock (INTL), and various geographic regions, such as Europe (EUROP) or the Pacific Basin (PACBN).

As you might expect, the **aggressive growth funds** take more risks in their investing; they do very well in bull markets and very poorly in bear markets.

Slightly less speculative are the so-called long-term growth (GRO) or growth funds. Some of these funds do relatively well in bear markets, as well as in bull markets.

The category of stock funds called **growth & income funds** (G&I) are more conservative, as they invest in stocks that pay reasonable dividends and thus carry less risk. Look at Figure 5-5 and note the current dividend yield of 2.2% for the growth & income funds versus a 0.4% yield for the much riskier aggressive growth funds.

So we have three general categories of domestic stock funds: aggressive growth, growth, and growth & income funds. Within each of these three groups, you'll find funds that specialize in small cap stocks, large cap stocks, value stocks, and/or growth stocks—as well as funds that hold a diversified basket of stocks. To round out

Figure 5-4

How Do Categories Perform in Typical Business Cycle?

NAME	OBJECTIVE	TYPE OF INVESTMENTS OWNED	BEST IN PHASE
Balanced	Current income plus modest appreciation	Fixed ratio of bonds and income oriented stocks	III
Corporate Bonds	Current income	Bonds issued by U.S. corporations	IV
Flexible Bonds	Current income	Combination of bonds; corporate, gov't, and/or foreign	IV
Global Bond	Current income, hedge the dollar	Bonds issued primarily by foreign gov'ts and corporations	IV
Global Stock	Capital appreciation	Stocks of both foreign and U.S. corporations	I
Gold	Aggressive capital appreciation, hedge inflation	Gold mining stocks, gold bullion	II
Growth & Income	Current income plus modest capital appreciation	Income–oriented stocks	III
International	Capital appreciation, hedge the dollar	Stocks of foreign corporations	I
Long–Term Growth	Capital appreciation with modest income	Stocks of large U.S. corporations	IV
Aggressive Growth	Aggressive capital appreciation	Stocks of small to medium sized U.S. corporations	I
Money Market	Safety, preservation of capital	Short–term (less than one year bonds, like T–bills)	III
Municipal Bond	Tax–free current income	Bonds issued by state and local gov'ts and agencies	IV
Sectors	Time the market, target special situations	Stocks in specific industries or geographic regions, like utilities	VARIOUS
U.S. Bonds	Low risk current income	Bonds issued by U.S. gov't and its agencies	IV
Small Cap Growth	Aggressive capital appreciation	Small growth companies with high P/E's	I
Small Cap Value	Moderate capital appreciation	Small cylical companies with low P/E's	II
Large Cap Value	Moderate capital appreciation	Large cylical companies with low P/E's	III
Large Cap Growth	Long–term capital growth	Large growth companies with high P/E's	IV

Figure 5-5

Vital Statistics on All Mutual Fund Categories*

	ABBREV	# OF FUNDS	TOTAL ASSETS $ BIL.	AVG. RISK	AVG REWARD TO RISK	AVG PORTFOLIO TURNOVER	AVG EXPENSE RATIO	AVG TOT COST 5 YR	AVG BULL	AVG BEAR	CURRENT 12 MO % YIELD	% PERF BEST YEAR	% PERF WORST YEAR	% AVG ANNUAL RETURN 5 YR	10 YR	15 YR	20 YR
STOCK FUNDS		**781**	**421.7**	**4**	**3.4**	**85**	**1.49**	**107**	**+—**	**+—**	**1.1**			**11.8**	**11.1**	**14.8**	**13.8**
Aggressive Growth	AGGRO	127	54.6	4	3.2	125	1.63	111	+	—	0.4	47.9	−29.7	13.9	10.2	15.8	14.7
Growth	GRO	263	157.4	4	3.3	76	1.37	99	+	—	0.8	43.9	−34.5	12.3	11.1	15.4	13.9
Growth & Income	G&I	156	142.3	3	3.1	66	1.22	95	+	—	2.2	30.4	−20.6	11.5	11.6	13.9	12.6
Gold	GOLD	27	2.9	5	3.8	128	1.82	128	—	+	0.4	148.5	−34.8	1.7	1.4	12.5	9.2
Sector	SECTR	88	25.1	4	3.1	110	1.65	118	+	—	1.2	27.8	−28.4	14.9	11.7	12.8	12.2
Global Stock	GLSTK	47	19.5	4	3.9	83	1.86	138	—	+	0.8	36.1	−24.0	6.6	10.9	14.1	12.3
International Stock	INTL	43	14.5	4	4.3	60	1.71	116	—	+	1.0	50.1	−19.6	7.6	13.4	11.9	9.9
Europe	EUROP	14	2.9	4	4.7	119	1.79	119	—	+	1.3	22.4	−7.3	4.4			
Pacific Basin	PACBN	15	2.5	4	3.8	127	1.81	127	—	+	0.6	71.1	−20.9	5.9	18.1	15.7	
HYBRID FUNDS		**118**	**81.7**	**3**	**2.7**	**94**	**1.28**	**95**	**—**	**+**	**3.5**			**11.0**	**11.7**	**13.4**	**12.4**
Asset Allocation	ASSET	17	8.9	3	2.8	74	1.51	109	—	+	3.0	28.0	−12.9	8.1	4.5		
Balanced	BAL	36	30.0	3	2.8	100	1.02	81	—	+	3.5	29.1	−15.8	10.7	12.0	13.5	11.7
Flexible income	FLEX	47	40.1	3	2.7	80	1.34	96	—	+	3.4	29.3	−11.4	11.7	12.1	13.6	12.1
Convertible	CONV	19	2.8	3	2.6	136	1.39	104	—	+	3.8	31.4	−11.0	11.5	9.7	12.1	11.7
BOND FUNDS		**574**	**380.5**	**2**	**2.6**	**109**	**0.96**	**79**	**—**	**++**	**6.2**			**9.4**	**10.1**	**9.4**	**9.5**
Corp Bond	C-BD	54	33.8	2	2.3	108	0.92	75	—	+++	6.5	31.1	−3.7	9.8	10.7	10.2	9.3
High Yield Corp	HY-CB	56	33.4	2	2.4	91	1.28	103	—	+++	9.4	36.0	−11.0	9.5	10.0	10.5	9.4
US Bond	US-BD	182	144.8	2	2.3	155	0.97	76	—	+++	6.0	26.5	−5.2	9.5	10.0	9.2	8.6
Flexible Bond	FLEXB	49	20.6	2	2.0	111	0.93	70	—	+++	6.4	31.6	−4.8	9.9	10.6	10.2	8.8
Global Bond	GLBND	44	11.7	3	3.5	170	1.53	103	—	+++	6.7	28.9	0.9	9.2	12.5		
Tax-Free	MUNI	189	136.2	2	2.9	55	0.79	72	—	++	5.4	35.7	−11.4	9.0	9.7	7.9	
CASH FUNDS		**794**	**403.9**	**0**			**0.61**				**2.7**			**5.9**	**6.0**	**8.7**	**8.3**
General		237	235.8	0			0.61				2.9	17.1	3.4	6.6	7.2	8.8	8.3
Government		95	37.4	0			0.66				2.9	15.9	3.3	6.4	6.9	8.5	
Tax-Free		323	102.3	0			0.59				2.3	6.8	2.6	4.5	4.7		
State Tax-Free		139	28.4	0			0.59				2.2			4.4			
TOTALS		**2267**	**1287.8**	**2**	**3.0**	**95**	**1.04**	**95**									
DJIA											2.9	45.0	−13.4	14.4	15.5	15.3	12.6
S&P 500											2.8	37.2	−26.5	14.2	14.4	15.6	12.2
CPI												1.1	13.3	4.2	3.8	5.5	6.1

*This table represents the stock and bond funds tracked by Schabacker Investment Management plus money market data from Money Fund Report, published by IBC Donoghue, Inc., Ashland, MA. These funds are available to the general public and are over 1 year old; therefore, the totals are less than those available from ICI.

the domestic funds, we must add some very targeted **sector funds** that have very specialized portfolios, such as health care funds, utility funds, natural resource funds, and even gold funds.

But wait, we're not finished with the stock funds yet! We also have all the overseas or **international stock funds** (INTL), that invest in the stocks of companies located overseas, such as T. Rowe Price International and Scudder International. Aside from the economic value of an overseas company and overseas mutual fund, international funds involve the added variable of movements between the U.S. dollar and the currency of the country or countries of the stocks within the fund. A rising U.S. dollar causes our international funds to suffer in performance, while a falling U.S. dollar causes our international fund to gain in performance. International funds can be rewarding, but they're tricky. Once again, the combination of diversification and balance is the answer.

In the ultimate attempt at diversification, we find global stock funds (GLSTK), which invest in both overseas companies *and* U.S. companies. Two such very diversified global stock funds are Janus Worldwide and Scudder Global.

Just in summary, stock funds are the most popular of all mutual funds. In total, their risks are above-average, but so are their returns. Over the last 20 years, the stock funds in my database have had an average annual total return of 13.8% per year!

Finding the Right Stock Funds. In my Directory of Mutual Funds, Appendix 4, I list every fund's category and specialty. In a fund's prospectus, you can also find out what type of investments a fund holds. Look under the heading marked Invest Style/Sector. You'll find out whether the fund invests in small, medium, or large companies, and whether it seeks out growth or value companies. (In subsequent figures in this chapter, I name for you my favorite stock mutual funds and indicate their style of investing.)

This is also the section of the prospectus in which you'll learn (if the name of the fund hasn't already made it clear) whether the fund invests in foreign securities versus U.S. stocks. Let me say that neither type of security is inherently better, but I generally prefer U.S. stocks because I like investing in what I understand. Foreign investing involves too many wild cards—including currency fluctuations and international politics. There are times when I see an international opportunity I just can't pass up, but most investors' portfolios should not overemphasize the internationals.

Bond Funds

Bond funds are second only to stock funds in importance and demand. A bond fund invests in the debt securities of corporations, governments, and municipalities. Bonds, as you know, represent *lending* to a company or government, whereas stock funds represent *ownership* in a company. Bonds and bond funds are important for investors because they provide current income or **yield.** Bond funds also represent a lower risk in the investment spectrum, and as such should have a place in almost any portfolio to provide balance and diversification.

With bond funds, there are two basic variables you want to consider and verify: the *quality* of the bonds (or of the government or corporation issuing them) and the *maturity* (or time length) of the bonds. Quality can range from super-safe government bonds to super-risky, low-rated, or unrated junk bonds issued by risky corporations. In the bond fund prospectus, read the section marked Investment Objectives and Programs. It may be long, but read it anyway; you'll be glad you did. The Investment Objectives and Programs section will spell out what types of bonds the fund holds and the maximum amount it can hold of any particular type of bond, such as low-rated bonds or foreign bonds.

The most popular group of bond funds is also the safest as to default risk: the **U.S. Bond fund** (US-BD) category. Subject only to interest rate risks, these funds invest in bonds issued by the U.S. government and its agencies. Interest payments from some government instruments and government funds, such as Vanguard Fixed Income Treasury-Long, are not subject to state taxes—an added plus.

Also in the bond fund arena are **corporate bond funds** (C-BD), which invest in bonds issued by U.S. corporations. These come in a wide variety of "quality," from AAA-rated investment grade bonds to high-yield, or **junk bonds.** Naturally, the lower the quality, the higher the risk—and so the higher the current yield. We list high-yield corporate bond funds (HY-CB) as a separate category.

The maturity of the bonds refers to the number of years before the average bond in the portfolio matures or comes due. This is often called **average portfolio maturity.** As discussed in Chapter

Four, there are phases of the business cycle when long-term bond funds (15 years or more) are best, and there are times when short-term bond funds (5 years or less) are best. If you're not a Business Cycle Market Timer, take the middle road and go with intermediate-term bond funds (6–14 years average maturity). Again, check the prospectus under Investment Objectives and Programs. Some have a nice little chart, some have the answer buried in the text, but it's there.

In our present interest rate environment, ordinary corporate bond funds yield 6–7%, while high-yield junk corporate bond funds yield 9–10%—3% (or 300 **basis points**) higher to compensate for the added risk. A couple of high-yield junk corporate bond funds are T. Rowe Price High Yield and Vanguard Fixed Income High Yield.

Flexible bond funds (FLEXB) are like flexible stock funds in that the portfolio manager may pick and choose among different investment opportunities. Hence, a flexible bond fund could contain a mixture of short-term corporates, long-term governments, and even overseas bonds, all to get the best performance possible. Two all-weather flexible bond funds are Fidelity Investment Grade Bond and Janus Flexible Income.

Rounding out the long list of available bond fund categories are **global bond funds** (GLBND), which invest primarily in bonds issued by foreign governments and corporations (and to a small degree in U.S. bonds for full diversification). Some of the global bond funds, such as Scudder International Bond, invest in medium- and long-term overseas bonds. Others, including Scudder Short-Term Global Income, purchase only the shortest-term fixed-income securities. Generally, in overseas investing, you get your lowest risk by using the short-term global income funds.

Lastly, for high–tax-bracket investors, there are tax-free bond funds that purchase bonds issued by state and local governments and agencies. The diversified **tax-free bond funds** or municipal bond funds (MUNI) yield interest that is free from federal income tax. And, if you buy a muni bond or a muni bond fund that owns only investments in your own state (or even city), then that yield is free from federal, state, and local income taxes. There are all kinds of tax-free bond funds, with two popular favorites being Scudder Managed Municipal Bonds and Vanguard Muni Bond Intermediate.

Cash Funds

Cash or money market funds are available at essentially no risk. Holding them is almost like having a savings account (not government-insured) with your mutual fund family, and many even offer limited check-writing privileges. The goal of money market funds (which are designed to always trade at $1 per share) is safety and preservation of capital. To reach this goal, a money market fund most often invests in very short-term (less than 30 days' maturity) corporate and government—even municipal—bond instruments. As such, there are many types of money market funds including **general money market funds, government money market funds, diversified tax-free money market funds,** and **single-state tax-free money market funds.**

Hybrid All-Weather Funds

It's not surprising that someone thought up **hybrid mutual funds,** which mix and match stocks, bonds, and cash into a single balanced portfolio. These hybrid funds are sometimes called **all-weather mutual funds** because they are designed to keep your nest egg safe in all kinds of cycles and markets. Often this is achieved by a fixed balance of investments, while other funds vary their balance of investments, depending on the investment climate.

An **asset allocation fund** (ASSET) spreads its portfolio among a wide variety of investments, including domestic and foreign stocks and bonds, government securities, gold bullion, and real estate stocks. The asset allocation is meant to lower risk while providing favorable total returns. With some funds, the allocation of assets remains relatively constant; with others, the mix is altered as market conditions change.

Balanced funds (BAL) use a relatively fixed mix of stocks and bonds in their portfolios. As an example, Vanguard Wellington uses a fixed mix of 60% stocks/40% bonds, while Vanguard Wellesley Income uses a fixed mix of 40% stocks/60% bonds. As you can expect, Wellington, with its higher stock content, carries slightly more risk, but it has also returned the greater performance over the long term.

Flexible funds (FLEX) do their own internal asset allocation.

They reallocate the proportion of stocks, bonds, and cash from time to time.

Convertible funds (CONV) essentially own convertible bonds and/or convertible preferred stocks. These convertible securities give their owners the right to exchange that security for common stocks issued by the same company. As such, these convertible funds also own regular common stocks (that have been converted) in their portfolios.

Three Types of Funds I Don't Much Like

No matter what type of fund you're considering, I encourage you to take advantage of the great safety margin built in to mutual funds by virtue of their size and diversification. Even for funds that invest in small companies, I like funds that have at least $50 million in invested assets. And I like those assets to be rather broad-based.

Which brings me to sector funds, gold funds, and index funds. None of these is a particular favorite of mine. **Sector funds** target their holdings to a particular industry, like health care or insurance. To me, this runs contrary to one of the best reasons for owning mutual funds: broad latitude by the portfolio manager to pursue investment diversification. The more narrowly defined a mutual fund's area, the thinner your layer of protection. Similarly, **gold funds** are very narrow, and much too volatile for most mutual fund investors.

Index funds present a different problem. Index funds are mutual funds whose portfolios match the makeup of a standard index, such as the S&P 500 Stock Index or the Wilshire 5000 Stock Index. You could say that they offer too much diversity. More to the point, they, too, ignore the skills of a portfolio manager. When you invest in a mutual fund that simply mimics an index, you've deprived yourself of the advantages of having an experienced professional picking stocks for you. You're just riding the waves with the rest of the market.

The Role of the Portfolio Manager

Just how important *is* the portfolio manager? How do you weigh this factor in choosing the best fund to buy? With bond funds, frankly, the portfolio manager isn't of extreme importance. In most cases, the fund has a clearly defined area of concentration, be it long-term treasuries, short-term corporate bonds, or municipal bonds. And one AAA-rated ten-year corporate bond is not all that different from another. So the portfolio manager acts more as a conscientious custodian than as an active investment picker. Furthermore, this type of fund is usually so big that one or two bad apples won't spoil the pie.

With a stock fund, however, the portfolio manager is vitally important. The better he or she is at finding opportunities and bargains, and at timing the market and trading shrewdly, the more money you'll make. I get to know the fund managers of the funds I recommend very well. I like to know their investment style, their investment philosophy, and what they currently think of the market and its risks and opportunities. I talk to the folks at Vanguard, T. Rowe Price, Fidelity, and a handful of other fund groups regularly to keep up with what they're buying and what they're selling inside their funds' portfolios.

So the simplest way to find a good fund manager is to follow my lead and go with the Schabacker 100 All Stars listed in Figure 5-6. Checking up on your own fund managers is a bit tougher. You can look at the fund track records (as long as you make sure the current portfolio managers have been there for the entire period), or you can call each fund and ask for details on the manager's experience. Quite often you can read interviews a portfolio manager has given to the news media, magazines, or newsletters. The key things to look for are *consistently high returns over the years* and a *commitment to the stated objectives of the fund.* In other words, if the prospectus says the fund will invest in blue-chip stocks, make sure that is indeed what the fund owns.

I don't like surprises. When I buy a fund, I like to know what I'm buying, and I like the fund to stick to its knitting. As I said, if it promises to invest in blue chips, that's what I want to find in its portfolio, not some brand new biotechnology firm, not some wildcat oil and gas drilling venture, but safe and secure blue-chip stocks. That gives me confidence in the portfolio manager and in the fund group.

So when you are shopping for funds for your own portfolio, make sure you're getting what you asked for. This is where an annual report really comes in handy. It spells out exactly which

Figure 5–6

Alphabetical Listing

Benham GNMA
Blanchard Short-Term Global Income
Brandywine Fund
CGM Mutual
Columbia Fixed Income Securities
Columbia Growth
Columbia Special
Dodge & Cox Balanced Fund
Dreyfus Intermediate Municipial Bond
Dreyfus Short Intermediate
  Government
Evergreen Foundation Fund
Fidelity Aggressive Tax-Free
Fidelity Asset Manager
Fidelity Balanced
Fidelity Capital and Income
Fidelity Contrafund
Fidelity Disciplined Equity
Fidelity Equity Income
Fidelity Equity Income II
Fidelity Global Bond
Fidelity Government Securities Fund
Fidelity Growth Company
Fidelity Intermediate Bond
Fidelity Investment Grade Bond
Fidelity Puritan
Fidelity Short-Term Bond
Fidelity Short-Term World Income
Fidelity Value
Harbor Bond
INVESCO High Yield
INVESCO Industrial Income Fund
INVESCO Select Income
INVESCO Tax-Free Long-Term Bond
Janus Flexible Income
Janus Fund

Janus Worldwide
Kaufmann Fund
Lexington GNMA Income
Lindner Dividend
Lindner Fund
Loomis Sayles Municipal Bond
Mainstay Value
Merger Fund
Mutual Beacon
Neuberger Berman Guardian Mutual
Neuberger Berman Limited Maturity
  Bond
Neuberger Berman Partners Fund
Neuberger Berman Ultra Short Bond
Nicholas Fund
Oakmark Fund
Royce Equity Income
Scudder Global
Scudder Growth and Income
Scudder High Yield Tax-Free
Scudder Income Fund
Scudder International Fund
Scudder International Bond
Scudder Managed Municipal Bonds
Scudder Medium Term Tax-Free
Scudder Short-Term Bond
Scudder Short-Term Global Income
Stein Roe Managed Municipals
Stein Roe Special Fund
Strong Advantage
Strong Discovery
Strong Government Securities
Strong Municipal Bond
Strong Opportunity
Strong Short-Term Bond
T. Rowe Price Balanced Fund

(continues)

Figure 5-6 Continued

T. Rowe Price Capital Appreciation	Vanguard Bond Index
T. Rowe Price Equity Income	Vanguard Equity Income
T. Rowe Price GNMA	Vanguard Fixed Income GNMA
T. Rowe Price High Yield	Vanguard Fixed Income High Yield
T. Rowe Price International Bond	Vanguard Fixed Income Short Corp.
T. Rowe Price International Stock	Vanguard Fixed Income Short Federal
T. Rowe Price New Income	Vanguard Fixed Income Treasury Long
T. Rowe Price Short-Term Bond	Vanguard Index 500 Trust
T. Rowe Price Tax-Free Income	Vanguard International Growth
T. Rowe Price Tax-Free Short	Vanguard Muni Bond Intermediate
Intermediate	Vanguard Muni Bond Limited Term
Twentieth Century Growth	Vanguard Muni Bond Long Term
Twentieth Century International	Vanguard U.S. Growth
Equity	Vanguard Wellesley Income
Twentieth Century Ultra	Vanguard Wellington
Vanguard Asset Allocation	Vanguard Windsor II

stocks the fund currently owns, how much, and what types of stocks they are. You get a complete breakdown, by industry, of the fund's portfolio, so you can easily see if the fund is indeed pursuing the course it promised.

Use Top-Notch No-Load Funds

Unlike stocks (and closed-end funds), mutual funds (sometimes referred to as *open-end investment companies*) are not traded on the New York Stock Exchange—or on any other exchange for that matter. Shares in mutual funds are bought and sold directly from the mutual fund company, although many investors still use a broker.

But I have found that you don't need to pay a commission to buy a great fund. In the vast majority of cases, you can use top-notch no-load funds and pay no commission at all.

What's a **no-load fund**? Quite simply, it's a fund that charges no direct fees—no sales commission and no redemption fee (where you pay a commission when you sell your shares).

I recommend you stick to funds that charge no sales commission (often referred to as a *front-end load*) or funds that charge a very modest front-end load. I'd never pay more than 3%.

Fees

Of course, mutual funds aren't charities, and the company has to get paid to stay in business. So every fund charges an annual management fee, along with such fees as shareholder services, custodial services, auditing, and transfers. These annual fees are grouped together as **annual operating expenses,** and are usually expressed as a percentage of assets. You may see them referred to as the **expense ratio.** Stick with stock funds that charge 1.5% or less for an annual expense ratio. You don't have to pay more to get good performance.

Other Fees to Watch Out For

Other fees to watch out for include 12b-1 fees, back-end loads, redemption fees, and transfer fees. **12b-1 fees** (sometimes called **market distribution fees**) are annual fees assessed to pay for marketing and related expenses above and beyond the annual fees mentioned above. In most cases, I don't mind a small (very small) 12b-1 fee if the fund is truly outstanding, but I would avoid funds with 12b-1 fees of more than 0.25% per year.

Redemption fees and **back-end loads** are charged to you when you sell your shares of a fund. The fund gets you in the door by claiming to be "no-load" (that is, you pay no commission when you *buy*) but socking you with a big back-end commission when you sell. In most cases, I really object to redemption fees, because they are a sneaky way of getting you to hold on to shares you would otherwise sell. I've found far too many investors stuck in losing funds because of redemption fees. A redemption fee is acceptable *only* if it disappears after 60–90 days. Some funds charge you a redemption fee if you sell your shares right after you bought them. Fair enough. You probably shouldn't buy a fund if you don't plan to hold on to it for at least six months, so a redemption fee that disappears after two to three months is not unreasonable. But avoid funds with redemption fees that never disappear.

Similarly, I don't like funds that charge **exchange fees,** i.e., fees charged when you switch from one fund to another fund in the same group. I want to be able to switch when I want, where I want, without cost impediment.

Finding the Fees in the Prospectus

So, how do you find out what you're really paying for a fund? It's all in the prospectus. Now, if this is the first time you've looked at a mutual fund prospectus, you're probably shaking your head right now, saying, "Well, Jay, if it's in there, I sure can't find it or understand it!"

Let me help. Turn to the section in the prospectus marked Summary of Fees and Expenses or Expense Information. You'll find two varieties of fees: Shareholder Transaction Expenses and Annual Operating Expenses. Under Shareholder Transaction Expenses, you'll find the front-end load (if any), as well as any back-end (or deferred) load, redemption fee, or transfer (exchange) fee.

To find the annual management fee and other yearly charges, look under the heading Annual Fund (Operating) Expenses. Here you'll find the management fee, the 12b-1 fee (if there is one), and custodial and auditing and shareholder services fees—typically labeled as Other Expenses. And you'll find them all added up for you on a line labeled Total Fund (Operating) Expenses.

My favorite no-load mutual funds have a lot of lines in this part of their prospectuses marked *none*. Such truly no-load companies include Vanguard, T. Rowe Price, Twentieth Century, Scudder, and a handful of others. We'll talk more about some of these families in a moment.

In my Directory of Mutual Funds (Appendix 4), you'll find two columns describing each fund's fees. The first column, called Sales Charge, shows the front-end load, if any. The second column, marked 5-yr. Cost, shows the total effect of all fees and loads charged by the fund. The more dollar signs ($), the more expensive the fund.

You can also spot funds that charge fees by looking in the newspaper. In *The Wall Street Journal*'s daily mutual fund listings (Section C), any fund with a small *r* after its name charges a redemption fee or back-end load. A small *p* means that it charges a 12b-1 fee. A small *t* indicates that the fund charges *both* a back-end fee and a 12b-1. Finally, the third column in the *Journal* listings shows whether or not the fund charges a front-end load. *N/L* means "no-load," which means you won't pay a commission to buy shares. Any number in this third column shows the price of one share, *including* the commission. Compare this to the number in the second column, and you can see the exact dollar amount of the sales fee per share (see Figure 5-7).

You Get What You Pay For, Right?

Many investors assume that paying high loads and fees is simply the necessary trade-off for owning top-performing funds. Not true! My 18 years of experience has proven to me that some of the very best performing funds are also those that charge you the least. Don't assume that low costs equals low quality.

Nor do you sacrifice good service. Again, some of lowest-cost mutual funds offer excellent customer service. I am particularly impressed by the service provided by INVESCO, Vanguard, T. Rowe Price, Fidelity, Scudder, Twentieth Century, Lexington, and Rushmore.

Three Key Services to Look For

One of the key services to look for when choosing a fund is **telephone switching.** That means you can sell shares or switch to another fund with a simple telephone call, making your whole investment program safer (no time delays in executing your trades) and simpler. Look in the fund's prospectus under How to Exchange Shares or Exchange Privileges.

Another service to look for when buying a money market mutual fund is **check-writing privileges.** You want your money market to be as good as a checking account, only better. Most good fund groups offer this feature. Check the prospectus under Money Market Services.

And when you invest in a fund for your retirement savings plan, demand one that offers *free* **automatic reinvestment of dividends.** That means any dividends from the fund are automatically used to buy you more shares—one of the best ways to build your nest egg steadily and reliably through the years with almost no effort. Check the section of the prospectus entitled Dividends and Distributions to make sure your dividends will be reinvested automatically. *Then,* check under the Fees and Expenses section to be sure *no* sales load is charged for reinvested dividends. Franklin Resources

Figure 5-7

Reading The Mutual Fund Listings

LIPPER INDEXES

Friday, October 15, 1993

Indexes	Prelim. Close	Percentage chg. since		
		Prev.	Wk ago	Dec. 31
Capital Appreciation .	434.01	+ 0.44	+ 2.53	+ 15.77
Growth Fund	770.29	+ 0.29	+ 2.02	+ 14.78
Small Co. Growth	442.38	+ 0.43	+ 3.09	+ 16.74
Growth & Income Fd	1153.65	+ 0.30	+ 1.23	+ 14.13
Equity Income Fd	739.71	+ 0.27	+ 0.95	+ 13.91
Science & Tech Fd	335.30	+ 0.64	+ 4.68	+ 25.47
International Fund ...	443.20	+ 0.94	+ 1.28	+ 31.74
Gold Fund	187.40	− 0.54	+ 1.84	+ 58.91
Balanced Fund	867.20	+ 0.32	+ 0.99	+ 12.14

OVERSEAS FUND INDEXES-a
Friday, October 15, 1993

LOFT Global Bond ...+	169.13	N/A	+ 0.69	+ 11.43
LOFT Global Eqty ....+	396.90	N/A	+ 1.30	+ 21.60

a-Foreign Registered
Source: Lipper Analytical Services, Inc.

Friday, October 15, 1993

Ranges for investment companies, with daily price data supplied by the National Association of Securities Dealers and performance and cost calculations by Lipper Analytical Services Inc. The NASD requires a mutual fund to have at least 1,000 shareholders or net assets of $25 million before being listed. Detailed explanatory notes appear elsewhere on this page.

	Inv. Obj.	NAV	Offer Price	NAV Chg.	%Ret YTD	Max Initl Chrg.	Total Exp Ratio R
AAL Mutual:							
Bond p	BND	10.83	11.37	+0.02	+10.7	4.750	1.030 ..
CaGr p	GRO	15.32	16.08	+0.13	+5.9	4.750	1.200 ..
MuBd p	GLM	11.44	12.01	+0.02	+11.0	4.750	1.000 ..
SmCoStk p	SML	11.06	11.61	+0.04	NS	4.750	NA ..
AARP Invst:							
CaGr	GRO	37.92	NL	+0.03	+18.2	0.000	1.130 ..
GinIM	BND	15.94	NL	−0.02	+5.7	0.000	0.720 ..
Gthinc	G&I	33.22	NL	+0.08	+14.4	0.000	0.910 ..
HQ Bd	BND	17.45	NL	+0.09	+13.5	0.000	1.130 ..
TxFBd	ISM	19.22	NL	+0.09	+13.3	0.000	0.740 ..
ABT Funds:							
Emrg p	CAP	14.77	15.51	+0.18	+15.5	4.750	1.440 ..
FL HI	HYM	10.83	11.37	+0.05	+13.6k	4.750	0.000 ..
FL TF	MFL	11.75	12.34	+0.06	+12.8	4.750	0.580 ..
Gthin p	G&I	11.08	11.63	...	+4.9	4.750	1.230 ..
Utilin p	SEC	14.35	15.07	+0.04	+15.9	4.750	1.170 ..
Acc Mortg	BND	12.41	12.41	−0.01	+6.8	0.000	0.840 ..
Acc Sht Int	BST	12.52	12.52	+0.01	+6.0	0.000	0.830 ..
AHA Funds:							
Balan	S&B	13.32	NL	+0.03	+12.1	0.000	0.380 ..
Full	BND	11.13	NL	+0.03	+13.3	0.000	0.420 ..
Lim	BST	10.58	NL	...	+5.5	0.000	0.290 ..
AIM Funds:							
AdiGv p	BST	9.90	10.00	...	+3.9	1.000	0.140 ..
Agrsv p	SML	24.13	25.53	+0.12	+30.3	5.500	1.250 ..
Chart p	G&I	9.55	10.11	...	+12.9	5.500	1.170 ..
Const p	CAP	17.33	18.34	+0.05	+16.2	5.500	1.200 ..
CvYld p	S&B	16.77x	17.61	+0.06	+19.8	4.750	2.120 ..
GoScA p	BND	10.44	10.96	+0.01	+8.1k	4.750	0.980 ..
GrthA p	GRO	13.32	14.10	+0.03	+8.5	5.500	1.170 ..
HIYld p	BHI	5.97	6.27	...	+14.0k	4.750	1.530 ..
HYIdC p	BHI	10.02	10.52	+0.01	+15.5k	4.750	1.150 ..
IncoA p	BND	9.01	9.46	+0.06	+18.6k	4.750	0.990 ..
IntlE p	ITL	12.09	12.79	+0.16	+34.9	5.500	1.800 ..
LimM p	BST	10.20	10.30	...	+4.1	1.000	0.480 ..
MunlA p	GLM	8.83	9.27	+0.03	+11.8k	4.750	0.900 ..
Sumit	GRO	10.54	NA	−0.02	+9.3	8.500	0.760 ..
TeCt p	SSM	11.40e	11.97	+0.01	+11.9	4.750	0.250 ..
TF Int	IDM	11.07	11.18	...	+8.3	1.000	0.020 ..
UtilA p	SEC	15.22	16.11	+0.07	+18.2k	5.500	1.170 ..
ValuA p	G&I	21.98	23.26	+0.06	+20.5	5.500	1.160 ..
Weing p	GRO	17.75	18.78	+0.01	+		
AMCORE Vintage Fds:							
Equity	GRO	10.32	10.78				
FxIncome	BIN		11.0				
IntdtTF							
AMF F							

*Reprinted by permission of Barron's
© 1993 Dow Jones & Company, Inc.
All rights reserved worldwide.*

Group, for one, charges a sales load for reinvestment of dividends for at least some of its funds.

Telephone switching, check-writing privileges on a money market, and automatic reinvestment of dividends are three key features I look for when buying a mutual fund. I'll talk about other useful services and how to get the very best service possible from any fund you own in Chapter Five.

Keeping Risks Under Control

No one wants expensive fees or bad service. But when it comes to risk, personal preferences are not so clear-cut. As we saw in Chapter One, some of us can withstand a great deal of risk in order to meet our goals, while others abhor any risks whatsoever and prefer the slow and steady course.

But what I am talking about here is volatility, a bumpy ride. No one wants a fund that's just as likely to go down as up, but some investors are willing to take a bumpy ride if the final outcome is very likely to be positive. That's why I look at risk in two different ways. First, I look at pure volatility, then I look at how well you get paid for that volatility.

Perhaps you've heard of the term **Beta,** which many investment experts use to measure volatility. Beta is the degree of correlation between a given investment and the stock market. Thus, a fund with a Beta of 1 has the same volatility as the market, while a fund with a Beta of 0.50 has half the volatility of the market. A fund with a Beta of 2 is twice as volatile as the market.

My experience has been that Beta doesn't work as well for mutual funds as it does for individual stocks, and it doesn't really have much relevance at all for funds that hold bonds, gold, international securities, and other non–U.S.-stock investments. A zero coupon bond fund can be quite volatile, for example, and yet have almost no correlation with the stock market (thus earning it a low Beta). Gold funds, which are notoriously volatile, often react *opposite* to the market and receive low Betas.

So, for about the past 15 years, I've been using and refining my own risk-rating system, which analyzes a fund's internal volatility. My approach shows exactly how bumpy or smooth a ride you'll get from any given fund, regardless of whether its volatility tracks with the stock market. By looking at each fund's track record and its history of gains and setbacks, I assign each fund in my database (over 1,400 funds in all) a risk rating from 1 (least volatile) to 5 (most volatile). With this rating, you can see at a glance how volatile a fund has been—and how volatile it's likely to be in the future. In the Directory of Mutual Funds (Appendix 4), you'll find the risk rating for every fund in my database.

Now, some 5-rated funds make their volatility worth your while: They take a rocky road but go up a steep incline. Other funds take you through some choppy waters with little forward progress. So in addition to my 1–5 ratings, I also measure a fund's volatility *compared with the returns it has given*. I call this my **reward-to-risk rating.** I like to buy funds with a superior reward-to-risk rating, which means that the more risk it entails, the more reward it must eventually bring. A 1 rating indicates the best (highest) reward to risk, and a 5 rating indicates the poorest (lowest). By looking at risk in this way, I cast a net that sweeps the entire universe of funds and brings home those that don't ask you to take risks without making those risks well worth your while.

Believe me, there are plenty of funds out there, *hundreds* of funds out there, that impose grave risks without giving investors even modest long-term gains. My favorites, on the other hand (see Figure 5-6), offer superior reward-to-risk ratings. In the Directory in Appendix 4, I list every fund's risk rating and *reward-to-risk rating*. By looking at both ratings, you can be sure to invest in funds with which you'll be comfortable in the short term, and which won't disappoint you in the longer term.

Are Bonds Safer Than Stocks?

Most investors believe that stocks and stock mutual funds are riskier than bonds and bond mutual funds, and in general, that is true. Particularly in the short run, the average stock fund tends to be more volatile than the average bond fund. But that doesn't mean you can't lose money in bonds—you certainly can! When interest rates are on the rise, long-term bond funds can be very risky indeed. As I showed you in Chapter Four, a 1% rise in interest rates can translate into an 8.7% loss in the value of your long-term bond! And junk bonds can lose you a great deal of money if the corporate issuers of the bonds default on their debt. That's why I avoid long-term bonds when interest rates are low or rising and avoid low-rated or junk bond funds at *all* times. This keeps my risks in bond funds low, and my likelihood of pleasing results quite high.

That Ugly Word: Taxes

In Chapter Seven, I'll talk about the taxes you must pay as a mutual fund investor, and I'll give you several tax-reduction strategies. But here, let me briefly raise the issue of taxes as it relates to choosing a good fund. First, let me say that tax considerations should *not* come in your selection process. They should not solely dictate what you buy and sell, or when you should do so.

Having said that, however, if you are choosing between two equally good funds, you might as well choose the one that will entail paying less to the IRS. To do that without making less, you want to look at **portfolio turnover.** I'll explain this more fully in Chapter Seven, but suffice it to say here that the lower the turnover, the lower the capital gains distribution taxes (all other things being equal).

Now, certain types or categories of funds naturally have more turnover. So you want to compare a fund's turnover to another fund *in the same category*, or to the *average* turnover for the category as a whole. In Figure 5-5, I list the average turnover for each major fund category. As you choose funds to buy, take a quick look at each fund's prospectus and compare the portfolio turnover to its category average.

Making Money Is Where It's At

After all is said and done, though—fees, services, risk, and taxes aside—what we all really want to do is to make money. How do we find the funds that will do that for us? We start with what the funds have done in the past.

Most funds will quote you their track record, usually in percentage terms, for various time periods. For example, a fund that claims a "12.5% return for the past 12 months" is stating that your starting investment of $1,000 was worth $1,125 by the end of the period.

I produce a *Mutual Fund Shopping Guide* (formerly called *Mutual Fund Yearbook*) that shows the performance of more than 1,500 major mutual funds for the year and for the past 5, 10, and 15 years. You can also pick up a copy of *Financial World*'s February or March issue, *Money* magazine's February or March issue, *Forbes* magazine's August Annual Mutual Fund issue, or *Barron's* quarterly mutual fund pull-out section to get a recap of recent fund performances.

But there are many traps in past performance ratings and statistics. The most common pitfall is that they only reflect recent past performances. My analysis shows that a good percentage of funds that outperformed the averages in a given year turned around and *under*performed in the following year. How many instances do you yourself know of (perhaps all too personally) where last year's "hot" fund turned into this year's big loser? *It is very dangerous to base your decision to buy a fund solely on recent past performance.* I, myself, look not only at recent performance numbers but at the last 5-, 10-, and 15-year performances as well. I want to buy a fund that has proved to me that it can *sustain* a track record of excellence, and is not just a flash in the pan.

Every fund's prospectus gives you its track record. Look for the section marked Per Share Income and Capital Changes or Per Share Data and Ratios. This is the most confusing part of any prospectus, but you really only need to focus on a few key numbers. The column marked Ratio of Net Investment Income (Loss) to Average Net Assets refers to the fund's annual dividends. These are expressed as a percentage, much as a bond will sport a percentage yield.

Capital gains are shown in dollar figures (per share) in the column marked Net Increase (Decrease) in Net Asset Value or Net Realized and Unrealized Gain (Loss) on Investments. Quite simply, this figure tells you how much the share price went up or down in a given year. To get a percent performance figure, divide this number by the Net Asset Value at the Beginning of the Period. If the fund, for example, started the period at $15.00 and the net increase was $2.50, the percent performance was $2.50 ÷ 15.00 = 0.1666 or a 16.7% gain for the period.

A look at these figures for *all* the years listed in the prospectus will give you a good idea of the steadiness of the fund's performance over time. You can expect a bond fund to be more consistent year-to-year than a stock fund. And watch out for stock funds with several years of losing performance.

Comparing Apples to Oranges

Once you determine a fund's past performance, how do you judge whether that track record is good or bad? Obviously, a negative performance number is not very promising. But beyond that, how do you know? By doing a little comparison shopping.

The mistake most often made in comparing past performances is comparing apples to oranges. In other words, comparing the performance of two different *types* of funds, or comparing a fund to an irrelevant index. For starters, a good rule of thumb is to compare stock funds to stock funds and bond funds to bond funds. Then go one step further: On the bond side, compare short-term bond funds to other short-term bond funds, long-term bond funds to other long-term bond funds, government bond funds to other government bond funds, and junk bond funds to other junk bond funds.

On the equities side, compare aggressive growth stock funds to other aggressive growth stock funds, equity income funds to other equity income funds, blue-chip stock funds to other blue-chip stock funds. In this way, at least you will have a fair idea of whether a given fund did better or worse than its peers—and whether you can easily find a superior fund.

You can also compare stock funds to the S&P 500 Index (listed daily in Section C of *The Wall Street Journal*). Compare corporate bond fund yields to the Merrill Lynch corporate index (also in the *Journal*); compare long-term government bond fund yields to the Lehman Brothers Long T-bond (also in the *Journal*).

What should you look for in these comparisons? Don't be swayed by short-term spurts. I look for funds that have beaten their peers and the corresponding market averages over the long term (five years or more).

I've made comparing funds easy for you. Figure 5-5 shows the average performance, risk, fees, size, and so on for each different category of funds. Compare this to the individual fund listings in Appendix 4, my fund directory. There you'll find my quality rating (A + through D) for each fund, which shows at a glance how well the fund performed against its peers. As you would expect, A is excellent while D denotes the poorest fund. You can also see how well each fund takes advantage of a rising stock market (bull market performance) and how well it protects you in a down market (bear market performance).

That Was Then, This Is Now

Make sure, too, that you are comparing figures from the same time periods. Even a difference of a month or two can have dramatic effects on fund performance results, particularly when you're using short-term figures, so when you look at a stock fund's performance for the first six months of 1994, make sure that you are comparing that figure to the S&P 500's return for the same period (i.e., January 1–June 30, 1994).

Another pitfall is to confuse gains with total return. The term **gains** often refers only to the capital gains made by the fund, the difference between the share price at the beginning of the period and its price at the end of the period. But **total return** is the more important figure. This represents your *total* reward for owning the fund, including capital gains and dividends. Particularly with a bond fund, which may offer little in the way of capital gains, you want to be sure to look at total return when analyzing performance. And make sure, once again, that when you compare two different funds, you are comparing gains to gains and total return to total return.

A Tour of My Hall of Fame All Star Mutual Funds: My Schabacker 100 All Stars

Now you have some insight into how I choose a fund. I look at fees and try to keep them as low as possible. I look at risks and again try to keep them as low as possible. I look at the services a fund group provides and demand telephone switching, automatic dividend reinvestment, and check-writing privileges on the money-market fund. I look at performance in several different ways and try to ensure that I am buying the cream of the crop. I look carefully at the prospectus and annual report to make sure I know what I am buying and that the fund matches my needs and desires. With bond funds, I make sure any bond fund I buy owns high-quality bonds. With stock funds, I look for a portfolio that's large and diversified enough to weather storms, for an experienced portfolio manager with proven success, and for different types of stock funds for each stage of the business cycle.

Once I put the 2,800 stock, bond, and hybrid mutual funds that exist today through this battery of tests, I'm left with a short list of winners that I have picked from among the major categories of funds. I call them my Schabacker 100 All Stars (see Figure 5-6).

The Schabacker 100 is a well-researched list of funds that have made the cut. I have tried to cull the also-rans from the all stars. From my large database of funds, I have selected the very best in each category: the best stock funds, hybrid funds, and bond funds. You can buy any of these funds with confidence. Of course, if you keep your portfolio balanced and stick to the strategies recommended in earlier chapters, you should do fine. I've left out the sector funds because they are so specialized and time-dependent, and have not included the cash or money market funds in my Schabacker 100. I have included the major categories in my Schabacker 100, and you can see my breakdown by category in Figure 5-8.

Appendix 4, my Directory of Mutual Funds, covers all the stock, hybrid, and bond funds I track on my computer—about 1,000 funds which are of sufficient asset size and length of performance that they can be adequately reviewed. I have highlighted those that appear in my Schabacker 100 All Stars (Figure 5-6).

I have also included an innovation: "quads" on 30 of my Schabacker 100 funds to give you more of a graphic look at how the funds in various categories differ and how they have performed in the past. Each quad has four quadrants, or general areas of information. One area gives details such as fund name, address, and phone numbers. Another presents a graph of the fund's past performance. The third gives numeric past performance statistics. And the fourth section gives examples of the investments that the fund uses in its portfolio (see Figure 5-9). With these 30 quads, you can really get to know the funds.

(text continues on page 115)

Figure 5-8

SCHABACKER 100

By Category

STOCK FUNDS

Aggressive Growth

SMALL CAP GROWTH	DIVERSIFIED AGGRESSIVE GROWTH
Columbia Special	Brandywine Fund
Kaufmann Fund	Fidelity Growth Company
Strong Discovery	Stein Roe Special
Twentieth Century Ultra	

Growth

SMALL CAP VALUE	LARGE CAP GROWTH	DIVERSIFIED GROWTH
Fidelity Value	Janus Fund	Columbia Growth
Lindner Fund	Twentieth Century Growth	Fidelity Contrafund
Mutual Beacon	Vanguard U.S. Growth	Fidelity Disciplined Equity
Oakmark		Merger Fund
		Neuberger Berman Partners
		Nicholas Fund
		Strong Opportunity
		T. Rowe Price Capital Appreciation

Growth & Income

LARGE CAP VALUE	SMALL CAP VALUE	DIVERSIFIED GROWTH & INCOME
Neuberger Berman Guardian	Royce Equity Income	Fidelity Equity Income
Mutual		Fidelity Equity Income II
Scudder Growth & Income		INVESCO Industrial Income
T. Rowe Price Equity Income		Mainstay Value
Vanguard Equity Income		Vanguard Index 500
Vanguard Windsor II		

International & Global Stock

INTERNATIONAL STOCK	GLOBAL STOCK
Scudder International	Scudder Global
T.Rowe Price International	Janus Worldwide
Twentieth Century International	
Vanguard International Growth	

HYBRID FUNDS

Asset Allocation

Fidelity Asset Manager   Vanguard Asset Allocation

Balanced

CGM Mutual	T. Rowe Price Balanced
Dodge & Cox Balanced	Vanguard Wellesley Income
Fidelity Balanced	Vanguard Wellington

Flexible

Evergreen Foundation   Fidelity Puritan   Lindner Dividend

BOND FUNDS

Corporate Bond

Fidelity Intermediate Bond	Strong Advantage
Fidelity Short Term Bond	Strong Short Term Bond
Neuberger Berman Ultra Short Bond	T. Rowe Price Short Term Bond
Scudder Short Term Bond	Vanguard Fixed Income Short Corp.

High Yield Corporate

Fidelity Capital and Income	T. Rowe Price High Yield
INVESCO High Yield	Vanguard Fixed Income High Yield

U.S. Government Bond

Benham GNMA Income	Strong Government Securities
Dreyfus Short-Intermediate Government	T. Rowe Price GNMA
Fidelity Government Securities Fund	Vanguard Fixed Income–GNMA
Lexington GNMA Income	Vanguard Fixed Income–Short Federal
	Vanguard Fixed Income–Treas. Long

Flexible Bond

Columbia Fixed Income Seciurities	Nerberger Berman Limited Maturitiy Bond
Fidelity Investment Grade Bond	Scudder Income Fund
Harbor Bond	T. Rowe Price New Income Fund
INVESCO Select Income	Vanguard Bond Index Fund
Janus Flexible Income	

Global Bond

Blanchard Short–Term Global Income	Scudder International Bond
Fidelity Global Bond	Scudder Short–Term Global Income
Fidelity Short–Term World Income	T. Rowe Price International Bond

Tax–Free Bond

Dreyfus Intermediate Municipal	Stein Roe Managed Municipals
Fidelity Aggressive Tax–Free	Strong Municipal Bond
INVESCO Tax–Free Long–Term Bond	T. Rowe Price Tax–Free Income
Loomis Sayles Municipal Bond	T. Rowe Price Tax–Free Short Intermediate
Scudder High Yield Tax–Free	Vanguard Muni Bond–Intermediate
Scudder Managed Municipal Bonds	Vanguard Muni Bond Limited–Term
Scudder Medium Term Tax–Free	Vanguard Muni Bond–Long Term

Figure 5-9

STOCK FUNDS

STRONG DISCOVERY
P.O. Box 2936 Milwaukee, WI 53201 (414)359–1400 (800)368–3863   *Quality Rating:* **B+**

Category:	**Aggressive Growth**
Portfolio Manager:	**Richard Strong**
Since:	**1988**
Ticker symbol:	**STDIX**
Size of fund ($Mil.):	**$220.6**
Minimum initial purchase:	**$1000**
Minimum subsequent purchase:	**$50**
Initial sales charge:	**N/L**
12B–1:	**No**
Management fees:	**1.00%**
Expense ratio:	**1.50**
Telephone switching:	**Yes**

Jun–88   Jun–90   Jun–92

Fund Style/Specialty:	Last 12 Months % Dividend Yield: **5.30%**
SMALL CAP GROWTH	**CHARACTERISTICS / PERFORMANCE SUMMARY** *(As of 9/30/93)*

Portfolio Statistics		Typical Holdings		
			BULL MARKET	**++**
			BEAR MARKET	**+**
Risk:	**4**	Magnetek		
Average P/E:	**22.7**	Walt Disney	1 YEAR PERF	**27.49%**
Price/Book:	**4.2**	Eastman Kodak	5 YEARS PERF, ANN	**17.03%**
Amount of cash:	**3%**	Magafoods Stores	10 YEARS PERF, ANN	**NA**
Turnover rate:	**1259%**	Canadaigua Wine CL A	15 YEARS PERF, ANN	**NA**

TWENTIETH CENTURY ULTRA
P.O. Box 419200 Kansas City, MO 64141 (816)531–5575 (800)345–2021   *Quality Rating:* **A–**

Category:	**Aggressive Growth**
Portfolio Manager:	**Management**
Since:	**1981**
Ticker symbol:	**TWCUX**
Size of fund ($Mil.):	**$6184.5**
Minimum initial purchase:	**$0**
Minimum subsequent purchase:	**$25**
Initial sales charge:	**N/L**
12B–1:	**No**
Management fees:	**1.00%**
Expense ratio:	**1.00**
Telephone switching:	**Yes**

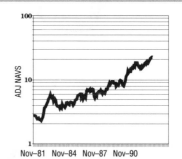

Nov–81   Nov–84   Nov–87   Nov–90

Fund Style/Specialty:	Last 12 Months % Dividend Yield: **0.00%**
SMALL CAP GROWTH	**CHARACTERISTICS / PERFORMANCE SUMMARY** *(As of 9/30/93)*

Portfolio Statistics		Typical Holdings		
		Cisco Systems	BULL MARKET	**+++**
		International Game	BEAR MARKET	**– – –**
Risk:	**5**	Technology		
Average P/E:	**33.1**	Tele–Communications CL A	1 YEAR PERF	**49.59%**
Price/Book:	**8.4**	Oracle Systems	5 YEARS PERF, ANN	**29.06%**
Amount of cash:	**11%**	Synoptics Communications	10 YEARS PERF, ANN	**15.52%**
Turnover rate:	**59%**		15 YEARS PERF, ANN	**NA**

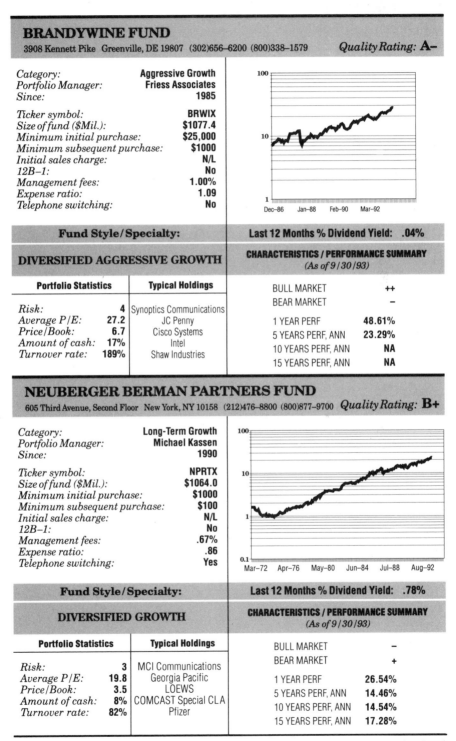

BRANDYWINE FUND

3908 Kennett Pike Greenville, DE 19807 (302)656–6200 (800)338–1579   *Quality Rating:* **A–**

Category:	**Aggressive Growth**
Portfolio Manager:	**Friess Associates**
Since:	**1985**
Ticker symbol:	**BRWIX**
Size of fund ($Mil.):	**$1077.4**
Minimum initial purchase:	**$25,000**
Minimum subsequent purchase:	**$1000**
Initial sales charge:	**N/L**
12B–1:	**No**
Management fees:	**1.00%**
Expense ratio:	**1.09**
Telephone switching:	**No**

Fund Style/Specialty:

DIVERSIFIED AGGRESSIVE GROWTH

Last 12 Months % Dividend Yield: .04%

CHARACTERISTICS / PERFORMANCE SUMMARY
(As of 9/30/93)

Portfolio Statistics		Typical Holdings
Risk:	**4**	Synoptics Communications
Average P/E:	**27.2**	JC Penny
Price/Book:	**6.7**	Cisco Systems
Amount of cash:	**17%**	Intel
Turnover rate:	**189%**	Shaw Industries

BULL MARKET	**++**
BEAR MARKET	**–**
1 YEAR PERF	**48.61%**
5 YEARS PERF, ANN	**23.29%**
10 YEARS PERF, ANN	**NA**
15 YEARS PERF, ANN	**NA**

NEUBERGER BERMAN PARTNERS FUND

605 Third Avenue, Second Floor New York, NY 10158 (212)476–8800 (800)877–9700   *Quality Rating:* **B+**

Category:	**Long-Term Growth**
Portfolio Manager:	**Michael Kassen**
Since:	**1990**
Ticker symbol:	**NPRTX**
Size of fund ($Mil.):	**$1064.0**
Minimum initial purchase:	**$1000**
Minimum subsequent purchase:	**$100**
Initial sales charge:	**N/L**
12B–1:	**No**
Management fees:	**.67%**
Expense ratio:	**.86**
Telephone switching:	**Yes**

Fund Style/Specialty:

DIVERSIFIED GROWTH

Last 12 Months % Dividend Yield: .78%

CHARACTERISTICS / PERFORMANCE SUMMARY
(As of 9/30/93)

Portfolio Statistics		Typical Holdings
Risk:	**3**	MCI Communications
Average P/E:	**19.8**	Georgia Pacific
Price/Book:	**3.5**	LOEWS
Amount of cash:	**8%**	COMCAST Special CL A
Turnover rate:	**82%**	Pfizer

BULL MARKET	**–**
BEAR MARKET	**+**
1 YEAR PERF	**26.54%**
5 YEARS PERF, ANN	**14.46%**
10 YEARS PERF, ANN	**14.54%**
15 YEARS PERF, ANN	**17.28%**

(continues)

Figure 5–9 Continued

LINDNER FUND

P.O. Box 11208   St. Louis, MO 63105   (314)727–5305   (800)995–7777   *Quality Rating:* **B+**

Category:	**Long-Term Growth**
Portfolio Manager:	**Lange/Ryback/Calahan**
Since:	**1977**
Ticker symbol:	**LDNRX**
Size of fund ($Mil.):	**$1266.4**
Minimum initial purchase:	**$2000**
Minimum subsequent purchase:	**$100**
Initial sales charge:	**N/L**
12B–1:	**No**
Management fees:	**0.55%**
Expense ratio:	**.80**
Telephone switching:	**No**

Fund Style/Specialty:	**Last 12 Months % Dividend Yield: 2.22%**

SMALL CAP VALUE	**CHARACTERISTICS / PERFORMANCE SUMMARY** *(As of 9/30/93)*

Portfolio Statistics		Typical Holdings
Risk:	**3**	Old Republic
Average P/E:	**16.8**	International
Price/Book:	**2.0**	Entergy Corp.
Amount of cash:	**8%**	Minorco
Turnover rate:	**11%**	Arkla
		Phillips Petroleum

BULL MARKET	–
BEAR MARKET	+++
1 YEAR PERF	**22.04%**
5 YEARS PERF, ANN	**12.62%**
10 YEARS PERF, ANN	**13.44%**
15 YEARS PERF, ANN	**17.75%**

MUTUAL BEACON

P.O. Box 15095   Worcester, MA 01653   (800)553–3014   *Quality Rating:* **B+**

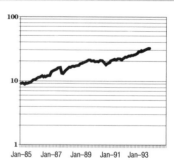

Category:	**Long-Term Growth**
Portfolio Manager:	**Michael Price**
Since:	**1985**
Ticker symbol:	**BEGRX**
Size of fund ($Mil.):	**$758.6**
Minimum initial purchase:	**$5000**
Minimum subsequent purchase:	**$100**
Initial sales charge:	**N/L**
12B–1:	**No**
Management fees:	**.60%**
Expense ratio:	**.81**
Telephone switching:	**No**

Fund Style/Specialty:	**Last 12 Months % Dividend Yield: 1.59%**

SMALL CAP VALUE	**CHARACTERISTICS / PERFORMANCE SUMMARY** *(As of 9/30/93)*

Portfolio Statistics		Typical Holdings
Risk:	**3**	Sunbeam Oster
Average P/E:	**20.2**	Multimedia, Inc.
Price/Book:	**2.0**	Pacific Telesis
Amount of cash:	**20%**	Salomon
Turnover rate:	**58%**	Fund American

BULL MARKET	–
BEAR MARKET	+
1 YEAR PERF	**26.67%**
5 YEARS PERF, ANN	**13.56%**
10 YEARS PERF, ANN	**NA**
15 YEARS PERF, ANN	**NA**

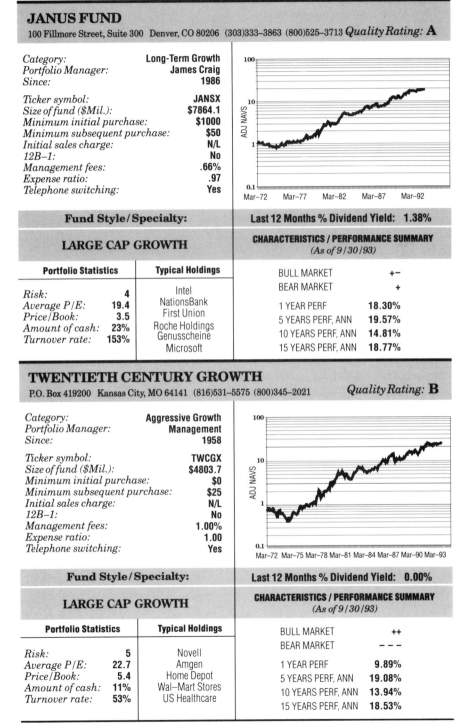

JANUS FUND

100 Fillmore Street, Suite 300   Denver, CO 80206   (303)333–3863   (800)525–3713 *Quality Rating:* **A**

Category:	**Long-Term Growth**
Portfolio Manager:	**James Craig**
Since:	**1986**
Ticker symbol:	**JANSX**
Size of fund ($Mil.):	**$7864.1**
Minimum initial purchase:	**$1000**
Minimum subsequent purchase:	**$50**
Initial sales charge:	**N/L**
12B–1:	**No**
Management fees:	**.66%**
Expense ratio:	**.97**
Telephone switching:	**Yes**

Fund Style/Specialty:

LARGE CAP GROWTH

Last 12 Months % Dividend Yield: 1.38%

CHARACTERISTICS / PERFORMANCE SUMMARY
(As of 9/30/93)

Portfolio Statistics		Typical Holdings
Risk:	**4**	Intel
Average P/E:	**19.4**	NationsBank
Price/Book:	**3.5**	First Union
Amount of cash:	**23%**	Roche Holdings
Turnover rate:	**153%**	Genusscheine
		Microsoft

BULL MARKET	+−
BEAR MARKET	+
1 YEAR PERF	**18.30%**
5 YEARS PERF, ANN	**19.57%**
10 YEARS PERF, ANN	**14.81%**
15 YEARS PERF, ANN	**18.77%**

TWENTIETH CENTURY GROWTH

P.O. Box 419200   Kansas City, MO 64141   (816)531–5575   (800)345–2021   *Quality Rating:* **B**

Category:	**Aggressive Growth**
Portfolio Manager:	**Management**
Since:	**1958**
Ticker symbol:	**TWCGX**
Size of fund ($Mil.):	**$4803.7**
Minimum initial purchase:	**$0**
Minimum subsequent purchase:	**$25**
Initial sales charge:	**N/L**
12B–1:	**No**
Management fees:	**1.00%**
Expense ratio:	**1.00**
Telephone switching:	**Yes**

Fund Style/Specialty:

LARGE CAP GROWTH

Last 12 Months % Dividend Yield: 0.00%

CHARACTERISTICS / PERFORMANCE SUMMARY
(As of 9/30/93)

Portfolio Statistics		Typical Holdings
Risk:	**5**	Novell
Average P/E:	**22.7**	Amgen
Price/Book:	**5.4**	Home Depot
Amount of cash:	**11%**	Wal–Mart Stores
Turnover rate:	**53%**	US Healthcare

BULL MARKET	++
BEAR MARKET	− − −
1 YEAR PERF	**9.89%**
5 YEARS PERF, ANN	**19.08%**
10 YEARS PERF, ANN	**13.94%**
15 YEARS PERF, ANN	**18.53%**

(continues)

Figure 5-9   Continued

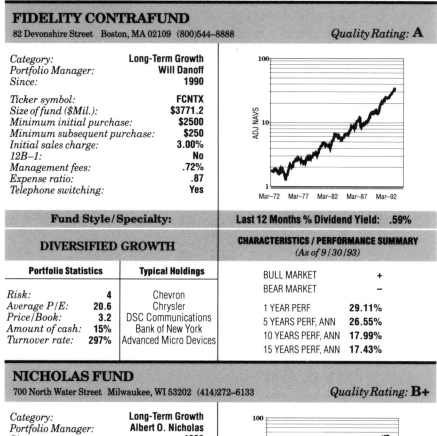

FIDELITY CONTRAFUND

82 Devonshire Street   Boston, MA 02109   (800)544-8888   *Quality Rating:* **A**

Category:	**Long-Term Growth**
Portfolio Manager:	**Will Danoff**
Since:	**1990**
Ticker symbol:	**FCNTX**
Size of fund ($Mil.):	**$3771.2**
Minimum initial purchase:	**$2500**
Minimum subsequent purchase:	**$250**
Initial sales charge:	**3.00%**
12B–1:	**No**
Management fees:	**.72%**
Expense ratio:	**.87**
Telephone switching:	**Yes**

Fund Style/Specialty:	Last 12 Months % Dividend Yield: .59%

DIVERSIFIED GROWTH

CHARACTERISTICS / PERFORMANCE SUMMARY
(As of 9/30/93)

Portfolio Statistics		Typical Holdings
Risk:	**4**	Chevron
Average P/E:	**20.6**	Chrysler
Price/Book:	**3.2**	DSC Communications
Amount of cash:	**15%**	Bank of New York
Turnover rate:	**297%**	Advanced Micro Devices

BULL MARKET	+
BEAR MARKET	–
1 YEAR PERF	**29.11%**
5 YEARS PERF, ANN	**26.55%**
10 YEARS PERF, ANN	**17.99%**
15 YEARS PERF, ANN	**17.43%**

NICHOLAS FUND

700 North Water Street   Milwaukee, WI 53202   (414)272-6133   *Quality Rating:* **B+**

Category:	**Long-Term Growth**
Portfolio Manager:	**Albert O. Nicholas**
Since:	**1969**
Ticker symbol:	**NICSX**
Size of fund ($Mil.):	**$3076.4**
Minimum initial purchase:	**$500**
Minimum subsequent purchase:	**$100**
Initial sales charge:	**N/L**
12B–1:	**No**
Management fees:	**.65%**
Expense ratio:	**.76**
Telephone switching:	**Yes**

Fund Style/Specialty:	Last 12 Months % Dividend Yield: 1.30%

DIVERSIFIED GROWTH

CHARACTERISTICS / PERFORMANCE SUMMARY
(As of 9/30/93)

Portfolio Statistics		Typical Holdings
Risk:	**3**	Philip Morris
Average P/E:	**17.5**	Mercury General
Price/Book:	**3.3**	FHLMC
Amount of cash:	**9%**	UNIFI
Turnover rate:	**10%**	Heilig Meyers

BULL MARKET	+
BEAR MARKET	+
1 YEAR PERF	**13.80%**
5 YEARS PERF, ANN	**14.27%**
10 YEARS PERF, ANN	**13.40%**
15 YEARS PERF, ANN	**17.36%**

SCUDDER GROWTH & INCOME FUND

160 Federal Street   Boston, MA 02110   (617)951–1828   (800)225–2470   *Quality Rating:* **A–**

Category:	**Growth and Income**
Portfolio Manager:	**Hoffman/Thorndike**
Since:	**1987**
Ticker symbol:	**SCDGX**
Size of fund ($Mil.):	**$1390.9**
Minimum initial purchase:	**$1000**
Minimum subsequent purchase:	**$100**
Initial sales charge:	**N/L**
12B–1:	**No**
Management fees:	**.60%**
Expense ratio:	**.97**
Telephone switching:	**Yes**

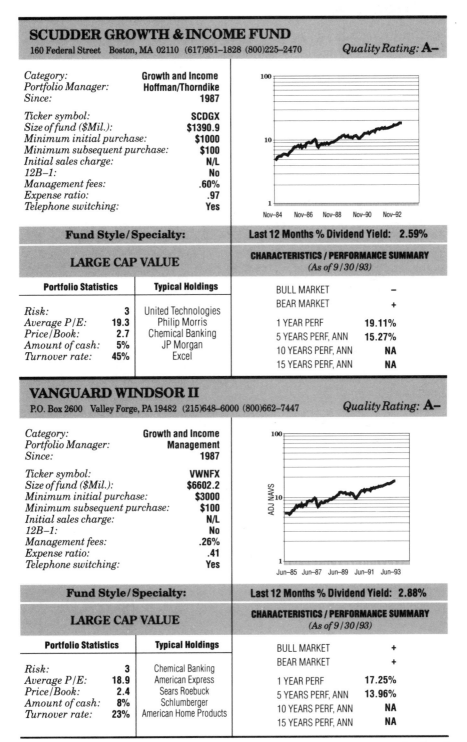

Fund Style/Specialty:	Last 12 Months % Dividend Yield: 2.59%
LARGE CAP VALUE	**CHARACTERISTICS / PERFORMANCE SUMMARY** *(As of 9/30/93)*

Portfolio Statistics		Typical Holdings			
Risk:	**3**	United Technologies	BULL MARKET	–	
Average P/E:	**19.3**	Philip Morris	BEAR MARKET	+	
Price/Book:	**2.7**	Chemical Banking	1 YEAR PERF	**19.11%**	
Amount of cash:	**5%**	JP Morgan	5 YEARS PERF, ANN	**15.27%**	
Turnover rate:	**45%**	Excel	10 YEARS PERF, ANN	**NA**	
			15 YEARS PERF, ANN	**NA**	

VANGUARD WINDSOR II

P.O. Box 2600   Valley Forge, PA 19482   (215)648–6000   (800)662–7447   *Quality Rating:* **A–**

Category:	**Growth and Income**
Portfolio Manager:	**Management**
Since:	**1987**
Ticker symbol:	**VWNFX**
Size of fund ($Mil.):	**$6602.2**
Minimum initial purchase:	**$3000**
Minimum subsequent purchase:	**$100**
Initial sales charge:	**N/L**
12B–1:	**No**
Management fees:	**.26%**
Expense ratio:	**.41**
Telephone switching:	**Yes**

Fund Style/Specialty:	Last 12 Months % Dividend Yield: 2.88%
LARGE CAP VALUE	**CHARACTERISTICS / PERFORMANCE SUMMARY** *(As of 9/30/93)*

Portfolio Statistics		Typical Holdings			
Risk:	**3**	Chemical Banking	BULL MARKET	+	
Average P/E:	**18.9**	American Express	BEAR MARKET	+	
Price/Book:	**2.4**	Sears Roebuck	1 YEAR PERF	**17.25%**	
Amount of cash:	**8%**	Schlumberger	5 YEARS PERF, ANN	**13.96%**	
Turnover rate:	**23%**	American Home Products	10 YEARS PERF, ANN	**NA**	
			15 YEARS PERF, ANN	**NA**	

(continues)

Figure 5–9   Continued

FIDELITY EQUITY INCOME II

82 Devonshire Street   Boston, MA 02109   (800)544–8888

Quality Rating: **A**

Category:	**GROWTH & INCOME**
Portfolio Manager:	**Brian Posner**
Since:	**1992**
Ticker symbol:	**FEQTX**
Size of fund ($Mil.):	**$3628.4**
Minimum initial purchase:	**$2500**
Minimum subsequent purchase:	**$250**
Initial sales charge:	**N/L**
12B–1:	**No**
Management fees:	**.53%**
Expense ratio:	**1.01**
Telephone switching:	**Yes**

Aug–90   Sep–91   Oct–92

Fund Style/Specialty:	**Last 12 Months % Dividend Yield: 2.14%**
DIVERSIFIED GROWTH & INCOME	**CHARACTERISTICS / PERFORMANCE SUMMARY** *(As of 9/30/93)*

Portfolio Statistics		Typical Holdings
Risk:	**3**	British Petroleum
Average P/E:	**16.8**	Primerica
Price/Book:	**2.2**	Bank of New York
Amount of cash:	**14%**	Reynolds Metals
Turnover rate:	**89%**	Entergy

BULL MARKET	++
BEAR MARKET	NA
1 YEAR PERF	24.32%
5 YEARS PERF, ANN	NA
10 YEARS PERF, ANN	NA
15 YEARS PERF, ANN	NA

INVESCO INDUSTRIAL INCOME FUND

P.O. Box 2040   Denver, CO 80201   (800)525–8085

Quality Rating: **A**

Category:	**Growth & Income**
Portfolio Manager:	**Kaweske/Lout/Mayer**
Since:	**1985**
Ticker symbol:	**FIIIX**
Size of fund ($Mil.):	**$3338.1**
Minimum initial purchase:	**$1000**
Minimum subsequent purchase:	**$50**
Initial sales charge:	**N/L**
12B–1:	**.25**
Management fees:	**.53%**
Expense ratio:	**.98**
Telephone switching:	**Yes**

Mar–72   Mar–77   Mar–82   Mar–87   Mar–92

Fund Style/Specialty:	**Last 12 Months % Dividend Yield: 2.62%**
DIVERSIFIED GROWTH & INCOME	**CHARACTERISTICS / PERFORMANCE SUMMARY** *(As of 9/30/93)*

Portfolio Statistics		Typical Holdings
Risk:	**3**	Contrywide Credit Industry
Average P/E:	**15.4**	McDonnel Douglas
Price/Book:	**2.7**	Telefonos De Mexico CL L
Amount of cash:	**9%**	Telefonos De Chile
Turnover rate:	**119%**	Chase Manhattan

BULL MARKET	+–
BEAR MARKET	+
1 YEAR PERF	20.79%
5 YEARS PERF, ANN	17.73%
10 YEARS PERF, ANN	16.22%
15 YEARS PERF, ANN	16.60%

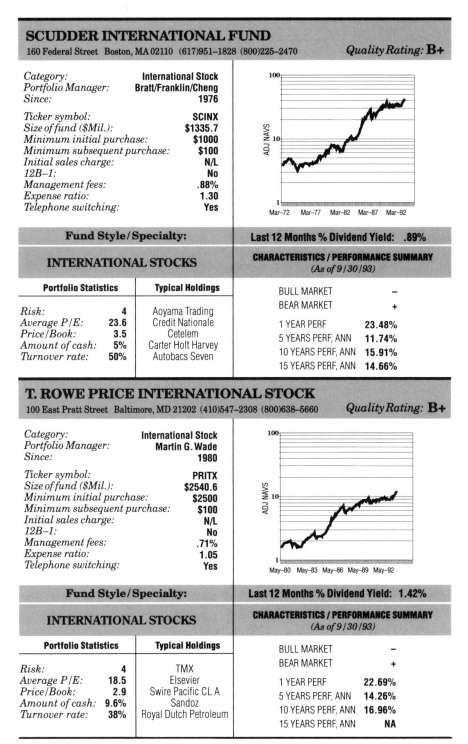

SCUDDER INTERNATIONAL FUND

160 Federal Street Boston, MA 02110 (617)951–1828 (800)225–2470   *Quality Rating:* **B+**

Category:	International Stock
Portfolio Manager:	Bratt/Franklin/Cheng
Since:	1976
Ticker symbol:	SCINX
Size of fund ($Mil.):	$1335.7
Minimum initial purchase:	$1000
Minimum subsequent purchase:	$100
Initial sales charge:	N/L
12B–1:	No
Management fees:	.88%
Expense ratio:	1.30
Telephone switching:	Yes

ADJ NAVS
Mar–72   Mar–77   Mar–82   Mar–87   Mar–92

Fund Style/Specialty:

INTERNATIONAL STOCKS

Last 12 Months % Dividend Yield: .89%

CHARACTERISTICS / PERFORMANCE SUMMARY
(As of 9/30/93)

Portfolio Statistics		Typical Holdings
Risk:	4	Aoyama Trading
Average P/E:	23.6	Credit Nationale
Price/Book:	3.5	Cetelem
Amount of cash:	5%	Carter Holt Harvey
Turnover rate:	50%	Autobacs Seven

BULL MARKET	–
BEAR MARKET	+
1 YEAR PERF	23.48%
5 YEARS PERF, ANN	11.74%
10 YEARS PERF, ANN	15.91%
15 YEARS PERF, ANN	14.66%

T. ROWE PRICE INTERNATIONAL STOCK

100 East Pratt Street Baltimore, MD 21202 (410)547–2308 (800)638–5660   *Quality Rating:* **B+**

Category:	International Stock
Portfolio Manager:	Martin G. Wade
Since:	1980
Ticker symbol:	PRITX
Size of fund ($Mil.):	$2540.6
Minimum initial purchase:	$2500
Minimum subsequent purchase:	$100
Initial sales charge:	N/L
12B–1:	No
Management fees:	.71%
Expense ratio:	1.05
Telephone switching:	Yes

ADJ NAVS
May–80   May–83   May–86   May–89   May–92

Fund Style/Specialty:

INTERNATIONAL STOCKS

Last 12 Months % Dividend Yield: 1.42%

CHARACTERISTICS / PERFORMANCE SUMMARY
(As of 9/30/93)

Portfolio Statistics		Typical Holdings
Risk:	4	TMX
Average P/E:	18.5	Elsevier
Price/Book:	2.9	Swire Pacific CL A
Amount of cash:	9.6%	Sandoz
Turnover rate:	38%	Royal Dutch Petroleum

BULL MARKET	–
BEAR MARKET	+
1 YEAR PERF	22.69%
5 YEARS PERF, ANN	14.26%
10 YEARS PERF, ANN	16.96%
15 YEARS PERF, ANN	NA

(continues)

Figure 5-9   Continued

HYBRID FUNDS/ALL WEATHER FUNDS

FIDELITY BALANCED

82 Devonshire Street   Boston, MA 02109   (800)544-8888   *Quality Rating:* **A+**

Category:	**Balanced**
Portfolio Manager:	**Bob Haber**
Since:	**1988**
Ticker symbol:	**FBALX**
Size of fund ($Mil.):	**$2996.9**
Minimum initial purchase:	**$2500**
Minimum subsequent purchase:	**$250**
Initial sales charge:	**N/L**
12B–1:	**No**
Management fees:	**.54%**
Expense ratio:	**.96**
Telephone switching:	**Yes**

(Chart: Nov–86 Nov–89 Nov–92)

Fund Style/Specialty:	**Last 12 Months % Dividend Yield: 4.68%**
VALUE	**CHARACTERISTICS / PERFORMANCE SUMMARY** *(As of 9/30/93)*

Portfolio Statistics		Typical Holdings
Risk:	**3**	Apple Computer
Average P/E:	**19.8**	General Motors CL H
Price/Book:	**2.3**	Williams Companies
Amount of cash:	**1%**	Ensearch
Turnover rate:	**242%**	Sante Fe Pacific

BULL MARKET	–
BEAR MARKET	+
1 YEAR PERF	**18.53%**
5 YEARS PERF, ANN	**13.89%**
10 YEARS PERF, ANN	**NA**
15 YEARS PERF, ANN	**NA**

VANGUARD WELLESLEY INCOME FUND

P.O. Box 2600 Valley Forge, PA 19482 (215)648–6000 (800)662–7447   *Quality Rating:* **A**

Category:	**Balanced**
Portfolio Manager:	**McEvoy/Ryan**
Since:	**1982**
Ticker symbol:	**VWINX**
Size of fund ($Mil.):	**$4281.0**
Minimum initial purchase:	**$3000**
Minimum subsequent purchase:	**$100**
Initial sales charge:	**N/L**
12B–1:	**No**
Management fees:	**.20%**
Expense ratio:	**.35**
Telephone switching:	**Yes**

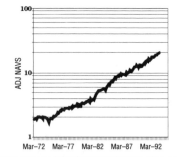

(Chart: ADJ NAVS; Mar–72 Mar–77 Mar–82 Mar–87 Mar–92)

Fund Style/Specialty:	**Last 12 Months % Dividend Yield: 5.95%**
LARGE CAP VALUE	**CHARACTERISTICS / PERFORMANCE SUMMARY** *(As of 9/30/93)*

Portfolio Statistics		Typical Holdings
Risk:	**3**	El DuPont DE Nemours
Average P/E:	**16.1**	Mobil
Price/Book:	**2.0**	Royal Dutch Petroleum
Amount of cash:	**2%**	Boatner's Bancshares
Turnover rate:	**40%**	Texaco

BULL MARKET	–
BEAR MARKET	+++
1 YEAR PERF	**17.07%**
5 YEARS PERF, ANN	**14.18%**
10 YEARS PERF, ANN	**14.32%**
15 YEARS PERF, ANN	**13.72%**

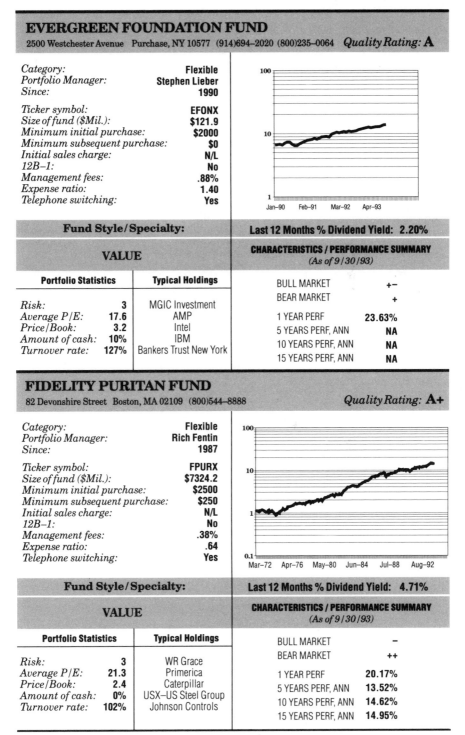

EVERGREEN FOUNDATION FUND

2500 Westchester Avenue   Purchase, NY 10577   (914)694–2020   (800)235–0064   *Quality Rating:* **A**

Category:	Flexible
Portfolio Manager:	Stephen Lieber
Since:	1990

Ticker symbol:	EFONX
Size of fund ($Mil.):	$121.9
Minimum initial purchase:	$2000
Minimum subsequent purchase:	$0
Initial sales charge:	N/L
12B–1:	No
Management fees:	.88%
Expense ratio:	1.40
Telephone switching:	Yes

Jan–90   Feb–91   Mar–92   Apr–93

Fund Style/Specialty:	Last 12 Months % Dividend Yield: 2.20%
VALUE	**CHARACTERISTICS / PERFORMANCE SUMMARY** (As of 9/30/93)

Portfolio Statistics		Typical Holdings
Risk:	3	MGIC Investment
Average P/E:	17.6	AMP
Price/Book:	3.2	Intel
Amount of cash:	10%	IBM
Turnover rate:	127%	Bankers Trust New York

BULL MARKET	+–
BEAR MARKET	+
1 YEAR PERF	23.63%
5 YEARS PERF, ANN	NA
10 YEARS PERF, ANN	NA
15 YEARS PERF, ANN	NA

FIDELITY PURITAN FUND

82 Devonshire Street   Boston, MA 02109   (800)544–8888   *Quality Rating:* **A+**

Category:	Flexible
Portfolio Manager:	Rich Fentin
Since:	1987

Ticker symbol:	FPURX
Size of fund ($Mil.):	$7324.2
Minimum initial purchase:	$2500
Minimum subsequent purchase:	$250
Initial sales charge:	N/L
12B–1:	No
Management fees:	.38%
Expense ratio:	.64
Telephone switching:	Yes

Mar–72   Apr–76   May–80   Jun–84   Jul–88   Aug–92

Fund Style/Specialty:	Last 12 Months % Dividend Yield: 4.71%
VALUE	**CHARACTERISTICS / PERFORMANCE SUMMARY** (As of 9/30/93)

Portfolio Statistics		Typical Holdings
Risk:	3	WR Grace
Average P/E:	21.3	Primerica
Price/Book:	2.4	Caterpillar
Amount of cash:	0%	USX–US Steel Group
Turnover rate:	102%	Johnson Controls

BULL MARKET	–
BEAR MARKET	++
1 YEAR PERF	20.17%
5 YEARS PERF, ANN	13.52%
10 YEARS PERF, ANN	14.62%
15 YEARS PERF, ANN	14.95%

(continues)

Figure 5–9   Continued

BOND FUNDS

FIDELITY INTERMEDIATE BOND

82 Devonshire Street Boston, MA 02109 (800)544–8888   *Quality Rating:* **B+**

Category:	**Corporate Bond**
Portfolio Manager:	**Michael Gray**
Since:	**1987**
Ticker symbol:	**FTHRX**
Size of fund ($Mil.):	**$1645.1**
Minimum initial purchase:	**$2500**
Minimum subsequent purchase:	**$250**
Initial sales charge:	**N/L**
12B–1:	**No**
Management fees:	**.33%**
Expense ratio:	**.63**
Telephone switching:	**Yes**

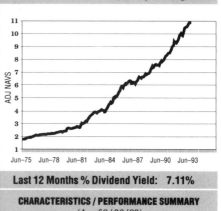

Fund Style/Specialty:	Last 12 Months % Dividend Yield: 7.11%
CORPORATE BOND	**CHARACTERISTICS / PERFORMANCE SUMMARY** *(As of 9/30/93)*

Portfolio Statistics		Typical Holdings			
Risk:	**2**	US Treasury Note	9.375%	BULL MARKET	– –
Average Maturity:	**9.2**	US Treasury Bond	8.125%	BEAR MARKET	+++
Avg. Wt. Coupon:	**8.7**	US Treasury Bond	8.875%	1 YEAR PERF	**11.38%**
Amount of cash:	**0%**	US Treasury Note	9.25%	5 YEARS PERF, ANN	**10.44%**
Turnover rate:	**80%**	US Treasury Bond	7.875%	10 YEARS PERF, ANN	**10.92%**
				15 YEARS PERF, ANN	**11.33%**

SCUDDER SHORT TERM BOND

160 Federal Street Boston, MA 02110 (617)951–1828 (800)225–2470   *Quality Rating:* **B+**

Category:	**Corporate Bond**
Portfolio Manager:	**Poor/Gootkind**
Since:	**1989**
Ticker symbol:	**SCSTX**
Size of fund ($Mil.):	**$2926.7**
Minimum initial purchase:	**$1000**
Minimum subsequent purchase:	**$100**
Initial sales charge:	**N/L**
12B–1:	**No**
Management fees:	**.55%**
Expense ratio:	**.44**
Telephone switching:	**Yes**

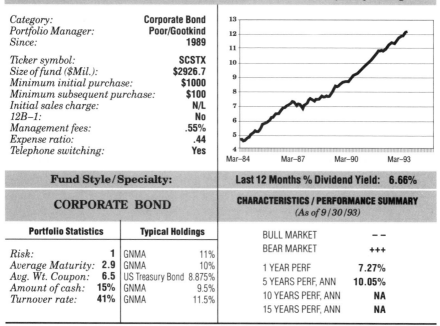

Fund Style/Specialty:	Last 12 Months % Dividend Yield: 6.66%
CORPORATE BOND	**CHARACTERISTICS / PERFORMANCE SUMMARY** *(As of 9/30/93)*

Portfolio Statistics		Typical Holdings			
Risk:	**1**	GNMA	11%	BULL MARKET	– –
Average Maturity:	**2.9**	GNMA	10%	BEAR MARKET	+++
Avg. Wt. Coupon:	**6.5**	US Treasury Bond	8.875%	1 YEAR PERF	**7.27%**
Amount of cash:	**15%**	GNMA	9.5%	5 YEARS PERF, ANN	**10.05%**
Turnover rate:	**41%**	GNMA	11.5%	10 YEARS PERF, ANN	**NA**
				15 YEARS PERF, ANN	**NA**

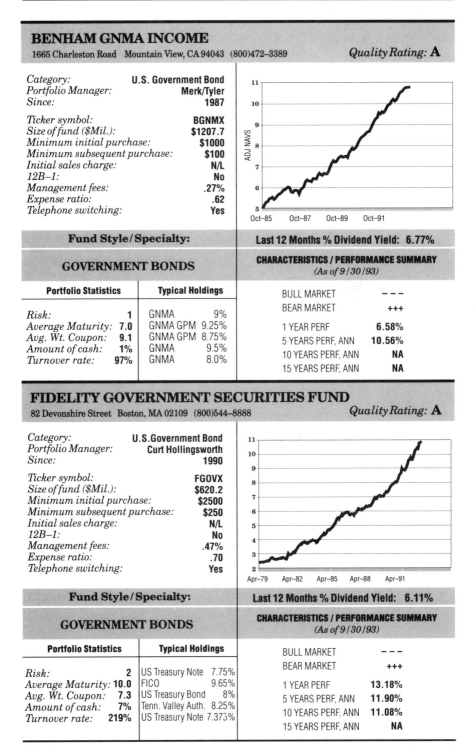

BENHAM GNMA INCOME

1665 Charleston Road   Mountain View, CA 94043   (800)472–3389   *Quality Rating:* **A**

Category:	U.S. Government Bond
Portfolio Manager:	Merk/Tyler
Since:	1987
Ticker symbol:	BGNMX
Size of fund ($Mil.):	$1207.7
Minimum initial purchase:	$1000
Minimum subsequent purchase:	$100
Initial sales charge:	N/L
12B–1:	No
Management fees:	.27%
Expense ratio:	.62
Telephone switching:	Yes

Fund Style/Specialty:

GOVERNMENT BONDS

Last 12 Months % Dividend Yield: 6.77%

CHARACTERISTICS / PERFORMANCE SUMMARY
(As of 9/30/93)

Portfolio Statistics		Typical Holdings	
Risk:	1	GNMA	9%
Average Maturity:	7.0	GNMA GPM	9.25%
Avg. Wt. Coupon:	9.1	GNMA GPM	8.75%
Amount of cash:	1%	GNMA	9.5%
Turnover rate:	97%	GNMA	8.0%

BULL MARKET	– – –
BEAR MARKET	+++
1 YEAR PERF	6.58%
5 YEARS PERF, ANN	10.56%
10 YEARS PERF, ANN	NA
15 YEARS PERF, ANN	NA

FIDELITY GOVERNMENT SECURITIES FUND

82 Devonshire Street   Boston, MA 02109   (800)544–8888   *Quality Rating:* **A**

Category:	U.S. Government Bond
Portfolio Manager:	Curt Hollingsworth
Since:	1990
Ticker symbol:	FGOVX
Size of fund ($Mil.):	$620.2
Minimum initial purchase:	$2500
Minimum subsequent purchase:	$250
Initial sales charge:	N/L
12B–1:	No
Management fees:	.47%
Expense ratio:	.70
Telephone switching:	Yes

Fund Style/Specialty:

GOVERNMENT BONDS

Last 12 Months % Dividend Yield: 6.11%

CHARACTERISTICS / PERFORMANCE SUMMARY
(As of 9/30/93)

Portfolio Statistics		Typical Holdings	
Risk:	2	US Treasury Note	7.75%
Average Maturity:	10.0	FICO	9.65%
Avg. Wt. Coupon:	7.3	US Treasury Bond	8%
Amount of cash:	7%	Tenn. Valley Auth.	8.25%
Turnover rate:	219%	US Treasury Note	7.375%

BULL MARKET	– – –
BEAR MARKET	+++
1 YEAR PERF	13.18%
5 YEARS PERF, ANN	11.90%
10 YEARS PERF, ANN	11.08%
15 YEARS PERF, ANN	NA

(continues)

Figure 5-9 Continued

FIDELITY INVESTMENT GRADE BOND

82 Devonshire Street Boston, MA 02109 (800)544-8888   *Quality Rating:* **A**

Category:	**Flexible Bond**
Portfolio Manager:	**Michael Gray**
Since:	**1987**
Ticker symbol:	**FBNDX**
Size of fund ($Mil.):	**$997.4**
Minimum initial purchase:	**$2500**
Minimum subsequent purchase:	**$250**
Initial sales charge:	**N/L**
12B–1:	**No**
Management fees:	**.38%**
Expense ratio:	**.70**
Telephone switching:	**Yes**

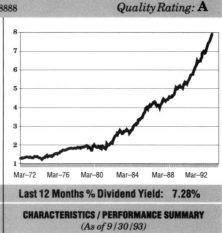

Fund Style/Specialty:	Last 12 Months % Dividend Yield: 7.28%

FLEXIBLE BOND

CHARACTERISTICS / PERFORMANCE SUMMARY
(As of 9/30/93)

Portfolio Statistics		Typical Holdings	
Risk:	**2**	US Treasury Bond 8.125%	
Average Maturity:	**13.2**	US Treasury Bond 8.875%	
Avg. Wt. Coupon:	**8.5**	GNMA	9%
Amount of cash:	**0%**	Gov't of Mexico ARM	
Turnover rate:	**77%**	US Treasury Bond 7.875%	

BULL MARKET	– –
BEAR MARKET	+++
1 YEAR PERF	**15.33%**
5 YEARS PERF, ANN	**12.40%**
10 YEARS PERF, ANN	**11.55%**
15 YEARS PERF, ANN	**10.27%**

JANUS FLEXIBLE INCOME

100 Fillmore Street Suite 300 Denver, CO 80206 (303)333–3863 (800)525–3713 *Quality Rating:* **A–**

Category:	**Flexible Bond**
Portfolio Manager:	**Ronald Speaker**
Since:	**1990**
Ticker symbol:	**JAFIX**
Size of fund ($Mil.):	**$358.6**
Minimum initial purchase:	**$1000**
Minimum subsequent purchase:	**$50**
Initial sales charge:	**N/L**
12B–1:	**No**
Management fees:	**.54%**
Expense ratio:	**1.00**
Telephone switching:	**Yes**

Fund Style/Specialty:	Last 12 Months % Dividend Yield: 7.64%

FLEXIBLE BOND

CHARACTERISTICS / PERFORMANCE SUMMARY
(As of 9/30/93)

Portfolio Statistics		Typical Holdings	
Risk:	**3**	US Treasury Note	7.65%
Average Maturity:	**14.0**	Orion Capital	9.125%
Avg. Wt. Coupon:	**10.2**	Warner Commun.	11.5%
Amount of cash:	**7%**	Oryx Energy	10.37%
Turnover rate:	**210%**	MEDIQ/PRN Life Support	
			11.125%

BULL MARKET	– –
BEAR MARKET	++
1 YEAR PERF	**14.25%**
5 YEARS PERF, ANN	**10.66%**
10 YEARS PERF, ANN	**NA**
15 YEARS PERF, ANN	**NA**

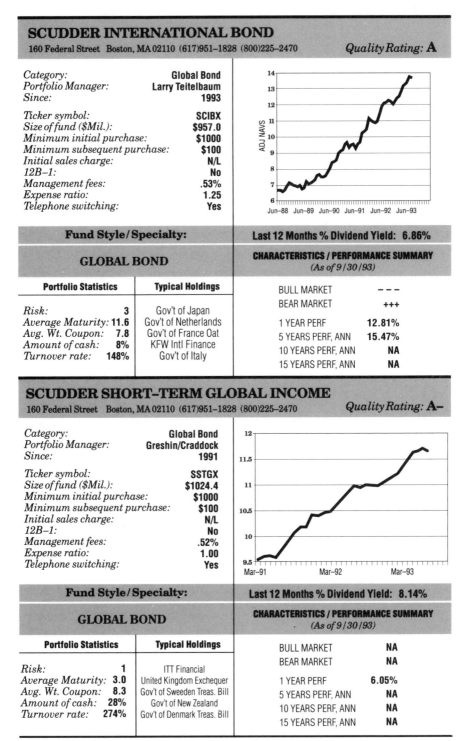

SCUDDER INTERNATIONAL BOND
160 Federal Street Boston, MA 02110 (617)951–1828 (800)225–2470   *Quality Rating:* **A**

Category:	**Global Bond**
Portfolio Manager:	**Larry Teitelbaum**
Since:	**1993**
Ticker symbol:	**SCIBX**
Size of fund ($Mil.):	**$957.0**
Minimum initial purchase:	**$1000**
Minimum subsequent purchase:	**$100**
Initial sales charge:	**N/L**
12B–1:	**No**
Management fees:	**.53%**
Expense ratio:	**1.25**
Telephone switching:	**Yes**

Fund Style/Specialty:

GLOBAL BOND

Portfolio Statistics	Typical Holdings
Risk: **3**	Gov't of Japan
Average Maturity: **11.6**	Gov't of Netherlands
Avg. Wt. Coupon: **7.8**	Gov't of France Oat
Amount of cash: **8%**	KFW Intl Finance
Turnover rate: **148%**	Gov't of Italy

Last 12 Months % Dividend Yield: 6.86%

CHARACTERISTICS / PERFORMANCE SUMMARY
(As of 9/30/93)

BULL MARKET	– – –
BEAR MARKET	+++
1 YEAR PERF	**12.81%**
5 YEARS PERF, ANN	**15.47%**
10 YEARS PERF, ANN	**NA**
15 YEARS PERF, ANN	**NA**

SCUDDER SHORT–TERM GLOBAL INCOME
160 Federal Street Boston, MA 02110 (617)951–1828 (800)225–2470   *Quality Rating:* **A–**

Category:	**Global Bond**
Portfolio Manager:	**Greshin/Craddock**
Since:	**1991**
Ticker symbol:	**SSTGX**
Size of fund ($Mil.):	**$1024.4**
Minimum initial purchase:	**$1000**
Minimum subsequent purchase:	**$100**
Initial sales charge:	**N/L**
12B–1:	**No**
Management fees:	**.52%**
Expense ratio:	**1.00**
Telephone switching:	**Yes**

Fund Style/Specialty:

GLOBAL BOND

Portfolio Statistics	Typical Holdings
Risk: **1**	ITT Financial
Average Maturity: **3.0**	United Kingdom Exchequer
Avg. Wt. Coupon: **8.3**	Gov't of Sweeden Treas. Bill
Amount of cash: **28%**	Gov't of New Zealand
Turnover rate: **274%**	Gov't of Denmark Treas. Bill

Last 12 Months % Dividend Yield: 8.14%

CHARACTERISTICS / PERFORMANCE SUMMARY
(As of 9/30/93)

BULL MARKET	**NA**
BEAR MARKET	**NA**
1 YEAR PERF	**6.05%**
5 YEARS PERF, ANN	**NA**
10 YEARS PERF, ANN	**NA**
15 YEARS PERF, ANN	**NA**

(continues)

Figure 5–9   Continued

SCUDDER MANAGED MUNICIPAL BONDS

160 Federal Street   Boston, MA 02110 (617)951–1828 (800)225–2470   *Quality Rating:* **A**

Category:	**Municipal Bond**
Portfolio Manager:	**Carleton/Condon**
Since:	**1986**
Ticker symbol:	**SCMBX**
Size of fund ($Mil.):	**$879.4**
Minimum initial purchase:	**$1000**
Minimum subsequent purchase:	**$100**
Initial sales charge:	**N/L**
12B–1:	**No**
Management fees:	**.51%**
Expense ratio:	**.64**
Telephone switching:	**Yes**

Fund Style/Specialty:	Last 12 Months % Dividend Yield: 5.07%
TAX–EXEMPT BONDS	**CHARACTERISTICS / PERFORMANCE SUMMARY** *(As of 9/30/93)*

Portfolio Statistics		Typical Holdings
Risk:	3	TX Rev. Muni Pwr Agency RFDC Ins
Average Maturity:	12.7	MA WTR Resource Auth
Avg. Wt. Coupon:	5.9	AK North Slope GO INS
Amount of cash:	12%	FL REV Homeownership MTG
Turnover rate:	32%	HSG FIN
		WA REV PUB PWR SPLY SYS Proj

BULL MARKET	– –
BEAR MARKET	+++
1 YEAR PERF	**14.63%**
5 YEARS PERF, ANN	**10.90%**
10 YEARS PERF, ANN	**10.70%**
15 YEARS PERF, ANN	**8.45%**

VANGUARD MUNI BOND–INTERMEDIATE

P.O. Box 2600   Valley Forge, PA 19482 (215)648–6000 (800)662–7447   *Quality Rating:* **B+**

Category:	**Municipal Bond**
Portfolio Manager:	**MacKinnon/Ryon**
Since:	**1981**
Ticker symbol:	**VWITX**
Size of fund ($Mil.):	**$4403.7**
Minimum initial purchase:	**$3000**
Minimum subsequent purchase:	**$100**
Initial sales charge:	**N/L**
12B–1:	**No**
Management fees:	**.12%**
Expense ratio:	**.23**
Telephone switching:	**Yes**

Fund Style/Specialty:	Last 12 Months % Dividend Yield: 5.16%
TAX–EXEMPT BONDS	**CHARACTERISTICS / PERFORMANCE SUMMARY** *(As of 9/30/93)*

Portfolio Statistics		Typical Holdings
Risk:	2	MA WTR Resource Auth
Average Maturity:	8.1	NY Triborough Bridge &
Avg. Wt. Coupon:	6.6	Tunnel Auth
Amount of cash:	10%	CA Los Angeles Transp
Turnover rate:	32%	Com Sales Tax
		GA State Go
		NJ Tpk Auth

BULL MARKET	– –
BEAR MARKET	+++
1 YEAR PERF	**12.56%**
5 YEARS PERF, ANN	**10.05%**
10 YEARS PERF, ANN	**10.15%**
15 YEARS PERF, ANN	**7.36%**

NOTE: The average P/E and Price/Book statistics, as well as the top holdings are provided by Morningstar, Inc.

What Makes a Fund an All-Star?

A lot goes into making a fund an All-Star. And a lot of research goes into my Schabacker 100. Some of my research comes from reading about the fund, some from checking statistics, and some from talking to the portfolio manager. I want a low risk (1 is lowest) and a high reward-to-risk history (1 is best). I also like funds with no sales charge and fees that are low so that the five-year cost is low ($ is best, $$$ is worst). Ordinarily, conservative me likes a fund with great performance in bear markets as well as in bull markets. In most cases, I favor a fund that has an experienced portfolio manager that has seen many cycles in the stock market, and if I can get a chance to chat with the portfolio manager about his or her views, that's even better.

I like a nonvolatile performance history for the fund, a low-portfolio price-to-earnings ratio, and a low-portfolio price-to-book ratio. Of course I want to understand the securities held and to feel that the fund's investment style makes sense.

Put it all together, and you get the 40 stock funds, 10 hybrid funds, and 50 bond funds that make up my Schabacker 100.

All-Weather Hall of Fame Funds

If you are a Buy and Hold investor, you'll want to choose funds that you can feel comfortable owning for the long haul (see Appendix 2 for model portfolios). And if you follow my Asset Allocation model, you'll also want good long-term holds—even if you vary your weighting in these funds with the ebb and flow of the market. For you, I recommend my Diversified Growth, Diversified Growth & Income, and my Hybrid All-Stars.

If you follow my Business Cycle Market Timing approach, you'll want to move from one type of fund to another, depending on where in the business cycle we are at any given time. At the same time, you'll want the very best funds in each of my four equity categories (small gap growth, small cap value, large cap value, and large cap growth) and in three bond fund categories (long-term bonds, intermediate-term bonds, and short-term bonds). Figure 5-9 shows which funds fall into each of these categories. And in Appendix 2, I show how you might put them together into a model portfolio.

My Seven Favorite Families

Among my favorite funds, I have found that seven mutual fund companies—or "families" of funds—tend to appear again and again. These seven families (Figure 5-10) have low fees, outstanding management, excellent customer service, and superior performance in many different funds. You'll be hearing even more about these cream-of-the-crop families throughout this book, but let me introduce you to them now in Figure 5-11. The figure lists vital statistics on these fund groups, including management fees, assets, number of funds, and more. You can easily see why these fund families rank in the top echelon of mutual funds. I hope this information makes our investing easier as well.

Summary of Chapter Five

- To choose winning funds from among the 2,800 mutual funds and 20 different categories of funds today, you must consider each fund's investment objective, portfolio manager, loads and fees, convenient services (like telephone switching and free automatic reinvestment of dividends), risk, and portfolio turnover.

- When it comes to performance, ignore the short-term stars and go for long-term winners. You also want to be sure you are comparing funds with others of the same style and across the same time periods.

- My favorite all-star funds make up my Schabacker 100, a list of the 100 top funds for reliability and all-around quality.

- Some of my Schabacker 100 are all-weather funds, others are tied to the four phases of the business cycle.

- I've also singled out seven favorite mutual fund companies (or families) for their excellent service and performance.

Figure 5–10

Seven Favorite Families

FIDELITY INVESTMENTS		
	Investment Advisor	Fidelity Management & Research Company
82 Devonshire Street Boston, MA 02109	*Custodians*	State Street Bank & Trust Company Boston, MA 02110
800•544•8888 801•534•1910	*Transfer Agent*	Fidelity Service Company 82 Devonshire Street Boston, MA 02109
	Qualified for Sale	In all states, DC and PR
	Switch Method	Telephone & Mail
INVESCO		
	Investment Advisor	INVESCO Funds Group, Inc.
7800 East Union Avenue Denver, Colorado 80237	*Custodians*	INVESCO Trust Co. 7800 East Union Avenue Denver, Colorado 80237
800•525•8085	*Transfer Agent*	INVESCO Trust Co. 7800 East Union Avenue Denver, Colorado 80237
	Qualified for Sale	In all states, DC and PR
	Switch Method	Telephone & Mail
SCUDDER, STEVENS & CLARK		
	Investment Advisor	Scudder, Stevens & Clark
160 Federal Street Boston, MA 02110	*Custodians*	Development & International Funds– Brown Brothers, Harriman Boston, MA 02109
800•225•2470 617•439•4640	*Custodians*	Growth and Income, Capital Growth, Income State Street Bank & Trust Company Boston, MA 02110
	Transfer Agent	Scudder Service Corporation Box 9046 Boston, MA 02205
	Distributor	Scudder Fund Distributors 160 Federal Street Boston, MA 02110
	Qualified for Sale	In all states, DC and PR
	Switch Method	Telephone & Mail

(continues)

Figure 5-10 Continued

STRONG		
P.O. Box 2936 Milwaukee, Wisconsin 53201 800•368•3863 414•359•1400	*Investment Advisor*	Strong/Corneliuson Capital Management, Inc.
	Custodians	Firstar Trust Comapny P.O. Box 701 Milwaukee, Wisconsin 53201
	Distributor	Strong/Corneliuson Capital Management, Inc. P.O. Box 2936 Milwaukee, Wisconsin 53201
	Qualified for Sale	In all states, DC and PR
	Switch Method	Telephone & Mail

T. ROWE PRICE		
100 East Pratt Street Baltimore, MD 21202 800•638•5660 410•547•2308	*Investment Advisor*	T. Rowe Price Associates, Inc.
	Custodians	State Street Bank & Trust Company P.O. Box 2357 Boston, MA 02107
	Distributor	T. Rowe Price Investment Services 100 East Pratt St. Baltimore, MD 21202
	Qualified for Sale	In all states, DC and PR
	Switch Method	Telephone & Mail

TWENTIETH CENTURY INVESTORS		
P.O. Box 419200 Kansas City, MO 64141–6200 800•345•2021 816•531•5575	*Investment Advisor*	Investors Research Corporation
	Custodians	United States Trust Company of NY New York, NY
	Transfer Agent	J. E. Stowers & Company P.O. Box 419200 Kansas City, MO 64141–6200
	Qualified for Sale	In all states and DC
	Switch Method	Telephone & Mail

VANGUARD GROUP		
P.O. Box 2600 Valley Forge, PA 19482 800•662•7447 215•648•6000	*Investment Advisor*	Wellington Management Company
	Custodians	Vanguard Marketing Corporation Valley Forge, PA 19482
	Qualified for Sale	In all states and DC
	Switch Method	Telephone & Mail

Figure 5–11

Fund Family Facts

FUND FAMILY	Average Mgmt. Fee (%)	Average Expense Ratio		Assets ($ Billion)	Number of Funds	Handled by These Discount Brokers*
		Equity	**Bond**			
Fidelity	.30 – 1.00	1.63	.80	149	113	F,J,S
INVESCO	.50–.75	1.30	1.08	8	22	F,J,S
Scudder	.50 –1.00	1.43	.92	15	28	J,S
Strong	.60–1.00	1.38	.74	14	14	F,J,S
T. Rowe Price	.25 –1.00	1.19	.90	25	43	F,J,S
20th Century	1.00	1.00	1.00	18	13	J,S
Vanguard	.10 –.50	0.43	.25	91	70	J,S

F = Fidelity Discount Brokerage   J = Jack White&Co.   S = Charles Schwab

Chapter Six

Buying and Selling Smart

Congratulations! You've made it to the fourth quadrant of our Mutual Fund Winners Circle. By now, you know what type of strategy suits you best, what to look for in any fund you buy, which funds are right for each stage of the business cycle, and which funds rank as my Hall of Fame All Stars.

Now that you're ready to invest, I'd like to share with you some of the secrets I've learned over the years for buying and selling smart. These simple habits and techniques can save you money and time, and can make your investing life a whole lot easier.

Watching the Fund Costs

When I buy a fund, I want to pay as little as I possibly can in fees and commissions. That's why my first choice among mutual funds is often a no-load fund. All other things being equal, I'll choose a fund with no up-front load, no redemption fee, no 12b-1, and low annual management fees. As we learned in Chapter Four, paying less doesn't mean you sacrifice anything in performance or service.

In Appendix 4, I list the up-front fees for every fund in my database, as well as whether or not the fund charges any redemption fee or 12b-1. And you'll note that my Hall of Famers are some of the lowest-cost funds around.

In fact, my first tip for buying smart is simply to realize that you don't have to pay high fees to get high quality. If you use a top no-load family like Vanguard or T. Rowe Price, you'll put less money into the funds' pocketbooks and more money toward your own bottom line.

Here are seven more ways to cut fees and expenses:

1. Avoid fund families and funds that charge high 12b-1 fees (greater than 0.25%).
2. Make sure you invest in a fund that charges *no fees* for reinvesting dividends.
3. If you use mutual funds in your IRA, use a single fund family for your custodian so that you pay only one custodial fee. (We'll discuss other retirement planning strategies in Chapter Eight.)
4. Use the no-transaction-fee funds offered through Schwab, Fidelity, and Jack White (see Figure 6-1).
5. Avoid funds with back-end loads and redemption fees (see my Directory, Appendix 4).
6. Look in the Directory for funds with one $ and avoid funds with $$$ to minimize costs when choosing between two similar funds.
7. Watch out for extra switching fees charged by your fund family. Find out what these fees are *before* you make a switch.

Buying Smart

Of course, in addition to saving money, you also want to make your purchase as simple, straightforward, and convenient as possible. Remember one of the advantages of mutual funds is that they are so convenient to buy and sell.

When You're First Starting Out

Take some time to set up your account just the way you want it. If you do it right from the outset, you're more likely to stay on track. Again, this is fairly easy. Back in Chapter Five, when you were choosing the funds you wanted to buy, you requested a prospectus from the funds you were interested in. Each prospectus should have come with an application form. If you didn't get one,

(text continues on page 125)

Figure 6–1

Discount Broker No-Transaction-Fee Funds

Schwab's
Mutual Fund OneSource™

Behnam CA Municipal High-Yield
Benham CA Tax-Free Intermediate
Benham CA Tax-Fee Long
Benham CA Tax-Free Short
Benham Equity Growth Fund
Benham European Government Bond Fund
Benham GNMA Income
Benham Gold Equities Index
Benham Income & Growth Fund
Benham National Tax-Free Intermediate-Term
Benham National Tax-Free Long-Term
Benham Target Maturities 1995
Benham Target Maturities 2000
Benham Target Maturities 2005
Benham Target Maturities 2010
Benham Target Maturities 2015
Benham Target Maturities 2020
Benham Treasury Note
Berger 100
Berger 101
Cappiello-Rushmore Emerging Growth
Cappiello-Rushmore Growth
Cappiello-Rushmore Utility Income
Cohen & Steers Realty Shares, Inc.
Dreyfus A Bonds Plus
Dreyfus Appreciation
Dreyfus Balanced Fund
Dreyfus CA Intermediate Municipal Bond
Dreyfus CA Tax-Exempt Bond
Dreyfus Capital Value (Closed to new accounts)
Dreyfus CT Intermediate Municipal Bond
Dreyfus FL Intermediate Municipal Bond
Dreyfus Fund
Dreyfus General CA Municipal Bond
Dreyfus General Municipal Bond
Dreyfus General NY Municipal Bond
Dreyfus GNMA
Dreyfus Growth & Income
Dreyfus Growth Opportunity
Dreyfus Insured Municipal Bond
Dreyfus Intermediate Municipal Bond
Dreyfus MA Intermediate Municipal Bond
Dreyfus MA Tax-Exempt Bond
Dreyfus Municipal Bond
Dreyfus New Leaders
Dreyfus NJ Intermediate Municipal Bond
Dreyfus NJ Municipal Bond
Dreyfus NY Insured Tax-Exempt Bond
Dreyfus NY Tax-Exempt Bond
Dreyfus NY Tax-Exempt Intermediate Bond
Dreyfus People's Index Fund, Inc.
Dreyfus People's S&P Midcap Index, Inc.
Dreyfus Short-Term Income
Dreyfus Short-Intermediate Government Bond
Dreyfus Short-Intermediate Tax-Exempt Bond
Dreyfus Third Century
Dreyfus-Wilshire Large Company Growth
Dreyfus-Wilshire Large Company Value
Dreyfus-Wilshire Small Company Growth
Dreyfus-Wilshire Small Company Value

Evergreen American Retirement
Evergreen Foundation
Evergreen Fund
Evergreen Limited Market Fund
Evergreen Real Estate Equity
Evergreen Total Return
Evergreen Value Timing
Federated ARMs Institutional Service
Federated GNMA Trust Institutional Service
Federated Growth Trust
Federated High-Yield Trust
Federated Income Trust Institutional Service
Federated Intermediate Government Trust
Federated Short-Intermediate Government Trust
Federated Short-Term Income Institutional
Federated Stock Trust
Federated Fortress Adjustable Rate U.S. Govt.
Federated Fortress Utility Income
Federated International Equity
Federated International Income
Founders Balanced
Founders Blue Chip
Founders Discovery
Founders Frontier
Founders Government Securities
Founders Growth
Founders Special
Founders Worldwide Growth
IAI Balanced
IAI Bond
IAI Emerging Growth
IAI Government
IAI International
IAI Midcap Growth
IAI Regional
IAI Reserve
IAI Stock
IAI Tax-Free
IAI Value
INVESCO Dynamics
INVESCO Emerging Growth
INVESCO European
INVESCO Growth
INVESCO High Yield
INVESCO Industrial Income
INVESCO Intermediate Gov't. Bond
INVESCO International Growth
INVESCO Pacific Basin
INVESCO Select Income
INVESCO Strategic Energy
INVESCO Strategic Environmental Services
INVESCO Strategic Financial Services
INVESCO Strategic Gold
INVESCO Strategic Health Sciences
INVESCO Strategic Leisure
INVESCO Strategic Technology
INVESCO Strategic Utilities
INVESCO Tax-Free Long Term Bond
INVESCO Total Return
INVESCO U.S. Government Securities

INVESCO Value Equity
Janus Balanced
Janus Enterprise
Janus Federal Tax-Exempt
Janus Flexible Income
Janus Fund
Janus Growth & Income
Janus Intermediate Government Securities
Janus Mercury
Janus Short-Term Bond
Janus Twenty (closed to new accounts)
Janus Venture (closed to new accounts)
Janus Worldwide
Kaufmann Fund
Lexington Convertible Securities
Lexington Corporate Leaders Trust
Lexington Global
Lexington GNMA Income
Lexington Goldfund
Lexington Growth & Income
Lexington Strategic Investments
Lexington Strategic Silver
Lexington Tax-Exempt Bond
Lexington Worldwide Emerging Markets
Liberty Municipal Securities
Montgomery Emerging Markets
Montgomery Global Communications
Neuberger & Berman Genesis
Neuberger & Berman Goverment Income
Neuberger & Berman Guardian
Neuberger & Berman Limited Maturity Bond
Neuberger & Berman Manhattan
Neuberger & Berman Municipal Securities Trust
Neuberger & Berman Partners
Neuberger & Berman Selected Sectors
Neuberger & Berman Ultra Short Bond
Oakmark International Fund
Rushmore American Gas Index
Rushmore U.S. Government Intermediate-Term
Rushmore U.S. Government Long-Term
Schwab 1000 Fund
Schwab CA Short/Intermediate Tax-Free Bond
Schwab California Long-Term Tax-Free Bond
Schwab Long-Term Government Bond
Schwab Long-Term Tax-Free Bond
Schwab Short/Intermediate Government Bond
Schwab Short/Intermediate Tax-Free Bond
Schwab Value Advantage
Skyline Europe Portfolio
Skyline Monthly Income Porfolio
Skyline Special Equities II
SteinRoe Capital Opportunities
SteinRoe Government Income
SteinRoe High-Yield Municipals
SteinRoe Income
SteinRoe Intermediate Bond
SteinRoe Intermediate Municipals
SteinRoe Managed Municipals
SteinRoe Prime Equities
SteinRoe Special

SteinRoe Stock
SteinRoe Total Return
Strong Advantage
Strong Discovery
Strong Government Securities Portfolio
Strong Income
Strong Insured Municipal Bond
Strong International Stock
Strong Investment
Strong Municipal Bond

Strong Opportunity
Strong Short-Term Bond
Strong Short-Term Municipal Bond
Strong Total Return
Twentieth Century Balanced Investors
Twentieth Century Growth Investors
Twentieth Century Heritage Investors
Twentieth Century International Equity
Twentieth Century Long-Term Bond
Twentieth Century Select Investors

Twentieth Century Ultra Investors
Twentieth Century U.S. Government
Twentieth Century Vista Investors
United Services European Income
United Services Global Resources
United Services Income
United Services Real Estate
United Services World Gold
Yacktman Fund

Jack White & Company
No–Transaction Fee Mutual Funds

Aetna Bond Fund
Aetna Fund
Aetna Growth & Income
Aetna International Fund
Alliance Balanced Fund - Class C
Alliance Corporate Bond - C
Alliance Counterpoint - C
Alliance Fund - C
Alliance Global Small Cap - C
Alliance Growth & Income - C
Alliance International - C
Alliance Mortgage Securities - C
Alliance Mortgage Strategy - C
Alliance Multi-Market Strategy - C
Alliance Muni California - C
Alliance Muni Income II FL - C
Alliance Muni Income II MN - C
Alliance Muni Income II NJ - C
Alliance Muni Income II OH - C
Alliance Muni Income II PA - C
Alliance Muni Insured CA - C
Alliance Muni Insured Nat'l - C
Alliance Muni National - C
Alliance Muni New York - C
Alliance New Europe - C
Alliance North American Gov't - C
Alliance Premier Growth - C
Alliance Quasar - C
Alliance Short-Term Multi Market-C
Alliance Technology - C
Alliance U.S. Gov't - C
ASM Fund
Baron Asset Fund
Bartlett Basic Value Fund
Bartlett Fixed Income Fund
Bartlett Value International
Berger 100
Berger 101
BJB Global Income Fund
Blanchard American Equity Fund
Blanchard Flexible Income Fund
Blanchard Global Growth Fund
Blanchard Precious Metals Fund
Blanchard Short Term Bond Fund
Blanchard Short Term Global Income Fund
Boston Company Asset Allocation
Boston Company California Tax Free
Boston Company Cap. Appreciation Fund
Boston Company Contrarian
Boston Company Intermediate Gov't
Boston Company International Fund
Boston Company Managed Income Fund
Boston Company Massachussetts Tax Free Bond

Boston Company National Tax Free Bond
Boston Company New York Tax Free Bond
Boston Company Short Term Bond
Boston Company Special Growth Fund
Bull & Bear FNCI Fund
Bull & Bear Global Income Fund
Bull & Bear Gold Investors
Bull & Bear Special Equities Fund
Bull & Bear Tax-Free Income
Bull & Bear U.S. & Overseas
Bull & Bear U.S. Government Securities
CIT California Investment Trust Fund Group
CIT California Tax-Free Income
CIT S&P 500 Index Fund
CIT S&P Mid Cap Index Fund
CIT U.S. Gov't Securities
Cappiello-Rushmore Emerging Growth Fund
Cappiello-Rushmore Growth Fund
Cappiello-Rushmore Utility Income Fund
Dreman Contrarian Fund
Dreman Fixed Income Fund
Dreman High Return Fund
Dreman Small Cap Value Fund
Dreyfus A Bond Plus
Dreyfus Appreciation
Dreyfus General CA Municipal Bond
Dreyfus General NY Municipal Bond
Dreyfus General Municipal Bond
Dreyfus GNMA
Dreyfus Insured Municipal Bond
Dreyfus New Leaders
Dreyfus NJ Municipal Bond
Dreyfus NY Insured Tax-Exempt Bond
Equifund-Wright Australia
Equifund-Wright Dutch
Equifund-Wright Hong Kong
Equifund -Wright Italy
Equifund-Wright Spain
Equifund-Wright United Kingdom
Evergreen Foundation
Evergreen Fund
Evergreen Limited Market Fund
Evergreen Real Estate Equity
Evergreen Total Return
Evergreen Value Timing
Fairmont Fund
Federated Arms Fund
Federated GNMA Trust
Federated Growth Trust
Federated High Yield Trust
Federated Income Trust Fund
Federated Inter. Gov't Trust
Federated Short-Intermediate Term Gov't Trust

Federated Short Term Income Fund
Federated Stock Trust
Flex-Fund Bond
Flex-Fund Growth
Flex-Fund Muirfield
Flex-Fund Short-Term Global Income
The Short-Term Global Income Fund
Fremont California Intermediate Tax Free Fund
Fremont Equity Fund
Fremont Multi-Asset Fund
Fundamental California Muni Fund
Fundamental High Yield Muni Bond Fund
Fundamental New York Muni Fund
Fundamental U.S. Gov't Strategic Income Fund
Gateway Gov't Bond Plus Fund
Gateway Growth Fund
Gateway Index Plus Fund
Gintel ERISA Fund
Gintel Fund
IAI Bond Fund
IAI Emerging Growth Fund
IAI International Fund
IAI Regional Fund
IAI Stock Fund
IAI Value Fund
Kaufmann Fund
Laurel Intermediate Income Fund
Laurel Stock Fund
Leeb Personal Finance Fund
Lexington Convertible Securities
Lexington Corporate Leaders Trust
Lexington Global
Lexington GNMA Income
Lexington Goldfund
Lexington Growth & Income
Lexington Tax Exempt Bond
LMH Fund, Ltd.
Loomis Sayles Bond Fund
Loomis Sayles Global Bond Fund
Loomis Sayles Growth Fund
Loomis Sayles Growth & Income Fund
Loomis Sayles International Equity Fund
Loomis Sayles Muni Bond Fund
Loomis Sayles Short-Term Bond Fund
Loomis Sayles Small Cap Fund
Loomis Sayles U.S. Gov't Securities Fund
Managers Balanced Fund
Managers Bond Fund
Managers Capital Appreciation
Managers Income Equity
Managers Intermediate Mortgage
Managers International Equity
Managers Municipal Bond

(continues)

Figure 6–1 Continued

Managers Short Gov't Fund
Managers Short & Intermediate Bond
Managers Short Term Municipal Fund
Managers Special Equity
Merger Fund
Merriman Asset Allocation Fund
Merriman Blue Chip Fund
Merriman Capital Appreciation Fund
Merriman Government Fund
Merriman Leveraged Growth Fund
Permanent Portfolio Aggressive Growth
Permanent Portfolio Fund
Permanent Portfolio Treasury Bill
Permanent Portfolio Versatile Bond
Perritt Capital Growth
PIMCO Foreign Fund
PIMCO Growth Stock Fund

PIMCO High Yield Fund
PIMCO Long-Term U.S. Government Fund
PIMCO Low Duration Fund
PIMCO Short Term Fund
PIMCO Total Return Fund
Reich & Tang Equity
Rushmore American Gas
Rushmore OTC Index Plus
Rushmore Precious Metal Index Plus
Rushmore Stock Market Index Plus
Rushmore U.S. Gov't Intermediate-Term
Rushmore U.S. Gov't Long-Term
State Street Research Capital Fund
State Street Research Government Income Fund
State Street Research Investment Trust
Sound Shore Fund
Toqueville Euro-Pacific Fund

Toqueville Fund
United Services European Income
Value Line Aggressive Income Trust
Value Line Convertible Fund
Value Line Fund
Value Line Income
Value Line Leverage Growth
Value Line Special Situations
Volumetric Fund
Wasatch Aggressive Equity Fund
Wasatch Growth Fund
Wasatch Income Fund
Wasatch Mid-Cap Fund
Wayne Hummer Growth Fund
William Blair Growth Shares
William Blair Income Shares
Yacktman Fund

Fidelity Fundsnetwork NTF Funds
No-Transaction Fee Mutual Funds

Benham Adjustable Rate Gov't Securities
Benham CA Municipal High Yield
Benham CA Tax-Free Insured
Benham CA Tax-Free Intermediate-Term
Benham CA Tax-Free Long-Term
Benham CA Tax-Free Short-Term
Benham Equity Growth Fund
Benham European Gov't Bond Fund
Benham GNMA Income
Benham Gold Equities Index
Benham Income & Growth Fund
Benham Long-Term Treas & Agency
Benham National Tax–Free Intermediate-Term
Benham National Tax–Free Long-Term
Benham Short Term Treas & Agency
Benham Target Maturities 1995
Benham Target Maturities 2000
Benham Target Maturities 2005
Benham Target Maturities 2010
Benham Target Maturities 2015
Benham Target Maturities 2020
Benham Treasury Note
Benham Utilities Income
Berger 100
Berger 101
Dreyfus A Bonds Plus
Dreyfus Appreciation
Dreyfus CA Intermediate Municipal Bond
Dreyfus CA Tax-Exempt Bond
Dreyfus CT Intermediate Municipal Bond
Dreyfus Florida Intermediate Municipal Bond
Dreyfus Fund
Dreyfus General CA Municipal Bond
Dreyfus General Municipal Bond
Dreyfus General NY Municipal Bond
Dreyfus Global Investing
Dreyfus GNMA
Dreyfus Growth & Income
Dreyfus Growth Opportunity
Dreyfus Insured Municipal Bond
Dreyfus Intermediate Municipal Bond
Dreyfus International Equity
Dreyfus MA Intermediate Municipal Bond
Dreyfus MA Tax-Exempt Bond
Dreyfus Municipal Bond
Dreyfus New Leaders

Dreyfus NJ Intermediate Municipal Bond
Dreyfus NJ Municipal Bond
Dreyfus NY Insured Tax-Exempt Bond
Dreyfus NY Tax-Exempt Intermediate Bond
Dreyfus NY Tax-Exempt Bond
Dreyfus Short-Intermediate Gov't Bond
Dreyfus Short-Intermediate Tax-Exempt Bond
Dreyfus Short-Term Income
Dreyfus Third Century
Evergreen American Retirement
Evergreen Foundation
Evergreen Fund
Evergreen Insured Natl Tax-Free
Evergreen Limited Market Fund
Evergreen Real Estate Equity
Evergreen Short-Intermediate CA Muni
Evergreen Short-Intermediate Muni
Evergreen Total Return
Evergreen US Government Securities
Evergreen Value Timing
Fidelity Aggressive Tax-Free
Fidelity Asset Manager
Fidelity Asset Manager Growth
Fidelity Asset Manager Income
Fidelity Balanced
Fidelity CA Tax-Free High Yield
Fidelity CA Tax-Free Insured
Fidelity Canada
Fidelity Capital & Income
Fidelity Convertible Securities
Fidelity Disciplined Equity
Fidelity Diversified International
Fidelity Dividend Growth
Fidelity Emerging Markets
Fidelity Equity-Income II
Fidelity Fund
Fidelity Global Balanced
Fidelity Global Bond
Fidelity GNMA
Fidelity Government Securities
Fidelity High Yield Tax-Free
Fidelity Insured Tax-Free
Fidelity Intermediate Bond
Fidelity International Growth & Income
Fidelity Investment Grade Bond
Fidelity Japan

Fidelity Latin America
Fidelity Limited Term Muni
Fidelity MA Tax-Free High Yield
Fidelity MI Tax-Free High Yield
Fidelity MN Tax-Free
Fidelity Mortgage Securities
Fidelity Municipal Bond
Fidelity New Markets Income
Fidelity NY Tax-Free High Yield
Fidelity NY Tax-Free Insured
Fidelity OH Tax-Free High Yield
Fidelity Puritan Fund
Fidelity Real Estate
Fidelity Retirement Growth
Fidelity Short-Intermediate Government
Fidelity Short-Term Bond
Fidelity Short-Term World Income
Fidelity Southeast Asia
Fidelity Spartan Aggressive Muni
Fidelity Spartan CA Muni High Yield
Fidelity Spartan CT Muni High Yield
Fidelity Spartan FL Muni Income
Fidelity Spartan GNMA
Fidelity Spartan Government Income
Fidelity Spartan High Income
Fidelity Spartan Intermediate Muni
Fidelity Spartan Investment Grade
Fidelity Spartan Limited Maturity Gov't
Fidelity Spartan Long-Term Gov't
Fidelity Spartan MD Muni Income
Fidelity Spartan Muni
Fidelity Spartan NJ Muni High Yield
Fidelity Spartan NY Muni High Yield
Fidelity Spartan PA Muni High Yield
Fidelity Spartan Short-Intermediate Gov't
Fidelity Spartan Short-Intermediate Muni
Fidelity Spartan Short-Term
Fidelity Stock Selector
Fidelity Trend
Fidelity Utilities Income
Fidelity Value Fund
Fidelity Worldwide
Founders Balanced
Founders Blue Chip
Founders Discovery
Founders Frontier

Founders Government Securities	Neuberger & Berman Genesis	SteinRoe Special
Founders Growth	Neuberger & Berman Gov't Income	SteinRoe Stock
Founders Special	Neuberger & Berman Guardian	SteinRoe Total Return
Founders Worldwide Growth	Neuberger & Berman Limited Maturity Bond	Strong Advantage
Janus Balanced	Neuberger & Berman Manhattan	Strong American Utilities Fund
Janus Enterprise	Neuberger & Berman Partners	Strong Discovery
Janus Federal Tax-Exempt	Neuberger & Berman Selected Sectors	Strong Government Securities Portfolio
Janus Flexible Income	Neuberger & Berman Ultra Short Bond	Strong Income
Janus Fund	SteinRoe Capital Opportunities	Strong Insured Municipal Bond
Janus Growth & Income	SteinRoe Government Income	Strong International Stock
Janus Intermediate Gov't Securities	SteinRoe High-Yield Municipals	Strong Investment
Janus Mercury	SteinRoe Income	Strong Municipal Bond
Janus Short-Term Bond	SteinRoe Intermediate Bond	Strong Opportunity
Janus Twenty	SteinRoe Intermediate Municipals	Strong Short-Term Bond
Janus Venture	SteinRoe Managed Municipals	Strong Short-Term Municipal Bond
Janus Worldwide	SteinRoe Prime Equities	Strong Total Return

call and request one. The phone numbers for all major mutual funds are in Appendix 4, the Directory.

Most application forms are quite straightforward. Frankly, the most common mistake people make is in not filling out the application completely. So here are a few pointers:

1. Make sure to *sign the application.*
2. Make sure to elect telephone switching, as well as dividend reinvestment if you don't need current income.
3. Some funds *automatically* reinvest dividends unless you instruct them not to, so make sure you read this part of the application carefully.
4. Make sure to enclose a check for the amount you wish to invest, plus any up-front fees.

Mail your signed application and check to the address indicated on the application. Don't be surprised if you are instructed to mail it to a transfer agent with a different name from the fund. That's OK. Just be sure to follow the directions on the application.

You should receive your confirmation materials from the fund in about one to two weeks. If you don't receive anything after two weeks, call. The sooner you do so, the less likely you are to lose a check or other paperwork.

Telephone Switching

Another way to buy shares is to switch money from a fund you already own into the new one you want to buy, and most major fund families allow you to make this type of transfer with a simple phone call (telephone switching). Just instruct the group to sell a certain number of shares (or a certain dollar amount) of one fund and use the money to buy shares in another fund in the same fund family.

There are certain limitations to how many times you can make this type of transfer within a given period, but most families give you ample room to move around within their family of funds.

(I'll come back to this in Chapter Seven, but let me point out here that transferring money from one fund to another is considered a sale and a subsequent purchase, and as such *it is a taxable event*.)

Building Your Wealth With More and More Shares

A third, and one of the simplest, way to invest is to take advantage of dividend reinvestment. Most funds will automatically reinvest your dividends for you. That means that whenever a fund declares a dividend (like a stock) or pays interest income (like a bond) or distributes capital gains (more on this in Chapter Seven), instead of sending you a check, the money is used to buy you more shares. This is a great way to make your money grow, because it doesn't require taking money out of your paycheck.

In fact, a common misconception is that simply because your share price hasn't gone up much, you're not making money. What you are overlooking is the fact that you have more shares than when you started. *Owning double the number of shares at the same price is just as good as owning the same number of shares at double the price.*

Telephone switching and dividend reinvestment make it possible to do all your mutual fund investing with a single fund family. That's why I recommend using a large no-load family like Vanguard, T. Rowe Price, or Fidelity. You can choose from a nice selection of quality funds, pay low or no loads, make all your trades with a simple phone call, and build your wealth steadily with very little effort.

Discount Brokers

In some cases, you may want to go outside your regular fund family to find just the right fund. That's when you should consider using a discount broker. I do not recommend buying mutual funds through a full-service broker because you can save a lot of time and paperwork using a discount broker to buy and sell shares from different fund families.

How to Trade

Through large discount brokers like Charles Schwab (800-526-8600), Jack White & Co. (800-233-3411), or Fidelity Discount Brokers (800-544-6767), you can easily trade money from one fund to another across family lines (see Figure 6-2). In effect, you get telephone switching among a huge pool of hundreds of funds. You'll

Figure 6–2

Vital Statistics on Three Major Discount Brokers

ACCOUNT NAME	Schwab & Co. Mutual Fund	Fidelity Brokerage Funds Network	Jack White & Co. Connect Marketplace
Account Fee	Regular: $0 IRA: $22 / yr.	Regular: $0 IRA: $20 / yr.	Regular: $0 IRA: $35 / yr.
# of Major Funds	700+	700+	1,000+
Automatic Gains/ Dividend Reinvest.	YES	YES	50% of funds
Trading Hours	24 hrs./day	24 hrs./day	5 A.M.–6 P.M. PST
Insurance Protection	up to $2.5 million	up to $2.5 million	up to $1 million (1,000,000 cash)
Consolidated Monthly Statements	YES	YES	YES

also get consolidated statements that show *all* your investments across various fund families, round-the-clock service, and a whole lot less paperwork!

How Much Do They Charge?

You will pay a modest commission for each trade, of course (see Figure 6-3 for sample fees), but the time and trouble you save may be worth the added cost. Furthermore, Schwab, Fidelity, and Jack White have created no-fee investing with hundreds of funds. With these funds, you pay *no* commission to the discount broker, only the load (if any) charged by the fund itself. The discount brokerage firms are always adding new funds to their lists, so check with them for recent additions. See Figure 6-1 for the current list of discount broker, no-transaction-fee funds.

Discount brokers tend to save you 50% or more compared to the fees you'd pay to a full-service broker. The three discount brokers I like offer competitive commission structures *and* good service. They also allow you to trade among several hundred different funds—an important criterion in choosing a discount broker. Even among these three major discount brokerage firms, fees vary depending on the size of the trade (see Figure 6-3).

Figure 6–3

Typical Fees From Major Discount Brokers

Transaction Amount	Schwab & Co. 800•526•8600		Fidelity Investments 800•544•6767		Jack White & Co. 800•233•3411	
	One–Way	Round–Trip	One–Way	Round–Trip	One–Way	Round–Trip
$1,000	$29	$58	$46.50	$93	$27	$54
$3,000	$29	$58	$75.30	$150	$27	$54
$5,000	$30	$60	$88.50	$177	$27	$54
$10,000	$60	$120	$109.50	$219	$40	$80
$50,000	$160	$380	$209.50	$419	$85	$170
$100,000	$260	$520	$246.50	$529	$135	$270
$250,000	$380	$760	$479.50	$959	$160	$320

Smart Switching Strategies

Whether you trade through a discount broker or within a single fund family, here are five tips for switching smarter:

1. When you switch from a sector fund to cash, switch to the sector money market to avoid paying the sector load twice should you later on want to get back into another sector fund.
2. Be familiar with the number of round-trips permitted *per year* by your fund family (see Figure 6-4).
3. Discount brokers limit switching on their no-transaction-fee funds—so watch out!
4. Remember, unless your funds are in an IRA or Keogh, every switch is a *taxable* event.
5. Sometimes, overactive switching can create a whipsaw effect and cause you to eat up your profits in transaction fees and taxes.

Redeeming Your Shares

The ability to sell mutual funds by phone makes them just about the most liquid investment I know of. You don't have to worry about finding a buyer, or about brokers' commissions, or about bid-and-asked spreads. You simply call, instruct the fund to sell as many shares as you want, and tell them to invest the proceeds of the sale in another fund or to park the money in a money market fund.

In fact, if you are ever ready to sell a fund, don't think you must wait to find a fund to buy before you can telephone switch. If you want to sell but don't know what to buy, sell now and move the proceeds into the fund family's money market fund. There, your money will be safe and will even earn a little interest while you look for better opportunities elsewhere. Not only will you probably earn more interest than you would in a bank savings account, your money will be right there ready to reinvest when you find a good fund you want to buy.

Of course, you can also sell a fund (called a **redemption** in mutual fund lingo) by written request. This is the best route when you

(text continues on page 132)

Figure 6-4

Fund Family Switching Policies and Fees

Fund	Fees	Rules
Benham Capital Management 800•472•3389	• No switching fees or 12b–1 fees charged	• Must wait until investment check clears before allowed to switch • Gold Equities Index, Target Maturities and Tax Frees limited to 6 switches out of variable price funds yearly • no limits on other funds
Blanchard Group 800•922•7771	• .25%–.78% 12b–1 fees	• No minimum, no limit to switches
Bull & Bear 800•847•4200	• .01% to 1.00% 12b–1 fees charged • $5 switch fee	• Minimum switch is $500
Dreyfus 800•645•6561	• .20% to .30% 12b–1 fee	• Minimum switch by phone is $500 • No minimum by mail • Strategic funds allow 2 free round-trips within 12-month period
Fidelity Investments 800•544•8888	• Switching fee of .75% charged on sector funds held less than 30 days • If held over 30 days then .75% or $7.50 switching fee, whichever is less • no 12b–1 fee	• 4 round-trips per year allowed in equity/bond funds • No limit on switches in the Select Portfolios
INVESCO 800•525•8085	• .25% 12b–1 fee charged except for Strategic funds and money market	• 4 switches per fund per year allowed
Founders 800•922•2173	• .25% 12b–1 fee	• Minimum switch is $1000 • 4 round-trips per year
Lexington 800•526•0056	• None	• Minimum phone switch is $500 ($250 for IRA) • 1 switch allowed every 7 days
Neuberger Berman 800•877•9700	• None	• Minimum switch by phone is $2,000 • 4 round-trips per year

Fund	Fees	Rules
Nicholas Company 414•272•6133	• $5 switch fee	• Minimum switch is $1,000 • $2,000 minimum to open money market account • Must maintain $1,000 minimum in money market • 2 round-trips allowed per year • No check writing allowed • No telephone switch with Limited Edition & Income • Must telephone switch Nicholas & Nicholas II into money market before switching into the other fund
Rushmore Group 800•343•3355	• None	• No minimum switch • Precious Metals unlimited telephone switching • Stock Market Index, OTC Index and American Gas Index limited to 5 redemptions per year
Scudder 800•225•5163	• $5 charge to wire funds to a bank	• 4 round-trips per year
Stein Roe 800•338•2550	• $5 fee for IRA terminations or distributions	• Minimum phone switch is $1,000 • 4 round-trip phone switches allowed annually • No limits on mail switches
Strong 800•368•3863	• None	• Minimum phone switch is $250 • No more than 3 switches per quarter.
T. Rowe Price 800•638•5660	• None	• Unlimited money market switching • Electronic switching available
20th Century 800•345•2021	• $10 fee for each account that falls below $1,000	• Switches must be $500 or more • Coded account necessary for telephone switching • No minimum purchase requirement • Shares must be held 30 days between switches
United Services 800•873•8637	• $5 telephone switch fee	• No minimum, no limit
USAA 800•531•8448	• $5 switch fee	• 1 exchange per fund per quarter (round-trip) except money market (16 allowed)

(continues)

Figure 6–4 Continued

Fund	Fees	Rules
Value Line 800•223•0818	• None	• Minimum phone switch is $1,000 • 8 switches allowed per year
Vanguard 800•662•7447	• 1% transaction fee for Index Extended Market, Small Capitalization and International Index Portfolios, 1% redemption fee for Specialized funds	• 2 round-trips per fund per year if involves 1/2 of portfolio or $500,000 whichever is less • 1 switch per 30-day period • Unlimited switching for lower amounts and money markets • No telephone switching for Bond Market, Explorer, Index 500, Index Extended Market, Quantitative, and Small Capitalization Stock

want to move money from one family to another *without* using a discount broker, or when you want to cash in your shares and not reinvest. A simple, one-page letter will do the trick. Use the format shown in Figure 6-5.

Note: Some mutual funds require a signature guarantee before they will honor written selling instructions. This is simply to ensure that no unauthorized person can sell your shares. Check your fund's prospectus (or call the fund and ask) to see if you need a signature guarantee. If you do, you can get one from your bank.

A Little at a Time

Dollar-Cost Averaging

Another nice feature of mutual funds is the ability to invest money gradually and steadily over time. Most of my favorite funds offer a feature called **dollar-cost averaging** (see Figure 6-6), which allows you to set up an automatic investment plan. You instruct the fund to invest a set amount of money for you each month or quarter. The fund will automatically take money from your money market or other checking account (per your instructions) and invest it in the fund you've chosen.

Figure 6–5

Dear Sirs,

Please redeem____shares of *(or completely liquidate my position in)* XYZ Fund. My account number is _____. Please send proceeds to _____ *(name and address)* as soon as possible.

Sincerely,

_____

(Make sure you use your full name as shown on your mutual fund statements.)

This is a great way to start small and build up your nest egg steadily, and to reduce the average price you pay for your shares. How does it reduce your buying price? By investing the same dollar amount each month, you buy more shares when the share price is low than when the price is high.

Say you set up a dollar-cost averaging program with Vanguard Windsor II. Each quarter, the fund invests $100 for you. It takes $100 out of your money market account or your bank checking account and buys as many shares as possible. In the first quarter, when the price is $10 per share, it buys 10 shares. Three months later, the price has risen to $20 per share, so your $100 buys just 5

Figure 6–6

Dollar-Cost Averaging Programs

Family/Phone Number		Program Name	Minimum Initial	Minimum Subseq.
Fidelity	800•544•8888	Automatic Account Builder	$2,500	$100
INVESCO	800•525•8085	Easi Vest	$250	$50
Janus	800•525•3713	Automatic Clearing House	$0	$50
Scudder	800•225•2470	Automatic Share Building	$1,000	$200
Strong	800•368•3863	Automatic Investment Plan	$0	$50
T. Rowe Price	800•638•5660	Automatic Asset Builder	$0	$50
20th Century	800•345•2021	Automatic Monthly Investment	$0	$25
Vanguard	800•662•7447	Fund Express	$3,000	$100

shares. In six months, you've bought 15 shares for $200. Your average price? Not the halfway point between $10 and $20 (or $15 per share), but $13^1/$_3$ ($200 ÷ 15) per share.

Automatic Withdrawal Plans

At the other end, you can also call on your fund to pay you money on a regular basis. This is called an **automatic withdrawal plan** (see Figure 6-7), and it's ideal for someone in retirement. Simply put, you instruct the fund to send you a check each month (or quarter) for a certain amount of money. No matter what the price or the performance of the fund for that period, the fund will sell enough of your shares each month (or quarter) to come up with your desired amount. You can withdraw as much as you want each year, but of course the more you take out, the faster you'll use up your money.

A strategy I like is to withdraw the average annual long-term gain of the fund each year. For example, if your fund has a long-term track record of growing by an average of 9% per year, you set up an automatic withdrawal plan that pays you 9% per year. If you want monthly checks, withdraw 0.75% each month (9 divided by 12). If you want quarterly checks, withdraw 2.25% per quarter

Figure 6–7

Automatic Withdrawal Plans

FUND FAMILY	Minimum Account Size	Minimum Withdrawal	Monthly Withdrawal Required	Are All Funds in Family Eligible?
Fidelity	$5,000/$10,000*	$25/$50	NO	Not Spartan Funds
INVESCO	$10,000	$100	NO	YES
Scudder	$10,000	$50	NO	YES
Strong	$5,000	$50	NO	YES
Vanguard	$10,000	$50	NO	YES
T. Rowe Price	$10,000	$50	NO	YES
20th Century	No Min.	$25	YES	YES

* $5,000 for quarterly withdrawal plan,
$10,000 for monthly withdrawal plan.

(9 divided by 4). That way you withdraw your gains in equal amounts and still keep your principal intact.

But even if you withdraw more than the fund is making, your nest egg can last quite a long time if you set up a reasonable withdrawal plan. And your income is predictable and automatic. I talk more about this strategy in Chapter Eight.

A Place for Everything and Everything in Its Place

Once you own shares in a fund, you will receive regular statements every month or quarter, as well as confirmations any time you make a trade (this includes any automatic reinvestment of dividends). One of the best tips I can give you is this: *Keep all your papers in one place.* It sounds obvious, but too many people don't do it. This will come as a lifesaver at tax time, and will help ensure that you don't lose anything that you might need when you want to buy or sell shares.

When you buy your first shares of a fund, you'll receive a confirmation for the specific transaction. Set up a simple folder or three-ring binder for each fund or fund family. It's not necessary to keep every letter and report you ever receive from your funds, but here is what you should keep:

- The prospectus and the most recent annual or semiannual report
- Every confirmation statement you receive from the fund, including records of your purchases, sales, transfers, and dividends—in chronological order
- Any 1099 forms you receive, along with the "explanation of tax information" that accompanies the 1099s

Another handy trick for keeping things simple and organized is to keep a master sheet with the phone numbers and account numbers of every fund you own. Just start a list on a yellow pad, and keep adding to it whenever you buy a new fund. Again, it sounds simple, but maybe that's why it works so well. You've got your vital numbers handy whenever you need them, and you don't have to go rummaging through desk drawers and lockboxes to make a simple phone call.

In Appendix 3, you'll find some sample worksheets to help you keep track of your holdings and activities.

Making Things Right

No matter how good a fund may be, and no matter how careful you are, at some point something will probably go wrong. Maybe it will be as simple as a persistent busy signal; maybe it will be a transaction incorrectly executed. Whatever the mishap, here's what to do to fix it.

If you have trouble getting through to a fund (which sometimes happens when a fund becomes very popular, often around the end of the year), here are *three insiders' tricks*:

1. *Use the toll number.* Most people call the 800 number, and the regular long-distance number goes unused. So if you keep getting a busy signal on the 800 line, do yourself a favor and pay for the call. It's worth it.
2. *Call early in the day.* Lunchtime and late in the business day

are the busiest times for mutual fund phone calls. Avoid "rush hour" and you may have better success.

3. *Call on Sunday morning.* Lots of fund families are open on weekends, but most investors don't call on Sundays.

If your problem is more complicated, here's what to do. If you suspect that something has gone wrong, if there's a mistake on your statement or if you don't receive confirmation of a trade, call immediately (see Figure 6-8). Have your account number (if you have one) and copies of any relevant letters or statements in hand. Refer to your folder or three-ring binder (where you're keeping all

---

Figure 6–8

Solving Problems with Fund Families

FUND FAMILY	Phone Service	When Calling. Have Your...	When Writing. Have Your...	When Purchasing/ Redeeming Shares. You get...	When Exchanging. Shares Priced at...	To Resolve Problems. Contact...
Fidelity 800•544•8888	*Best:* Early AM, late PM (24 hour phones) *Worst:* Noon 3–4 pm EST	• Customer T– account number • SS number	• Customer T– account number • SS number • Phone rep's name • Date of call • Pertinent details	• Next closing price • Wire checks sent next business day • Confirmation mailed same day	Day received by 4 pm EST or next business day	Customer Relations 82 Devonshire Mail Zone ZF3 Boston, MA 02109
INVESCO 800•525•8085	*Best:* Early AM *Worst:* Noon 3–4 pm	• Account number • SS number	• Account number • SS number • Date in question • Details	• Next closing price • Check sent next business day	Day rec'd by 4 pm or next business day	P.O. Box 173706 Denver, CO 80217–3706
Scudder 800•225•2470	*Best:* 8-11 am EST 4–6 pm *Fax service:* 800-821-6234	• Account number • SS number • Explanation of problem	• Name • Account number • Daytime phone number • Pertinent details • Signature	• Next closing price confirmation/check mailed next business day	Day received by 4 pm EST or next business day	Shareholder Svcs. 160 Federal St. Boston, MA 02110
Strong 800•368•3863	*Best:* Early AM	• Account number • SS number	• Account number • SS number • Date/time in question • Details	• Next closing price • Checks mailed next business day	Day rec'd by 4 pm or next business day	P.O. Box 2936 Milwaukee, WI 53201
T. Rowe Price 800•638•5660	*Best:* 8:30–9 am	• Account number • Fund name • Registration name and address	• Fund & account number • Registration infor. • Pertinent details	• Next closing price • Checks mailed next business day	Day received by 4 pm EST or next business day	Shareholder Svcs. 100 E. Pratt St. Baltimore, MD 21202
20th Century 800•345•2021	*Best:* Early AM *Worst:* 11–2 pm EST	• SS number • Tax ID number • Account number	• Transaction number • Date & time • Name of rep talked to • Pertinent details	• Next closing price • Checks mailed w/in 3-4 business days • Confirmations sent w/in 2 days	Day received by 4 pm EST or next business day	James E. Stowers, Jr. P.O. Box 419200 Kansas City, MO 64141
Vanguard 800•862•7447	*Best:* 2–3 T–Thu. *Worst:* Monday 1st week of month 3–4 pm no exch. after 4 pm EST	• Account name and address • Registration • Fund name • Fund number • Account number	• Account name and address • Registration • Fund name • Fund number • Account number	• Next closing price • Check/confirmation should be received 5-10 days later	Day received by 4 pm or next business day	*Call or write:* Jack Bogle, Pres. 215–669–1000 P.O. Box 2600 Valley Forge, PA 19482

your statements and confirmations, as well as copies of any letters you write to the fund).

Ask for customer service, customer relations, or shareholder services. Explain exactly what you think has gone wrong or why you suspect an error. If the person you first speak with is not able to help, ask for his or her supervisor. If you still are not satisfied, contact the Securities and Exchange Commission, Office of Consumer Affairs and Information Services, 450 Fifth Street, NW, Washington, D.C. 20001. Or you can contact a regional branch of the SEC (see Figure 6-9).

So there you have it . . . buying and selling smart, whether automatically or selectively, whether switching or cashing in, whether within a single fund family or across many fund families. Mutual fund investing doesn't have to be a chore, or a full-time job, if you follow these commonsense tips.

Mistakes I Know All Too Well

Let me close this chapter with a list of the most common mistakes investors make in buying and selling mutual funds. Just by avoiding these pitfalls, you will surely become a more successful mutual fund investor.

Most Common Mistakes in Buying a Fund

1. *Paying a full load.* No excuses here. In some cases, it may be worth a small load, say up to 3%, to buy a truly excellent and unique fund. But I would *never* buy a fund with an 8.5% load. You just don't need to pay that much to get an excellent fund.

2. *Buying last year's "hot" fund.* Beware of flash-in-the-pan funds. It's tempting to invest in a fund that blew the roof off last year, but if you do, you are more likely to buy at the top than if you buy a fund with a more steady, long-term track record of solid gains. It's not that I don't like winners—I love them. But make sure you're not buying yesterday's winner.

3. *Not considering how the fund fits into your overall portfolio.* Remember, a fund does not stand alone; it fits into an overall strategy that is keyed both to your comfort level and to the economic climate. So when you buy a fund, make sure it makes sense for *you* now.

Figure 6–9

Regional SEC Offices

New York Regional Office
26 Federal Plaza
New York, NY 10278
212–264–1636
(NY, NJ)

Boston Regional Office
John W. McCormick Post Office
and Courthouse Bldg.
90 Devonshire St., Suite 700
Boston, MA 02109
617–223–9900
(ME, NH, VT, MA, RI, CT)

Philadelphia Regional Office
600 Arch St., Room 2204
Philadelphia, PA 19106
215–597–3100
(PA, DE, MD, VA, WV, DC)

Atlanta Regional Office
1375 Peachtree St., N.E., Suite 788
Atlanta, GA 30367
404–347–4768
(TN, PR, NC, SC, GA, AL,MS, FL, east LA)

Miami Branch Office
Dupont Plaza Center
300 Biscayne Blvd, Way, Suite 500
Miami, FL 33131
305–536–5765

Detroit Branch Office
231 W. Lafayette
438 Federal Bldg. & U.S. Courthouse
Detroit, MI 48226
313-226-6070

Chicago Regional Office
Everett McKinley Dirksen Bldg.
219 S. Dearborn St., Room 1204
Chicago, IL 60604
312–353–7390
(MI, OH, KY, WI, IN, IA, IL, MN, MO)

Fort Worth Regional Office
411 W. Seventh St.
Fort Worth, TX 76102
817–334–3821
(OK, AR, TX, west LA, KS)

Houston Branch Office
7500 San Felipe St., Suite 550
Houston, TX 77063
713–226–3671

Denver Regional Office
410 17th St., Suite 700
Denver, CO 80202
303–844–2071
(ND, SD, WY, NE, CO, NM, UT)

Salt Lake City Branch Office
U.S. Post Office & Courthouse, Rm 505
350 S. Main St.
Salt Lake City, UT 84101
801–524–5796

Los Angeles Regional Office
5757 Wilshire Blvd., Suite 500 East
Los Angeles, CA 90036
213–468–3098
(NV, AZ, CA, HI, Guam)

San Francisco Branch Office
901 Market St. Suite 470
San Francisco, CA 94103
415–995–5165

Seattle Regional Office
3040 Jackson Federal Bldg.
915 Second Ave.
Seattle, WA 98174
206–442–7990
(MT, ID, WA, OR, AK)

4. *Reinvesting dividends in a loser.* Many investors reinvest dividends, and that's good. It helps build wealth painlessly, almost magically. You don't send any more money, yet you keep getting more shares. Great! But the hidden trap of reinvesting dividends is reinvestment in a poor fund. So watch what you're buying, even when "buying" is just reinvesting dividends. If you don't want to sell your existing shares of a poor fund for some reason, at least

stop buying more! Call the fund (or write, if necessary) and instruct it to start sending you the dividends and distributions in cash. Then channel that money into a superior fund.

5. *Buying a junk bond fund for high yields.* There are many good ways to increase your income, but junk bond funds are not one of them. Don't be tempted by the high yields these low-rated-bond funds offer. High yields aren't much help if your share price is sinking faster than the yield they're paying.

6. *Buying another fund instead of adding money to the good funds you already own.* I've seen far too many investors owning 2% of this and 3% of that. They wind up owning 40 or 50 funds in their portfolios. One way to avoid owning too many funds is to always ask yourself, "Rather than buy this new fund, can I simply buy more shares of a really great fund I already own?"

7. *Buying just before a fund declares its dividend.* If you buy right before a fund declares a dividend, you'll owe taxes on the dividend, even if you automatically reinvest it. If you wait until after the dividend is declared, you won't owe taxes right away (more about this in Chapter Seven).

8. *Buying a tax-free fund in a retirement account.* We'll discuss both tax strategies and retirement strategies in later chapters, but for now, take my word for it: You don't want a tax-free fund (like a municipal bond fund) in a retirement account. The account is already tax-sheltered, so you don't need a tax-free fund.

9. *Rushing into a decision.* Don't buy because of a hot tip, a high-pressure phone call from a broker, an article in a newspaper, or an ad on TV. Do your homework, and don't be pressured into a quick decision. If the fund is good today, it will still be good tomorrow.

10. *Never buying.* While I don't want you to rush, the one sure way to miss out on a great fund is to wait for the "perfect moment" to buy. There is no perfect moment, except perhaps on hindsight. So after you've carefully evaluated your own goals, the market's risks and opportunities, the funds you already own, how much time and money you have, the fund's prospectus and annual report—go ahead and *do it*.

Most Common Mistakes in Selling a Fund

1. *Switching from a sector fund to a regular money market.* Remember, most sector funds charge a small front-end load, and it's usu-

ally worth paying, because sector funds are so targeted and have little competition. But it's not worth paying the load twice, which is what you'll do if you switch to a regular money market and then switch back to another sector fund. Switch to the sector money market, and you'll pay the sector load just once.

2. *Jumping out for emotional reasons at the first sign of trouble.* We've talked about volatility, and I know that some of you are more able to stand short-term dips than others. So know yourself, and don't buy a volatile fund (check my risk ratings in Appendix 4) if you can't take the heat. But if you do buy, don't jump ship if the seas get a little choppy.

3. *Selling because the fund has one bad quarter.* Successful investors invest for the long term, not for a month or even a quarter. So don't bail out if you have a bad quarter.

4. *Selling a fund with a declining redemption fee before the fee disappears.* As we discussed earlier, some funds charge a back-end load (a commission when you sell your shares) for anyone who sells within a few months (or even years) of buying. Again, remember you are a long-term investor, so don't sell within two or three months of buying—especially if the fund charges a fee to sell so soon.

5. *Never selling.* Most investors will agree that it's easier to buy than to sell. When we buy, we can get all excited about how much money we're going to make and the whole world of possibilities that lies before us. When we sell, however, it seems we're never quite ready. If the fund has done well, we hate to pass up the future gains we might be missing. And if the fund has not done well, we want to hang on just long enough for the fund to turn around—at which point we don't want to give up a good thing. And so it goes. But you haven't really made money until you sell shares, it's as simple as that. Until you sell, it's all on paper. So don't be afraid to sell when your Back of the Envelope forecaster or Business Cycle economic clock tells you the time is right.

It's not difficult to be a smarter mutual fund investor. In many instances, it's simply a question of common sense. I hope the tips I've laid out for you here help remind you that the little things you do can really add up—and that buying and selling smart can open the door for you into the Mutual Fund Winners Circle.

Summary of Chapter Six

- There are many ways to save money when buying and selling mutual funds. They include avoiding hidden fees, such as 12b-1 fees and loads for reinvesting dividends, and using no-load funds at discount brokers and all-weather funds that can weather market turbulence.

- You can also save time, money, and aggravation by using high-service families, such as Vanguard, Fidelity, Invesco, T. Rowe Price, Scudder, Strong, and Twentieth Century.

- Make sure to follow up with your fund whenever you make a transaction, and keep all records of trades, distributions, and dividends.

- Use discount brokers for telephone switching among different fund families.

- Watch out for switching fees within the same family; look before you leap.

- To avoid mistakes and misunderstandings, use the form letter shown in Figure 6-5 when redeeming shares.

- For lowest-hassle investing, sign up for your fund's automatic dollar-cost averaging plan or automatic withdrawal plan.

- Avoid the common mistakes listed in this chapter.

Chapter Seven

Mutual Fund Tax Guide

You've now completed the Mutual Fund Winners Circle. You have the tools you need to craft a strategy that fits your needs and desires, that stays on the right side of the market, that chooses top-quality funds, and that enables you to buy and sell your funds easily and shrewdly.

There are two more areas of special interest: taxes and retirement. (Retirement is discussed in Chapter Eight.)

Taxes on mutual funds are a bit more complicated than taxes on other investments, but if you keep good records and understand the basic rules, you should be able to prevent a tax headache. And you may even be able to lower your taxes a bit while you're at it!

An Important Tax Difference

When it comes to taxes, the first important difference between individual stocks and mutual funds is this: Until you sell your individual stock shares, you face no capital gains taxes; with mutual funds, you must pay applicable capital gains taxes every year.

For example, suppose you buy 100 shares of IBM in January. During the year, the price goes from $95 per share to $100 per share. At the end of the year, you've made $5 per share, or $500 for owning your 100 shares. But until you sell those shares, you owe no taxes. If you've also received dividends, you do owe taxes on them, but you owe no capital gains taxes on the price gains made so far by your stock.

With a mutual fund, however, the story is somewhat different due to federal tax regulations relating to mutual funds. Say you purchase 100 shares of Vanguard Windsor II. You buy the shares at $10 per share, and at the end of the year, they are worth $15. Again, your share price has appreciated $5, or $500 for your 100 shares. But near the end of the year, you will probably also receive a statement or a check from the fund for capital gains distributions. These are the net gains (gains minus losses) that the fund itself realized during the year by buying and selling stocks within its portfolio. By law, a mutual fund must distribute 98% of its ordinary income *and net capital gains* to shareholders each year. And it is that money on which you must pay taxes.

Now, if the fund holds IBM all year without selling it, the fund, like our individual shareholder, does not have any capital gains. But if the fund buys IBM, then sells it sometime during the year and buys something else, there will be capital gains to distribute.

Since mutual funds are constantly buying and selling the stocks and bonds in their portfolios, there are almost always capital gains—as well as capital losses to offset some of those gains. The net gain per share is then given to each shareholder of the fund as a **capital gains distribution**.

Like dividends, these distributions are usually reinvested, so most investors don't actually receive a check. You just get a confirmation from the fund that your distribution was used to buy more shares in your account. But you still owe taxes on that distribution.

If your fund pays interest income, the way a bond does, these "dividends" are also taxable, whether or not you reinvest them. And, of course, when you sell shares, your gains are taxable, even if you switch the money into another mutual fund.

So, with mutual funds you have three taxable events:

1. *Annual capital gains distributions*—which are taxable even if you reinvest the distributions and even if you haven't sold any shares
2. *Annual dividends*—which are taxable even if you reinvest them
3. *Capital gains when you sell your shares*—even if you turn around and reinvest the money in a different fund

How can you minimize these taxes? Well, you obviously don't want to reduce your capital gains when you sell your shares—you want your shares to go up as much as possible. However, you can reduce capital gains taxes by choosing a fund with smaller annual capital gains distributions. That doesn't mean choosing a fund that doesn't make as much money; it means choosing a fund that doesn't buy and sell very often. Because, you see, the less "turnover" of merchandise within the fund's portfolio, the lower its capital gains distributions will be.

The Fund Portfolio's Turnover

You'll remember that I mentioned in Chapter Five the advantage of buying a fund with low portfolio turnover. Now you can see why, all other things being equal, you want a low-turnover fund rather than a high-turnover fund.

Certain types of funds tend to have higher turnover than others. Short-term bond funds generally have higher turnover than long-term bond funds, simply because short-term bonds mature more quickly than long-term bonds. Aggressive growth funds tend to have more turnover than growth & income funds.

Don't choose a fund *just* because it has low turnover. But check a fund's portfolio turnover before you buy, and realize that the higher the turnover, the higher your capital gains distributions (and related taxes) will probably be.

As for how to reduce taxes on dividend income, the simple answer is to reduce your dividend income. Seriously, if you are not depending on your fund for current income, look for a fund whose major payoff to investors is price appreciation. If you're simply going to reinvest the dividends anyway, go for growth right out of the starting block.

Careful Timing Can Reduce Taxes

You can also reduce your taxes by buying a fund after it goes **ex-dividend**—after it has just paid out its annual or semiannual dividends. That won't make a difference to your overall total return, but it can help take the bite out of your next tax bill.

Let's say Mr. Right wants to invest $2,500 in Vanguard Windsor II at the current price of $25 per share, giving him 100 shares. But Vanguard Windsor II is about to pay a $1.20 dividend. If he waits until after the dividend is paid, he can buy shares at $23.80 because the share price will fall to reflect the dividend payout. At that price, he can buy 105 shares for the same $2,500.

Meanwhile, Mr. Wrong buys his shares *before* the fund goes ex-dividend. He pays $25 per share and buys 100 shares. A few days later, he receives his dividend for $120 ($1.20 × 100 shares). He automatically reinvests those dividends at the new price of $23.80 (the same price Mr. Right paid), and he buys five shares with his $120.

As you can see, both Mr. Right and Mr. Wrong now own 105 shares at $23.80. And both invested $2,500. So what's the difference? Taxes. Mr. Right received no dividends; Mr. Wrong did. Come April 15, Mr. Wrong will owe taxes on that $120—even though he reinvested it—but Mr. Right will not.

That's why you're better off, all other things being equal, to wait until after a fund goes ex-dividend before you buy.

What About Tax-Free Funds?

Another strategy for reducing taxes on income is to invest in tax-free income funds such as municipal bond funds.

What Stage of the Business Cycle Are We In?

I like muni bond funds quite a bit—at certain stages in the business cycle. But while bond fund share prices are dropping, don't stay in a muni bond fund just to avoid taxes. That means when interest rates are rising, you probably don't want to own a muni bond fund regardless of the tax advantage. Remember, you want to look at total return—capital appreciation plus dividend income—to really get a grip on how your fund is treating you.

When interest rates are falling, however, muni bond funds can be an excellent choice for investors in the highest tax brackets. How do you know if they're right for you? Here's a simple formula to help you compare tax-free bond funds to taxable funds:

Take the tax-free yield of the muni bond you are considering, say 4%. Divide that yield by 1 minus your marginal tax bracket. If you're in the 31% bracket, divide your yield by 1 minus 0.31, or 0.69. A 4% yield divided by 0.69 equals 5.797%. That means you need to get a 5.797% taxable yield to net the same as a 4% tax-free yield.

So do your own comparison shopping. If you can find a tax-free fund (with the same quality and maturity) that beats a taxable fund, buy it!

Just remember that considerations of quality, maturity, and interest rate trends all come before the question of taxes.

When Is Tax-Free Not Tax-Free?

I want to alert you to a little "fine print" concerning muni bond funds that most investors don't know about: Your capital gains are fully taxable. That's right, your dividend income is tax-free, but any capital gains profit you make when you sell your shares is still fully taxable. That doesn't mean you shouldn't buy muni bond funds—just be aware that they are not 100% tax-free. In fact, even the yield is not 100% tax-free. It is free of federal taxes, but state and local taxes may still apply unless you live in a state with no income tax (Alaska, Florida, Nevada, New Hampshire, South Dakota, Texas, Washington, or Wyoming) or in a state in which dividends are not taxed. Check with your own state for current laws.

Which brings us to the subject of double– and triple–tax-free funds. There are, in fact, certain muni bond funds that *do* allow you to avoid state and even local taxes as well as federal taxes. These are muni bond funds made up of muni bonds exclusively from your state. A handful of large fund families offer single-state (and even single-city) muni bond funds from some of the most populous states (e.g., California, New York, Maryland, and Ohio). Check with the following fund families for more information on these double–tax-free funds: Dreyfus, Nuveen, T. Rowe Price, Vanguard, and Fidelity.

Warning: While I love cutting my taxes, I love safety more. So before you dive into a single-state muni bond fund and especially a single-city muni bond fund, check the state's safety rating. All states get a rating from Moody's, Standard & Poor's, and Duff & Phelps.

Treasuries Save Taxes, Too

While municipal bond funds offer income that's exempt from federal income tax, U.S. Treasury bond funds offer income that's exempt from state and local taxes (except in Tennessee). So for investors who live in high-tax states like New York, Treasury funds may actually give a higher after-tax yield than a comparable corporate bond fund. This tax break applies only to Treasury bills, notes, and bonds—not GNMAs, FNMAs, or other debt instruments from other government agencies.

Deducting Your Expenses

In addition to choosing funds that offer you tax advantages, there are other ways investors can lower their tax burdens. For example, Uncle Sam allows you to deduct from your income tax certain investment-related expenses, including:

- Fees for advisors and accountants who help with your investments or taxes
- Fees for investment managers (as long as they manage taxable investments)
- Custodial fees from mutual funds, IRA custodians, or brokers
- Eighty percent of entertainment or meals associated with investments or taxes
- Investment-related travel and transportation (excluding seminars)
- Legal costs involved in producing taxable investment income
- Office supplies and stamps used to generate taxable investment income
- A safe-deposit box
- Fees to banks, brokers, attorneys, or trustees paid to administer your investments

- Investment-related subscriptions, including *Mutual Fund Investing*
- Investment-related telephone expenses
- Computer equipment (depreciated over five years) used to manage your investments

You cannot deduct them all—only that portion that exceeds 2% of your annual gross income.

Winners Circle Tip: Since certain expenses crop up every year, I have found that it makes sense to use a little advance planning to really take advantage of this tax write-off. I call it my **two-year deduction plan,** and it goes like this: At the end of year one, delay paying certain yearly deductible expenses until next January. Then, at the end of year two, accelerate some early-year payments into December and pay all your annual payments before December 31. Because you bunch your expenses into the even years, you are able to deduct some of them, and in the odd years, you reduce your expenses to the bare minimum. That way, you're more likely to break through the 2% threshold every other year, and to spend less money that goes undeductible.

Consider this: If you typically spend 1.5% of your annual gross salary on these types of expenses, you would never be able to deduct any of those expenses if you paid them steadily each year; you would never get over the 2% threshold. But if you timed your expenses so that you paid only 0.25% in the odd years, and 2.75% in the even years, you would be able to deduct 0.75% of those expenses without paying a penny more!

Keeping It All Straight

The trickiest part of mutual fund taxes is simply figuring out how much you owe. And I have seen hundreds of people overpay their taxes just because they got fouled up in their calculations. So let me give you a few tips on keeping things straight.

I've already talked about reducing your taxes on annual capital gains distributions—by keeping portfolio turnover as low as possible. And I've talked about several strategies for reducing taxes on interest income, from investing in muni bond funds to bunching your deductions. Now let's talk about keeping your taxes to the minimum when you sell your shares.

When you sell shares of your fund, you owe taxes on the increase in the price. If you paid $15 per share and sell at $20, you owe taxes on your profit of $5 per share. So far, so good. The confusion starts when you try to figure out just what price you actually paid for your shares. Because, chances are very good that you did not buy them all at once, and so probably paid different prices for different shares.

"No, Jay," you say, "I bought 100 shares and now I'm selling them. I didn't buy any more along the way." But wait! What about your automatic dividend and distribution reinvestment? Not only are these annual distributions and dividends taxable in the year you receive them (even if you don't actually receive them but reinvest them instead), but each time you reinvest those dividends and/or distributions, you are buying more shares at a new price.

The solution really is to keep track. As long as you know how many shares you bought at each price, you're in the driver's seat. So, each time you receive notice from your fund that it has reinvested your dividends and/or distributions, keep a copy of the confirmation and keep a simple log yourself.

You don't need a fancy computer program to keep track; just a simple notebook will do. I like to keep a separate page for every fund I own. Just write down how many shares you buy originally, and at what price per share. Then, every time you buy more shares, sell some shares, or reinvest dividends/distributions, write down the date, number of shares, and price per share. That way, no matter when you sell your shares—whether this year or 20 years from now—you will have the magic number you need: your **cost basis**.

Calculating Your Cost Basis

Cost basis simply refers to your buy price. It is the starting point from which you calculate your profits and losses. As noted above, you can have many different purchase prices for the shares you own. Let me set up an example using Mr. Right to show you how calculating your cost basis carefully and shrewdly can save you a lot of money at tax time.

Mr. Right buys 200 shares of Vanguard Windsor II at $20 per share, for $4,000. A few months later, the price dips to $18, and he buys 300 more shares. Next, the fund pays a 4.6% dividend (or $1.15 per share) when it hits $25 per share. Since Mr. Right owns 500 shares, his dividend is $575. But Mr. Right has signed up for automatic reinvestment of dividends, so that $575 is used to buy more shares the next day when the price is $23 per share. His $575 buys 25 more shares.

Mr. Right now owns 525 shares. A few months later, he decides to buy another 100 shares, this time at $22 per share. Later that year, the fund declares a capital gains distribution of $0.90 per share. Mr. Right receives $562.50 for his 625 shares, which he immediately reinvests at $22.50 to buy another 25 shares.

When Vanguard Windsor II hits $26 per share, Mr. Right is ready to take some profits. But how much has he made? He has three ways to calculate this:

1. In simple terms, Mr. Right invested a total of $12,737.50, and he owns 650 shares. Thus, his *average price per share* is $19.59. Mr. Right can use this as his cost basis for all his shares. If he sells 100 shares today, his profit will be $6.41 per share ($26 minus $19.59).

2. But some funds will assume that Mr. Right is selling the first shares he bought. Now, remember, Mr. Right bought his first 200 shares at $20, so his profit on those shares is only $6 each. If Mr. Right elects the **first in/first out** method of calculating his cost basis, his taxes on this trade will be lower.

3. A third choice available with some (but not all) funds is to *sell specific shares bought at a specific time*. For example, if Mr. Right decides to sell the 100 shares he bought at $22 per share, his per-share profit is cut down to $4.

Each case, of course, is different, and you will have to judge which method of calculating your cost basis is most favorable. But you can do so only if you keep careful records along the way. Just remember, once you choose a method for calculating cost basis, you must use that method for all shares of that fund no matter when you sell.

The Double-Tax Trap

The most common tax mistake I see is to fall into the **double-tax trap:** paying taxes on reinvested dividends twice. It's easy to do! But it's also easy to avoid, once you know the pitfall.

The mistake comes when you forget that your dividends were reinvested at a different price from that of your original shares. For example, if Mr. Wrong buys 200 shares of Vanguard Windsor II at $20, for $4,000, then reinvests dividends of $460 at $23 per share, he winds up owning 220 shares. When the fund hits $24, Mr. Wrong is ready to sell.

But Mr. Wrong thinks his cost basis is $20, which means he has a taxable profit of $4 per share. After all, he paid $20 when he bought his shares. Those other shares sort of grew out of what he already had, right? Wrong! Mr. Wrong has already paid taxes on that $460 dividend. To avoid the double-tax trap, he must realize that 20 shares of his 220 were bought at $23. And that means his taxable gain when he sells his 220 shares is not $4 times 220, or $880, but $4 times 200, plus $1 times 20, or $800 plus 20, or $820. Why pay taxes on that extra $60 again?

Appendix 3 contains some worksheets to help you calculate your cost basis.

Record Keeping for Tax Time

As I mentioned, a key way to minimize tax bills and tax head-aches is proper record keeping. You'll get a blizzard of forms and statements. Figure 7-1 shows what each one means.

Avoid the Wash Sale Trap

When you *sell* shares, beware of the **wash sale rule,** used by the IRS to prevent investors from selling funds to take a tax loss and then rebuying the same fund. This rule states that if you sell shares of a fund at a loss and then buy back shares of the same fund within 30 days, you cannot claim a loss on your tax return. This is particularly problematic with bond funds, since dividends may be reinvested every month and this reinvestment of dividends is con-sidered a purchase. Thus, if you sell some shares of a bond fund at a loss and then reinvest dividends on your remaining shares, you will be prevented from claiming a legitimate loss on the shares you sold.

Here are two taxwise solutions for both stock and bond funds:

1. If you sell all shares of a stock or bond fund at a loss and want to reinvest within 30 days, buy a similar fund—rather

Figure 7–1

Keeping Track of Tax Forms

Form	What It's For	Who Gets It	Key Item
1099–DIV	Dividend, Capital Gain Distributions	All shareholders in funds (except IRAs) that have made distributions	Column 1a shows the total distibution (including dividends and capital gains). Report this amount on line 5 of Schedule B.
1099–B	Redemption Proceeds	Anyone who has sold or exchanged shares in a fund (including switches between funds)	Column 2 shows the gross proceeds from the sale. Report this amount on Schedule D.
1099–R	Retirement Plan Distributions	Anyone who has taken a distribution from an IRA or other qualified retirement plan account	Box 1 shows the total amount, including any income tax withheld. Report this amount on line 16a of Form 1040.
5498	IRA information (Not part of your tax return)	Anyone who has an IRA	Box 1 shows the total contributions you made to your IRA for 1992. Keep this form for your records.

than the same exact fund—and you'll still be able to deduct your loss.

2. If you sell only a portion of your shares in an income fund, instruct the fund to pay you cash dividends—rather than reinvest your dividends—for the two months following the sale. That way you can't be accused of buying more shares within 30 days of selling, and you can still deduct your loss.

We've covered a wide range of tax questions involving mutual funds in this chapter. Let's close with a quick hit list of tax-smart moves:

Checklist of Tax-Smart Moves

1. Keep clear and complete records of all your mutual fund transactions, including purchases, sales, transfers from one

fund to another, and all dividends and distributions—whether received or reinvested.

2. Consider bunching your tax-deductible investment expenses in even years to break through the 2% minimum threshold.
3. Avoid buying a fund right before it goes ex-dividend.
4. If you sell a fund for a tax loss, don't reinvest in that same fund within 30 days of the sale.
5. When choosing between similar funds with similar long-term track records and investment objectives, opt for the one with lower portfolio turnover.
6. Consider municipal bond funds for federal tax-free income, but watch out when interest rates are on the rise.
7. Consider U.S. Treasury bond funds if you live in a high-tax state.

Summary of Chapter Seven

- Mutual fund investing involves some special tax planning, which can cost a lot of time and money if you don't plan ahead carefully.

- With mutual funds, you have three taxable events: when you sell your shares, when you receive dividends, and when you receive annual capital gains distributions. The last two events occur even if you never sell any shares.

- The most important tax tip is to keep careful, complete, and detailed records of all your investing activity. One number you want to keep special track of is your cost basis—the starting point for each investment you make.

- Receiving dividends and distributions is a taxable event, even if you automatically reinvest the money. Keep track of these reinvestments so you don't pay taxes on them twice.

- Switching is also considered a sale and subsequent purchase, and as such is a taxable event.

- You can avoid federal taxes with municipal bond funds, but remember that any capital gains you make when you sell your shares are taxable. Only the dividends are tax-free.

- You can avoid state and local taxes with Treasury mutual

funds, but you'll still owe federal taxes (and again, taxes on any capital gains).

- Timing of buying and selling can affect your tax burden. In general, buy a fund after it pays its dividend; avoid rebuying a fund within 30 days of selling it.
- You can deduct your investment expenses, such as money management software or investment newsletters, to the extent that those expenses exceed 2% of your gross income.

Chapter Eight

Retirement Strategies

In Chapter Seven, we discussed several strategies for reducing your taxes when you invest in mutual funds. But there's one area of tax-free investing that deserves a chapter of its own: *investing for and in retirement.*

Individual Retirement Accounts

As with stocks and bonds, mutual funds within an individual retirement account (IRA) are allowed to grow tax-free. Some investors are even allowed to fund their IRAs with pre-tax dollars, which means that you can deduct the money you put *in* your IRA from your taxable income. This is true if neither you nor your spouse is eligible for a pension plan or 401(k)/403(b) at work or, even if you are eligible, if you earn under $40,000 as a couple or $25,000 as an individual. But whether you contribute with pre- or after-tax money, the great advantage of an IRA is that all the money inside it grows tax-free.

Now that doesn't mean you never pay taxes on your gains. You must pay taxes when you eventually withdraw your money once you retire. But being able to build your wealth without paying current taxes each year means your money will grow faster and larger.

Just look at the power of tax-free compounding. Say you're 40 years old. If you put $2,000 away each year for the next 25 years and allow it to compound tax-free, you will have $157,119 when you reach age 65, assuming a modest 8% annual increase. If your money had been in a regular, taxable account and you had been paying (28%) on your 8% gain each year, your money would have grown to $112,202 over the same period. That's a difference of $44,917. If you start earlier, the advantage is even more dramatic: In 30 years, the difference between an IRA and a taxable amount would be $243,532 vs. $160,326 (see Figure 8-1 for a complete comparison of tax-free and taxable accounts). I believe everyone should contribute the full $2,000 allowed per year to an IRA.

If you have a lump sum growing tax-free, the benefits are even greater. Figure 8-2 shows how a nest egg of $10,000 will grow over time at various rates of interest.

The sheer power of tax-free compounding is one of the reasons

Figure 8–1

How a $2,000 Annual IRA Contribution Grows

Year	Taxable (28%)	Tax Deferred	Year	Taxable (28%)	Tax Deferred
1	$ 2,115	$ 2,160	16	$ 53,242	$ 65,106
2	4,352	4,493	17	58,424	72,474
3	6,718	6,867	18	63,905	80,432
4	9,220	9,576	19	67,701	89,026
5	11,867	12,502	20	75,831	98,309
6	14,665	15,663	21	82,314	108,333
7	17,625	19,076	22	89,171	119,160
8	20,756	22,762	23	96,422	130,853
9	24,066	26,743	24	104,091	143,481
10	27,568	31,042	25	112,202	157,119
11	31,271	35,685	26	120,780	171,849
12	35,187	40,700	27	129,852	187,757
13	39,329	46,116	28	139,447	204,937
14	43,710	51,966	29	149,594	223,492
15	48,343	58,283	30	160,326	243,532

Assumptions:
- *8% investment gain per year*
- *28% federal tax bracket*
- *$2,000 invested at the start of each year*

Figure 8–2

The Magic of Compound Interest

This table shows how your money will GROW, assuming various rates of return with earnings reinvested and compounded annually, and no taxes taken out during the accumulation phase. The figures in this table are computed on a $10,000 nest egg.

$10,000 Nest Egg

%	5th Yr.	10th Yr.	15th Yr.	20th Yr.	25th Yr.	30th Yr.	35th Yr.
3	11,593	13,434	15,580	18,061	20,938	24,273	28,139
4	12,167	14,802	18,009	21,911	26,658	32,434	39,461
5	12,763	16,289	20,789	26,533	33,864	43,219	55,160
6	13,382	17,908	23,965	32,071	42,918	57,435	76,860
7	14,026	19,671	27,590	38,697	54,274	76,122	106,765
8	14,693	21,589	31,722	46,609	68,484	100,626	147,852
9	15,386	23,674	36,425	56,044	86,231	132,676	204,138
10	16,105	25,937	41,772	67,275	108,346	174,493	281,022
11	16,851	28,394	47,846	80,623	135,854	228,921	385,746
12	17,623	31,058	54,736	96,463	169,999	299,597	527,993
13	18,424	33,946	62,543	115,230	212,304	391,157	720,685
14	19,254	37,072	71,379	137,434	264,618	509,499	981,001
15	20,114	40,456	81,370	163,664	329,188	662,114	1,331,745
16	21,003	44,114	92,655	194,606	408,740	858,494	1,803,135
17	21,924	48,068	105,387	231,055	506,576	1,110,646	2,484,034
18	22,878	52,338	119,737	273,929	626,683	1433,700	3,279,972
19	23,864	56,947	135,895	324,293	773,878	1,846,753	4,407,006
20	24,883	61,917	154,070	383,375	953,959	2,373,763	5,906,682

I like IRAs so much. I also like them—and recommend that everyone use them—because they allow you to combine the magic of tax-free compounding with the many great benefits of mutual funds.

Within your IRA, you can own just about any mutual fund you wish. You can keep your IRA within a single fund family or group, or you can use a variety of fund families and house your IRA with a discount broker, such as Charles Schwab or Jack White.

Whichever route you choose, an individual retirement account using mutual funds is a great way to follow my Winners Circle strategy and get the added boost of *not* paying current taxes on your profits. Remember, there are a lot of ways in which you pay taxes on mutual funds in a regular account, even when you don't receive your money. When you trade from one regular fund to another, and when you reinvest dividends and distributions each year, you must pay taxes. But within your IRA, you can trade as much as you want and have all your profits reinvested without any tax penalty.

A Winners Circle Strategy for Retirement

So if IRAs and mutual funds are a terrific combination, how should you invest? In most cases, you will want to follow a long-term strategy. (long-term because you'll be heavily penalized if you withdraw your money before you reach age 59!). Until you get close to, or into, retirement, you shouldn't be concerned about short-term fluctuations in your account; your goal is maximum growth. Go back to Chapter Two and take the Investor Risk Profile again, this time with a view to your IRA account. I think you'll find that you score in the Moderate or Aggressive camp. Whatever your Profile, that's the path you should follow with the money you're saving up to live on in retirement.

The concepts of choosing top funds and allocating your assets and/or timing the market apply to your IRA investing as well. In addition, here are a few tips *especially* for retirement investing:

1. *Never own a tax-free fund in your IRA.* The tax benefit of a municipal bond fund is wasted in an IRA—your money is already tax-sheltered—so you're better off getting the higher yield of a regular bond fund in your IRA.
2. *Put your highest "portfolio turnover" funds in your IRA.* Remember, you are shielded from taxes on distributions within your IRA, so high portfolio turnover won't hurt you here.
3. *Consolidate.* You may have as many IRAs as you wish—as long as your combined total contribution doesn't exceed $2,000 per year. But to keep matters simple and less expensive, I suggest consolidating your IRA at one of my favorite large no-load fund families.
4. *Start early in the year.* You have until midnight April 15th to contribute to your IRA for the *previous* tax year. However, I recommend you fund your IRA as early as possible in the year to get the maximum wealth-building possible.
5. *Emphasize stock funds over bond funds in your IRA.* Even if you

are conservative by nature, your nest egg will grow faster and larger in equities. If you're nervous, stick to low-risk equities like utilities and other high-yield stock funds.

IRAs With My Favorite Fund Families

One of my favorite ways to set up a mutual fund IRA is with a large, no-load, high-quality mutual fund family, such as Fidelity, INVESCO, Scudder, Strong, T. Rowe Price, Twentieth Century, or Vanguard. As you can see from Figure 8-3, these seven families have a broad range of funds, low IRA fees, and flexible switching policies. They also have records of excellent long-term performance in most of their growth funds.

Each of these seven families has its own special strengths, and you may wish to base your choice according to these individual traits.

Vanguard is the best choice for conservative investors: Its special strength is in bond funds and income-oriented stock funds. *Twentieth Century*, on the other hand, excels in growth funds: Its best funds are all growth-oriented stock funds. *Fidelity* would have to be the choice for an investor who wanted a lot of choices; it has over 100 different funds, including the broadest array of sector funds in the business. However, as we've seen, Fidelity has begun to charge a number of fees and low loads on its funds. *T. Rowe Price* and *Scudder* are the best low-cost, all-round fund families; both offer excellent choices in growth, income, and international arenas.

If you want to own funds from a number of different fund families in your IRA, one of the best and easiest routes is to use a discount broker. For this, I would recommend Charles Schwab. Schwab is currently offering a no-fee lifetime IRA. Anyone who opens an IRA of $10,000 or more is assured of never paying an IRA custodial fee. Of course, you will pay a small commission on any trades you make.

Rolling Over Your IRA

Suppose you set up an IRA and you're not pleased with the service or performance. Or perhaps you already have an IRA that doesn't offer enough choices. What then?

It's quite easy to switch your IRA custodian. In fact, the *new*

Figure 8–3

IRA Accounts with Top Fund Families

	Set Up Fee $	Annual Maint. Fee $	# of Funds Avail.	Min. Invest./ Fund	Min. Subsequent Invest.	Special Services	Comments
Fidelity 800•544•8888	0	10	50+	500	100	• auto bank transfers • auto fund to fund exchanges • auto fund to IRA exchanges	• per fund ($30 max.) plus $10 liquidation fee/fund • some 3% load funds; • 4 transfers /yr.
INVESCO 800•525•8085	5	10	20	250	50	• auto bank transfers • auto fund to fund exchanges	• per IRA account • no limit to # of transfers
Scudder 800•225•2470	0	10	12	500	50	• auto bank transfers	• per fund • "account sweep" option.
Strong 800•368•3863	0	10	13	250	50	• auto invest	• per fund • $30 annual cap
T. Rowe Price 800•638•5660	0	10	25+	1,000	50	• auto bank transfers • auto fund to fund exchanges • auto fund to IRA exchanges	• per fund • offers CD Transfer Service.
20th Century 800•345•2021	0	10	8	500	100	• auto bank transfers • auto fund to fund exchanges	• per fund • $30 annual cap.
Vanguard 800•662•7447	0	10	30+	500	50	• auto bank transfers	• per fund • 4 transfers/yr.

custodian you've selected will be more than happy to do the transfer work for you. All you have to do is contact the group you want as your new custodian and tell them you want to do a **direct, custodian-to-custodian transfer.** They'll send you a form to fill out and send back to them, and they'll handle the rest. You never need undergo the uncomfortable experience of telling your old custodian you want to leave.

In fact, when you use this kind of direct **rollover,** where you never physically take possession of the money, you can change custodians more than once a year. You've probably been told that you can only make a rollover once every 12 months. But when you use this custodian-to-custodian method, the once-a-year rule does not apply. In general, I don't recommend switching often—once you find a good custodian, you should stay put. But there may be circumstances in which you'll need to switch more than once, and it's nice to know you have the freedom to do so.

You can also use the **60-day rollover** to transfer from one IRA custodian to another. With the 60-day rollover, you physically take possession of your IRA money, withdrawing it from one custodian and then depositing it with another. Its name comes from the fact that you must redeposit or reinvest the money in another IRA within 60 days of withdrawal—or face stiff IRS penalties and taxes.

As of January 1993, 60-day rollovers of retirement money in company plans have been actively discouraged by the IRS. When you leave an employer before age 59, for example, the IRS withholds 20% of your pension money before letting your employer pay you the rest. The IRS is trying to encourage you to set up direct custodian-to-custodian transfers of retirement savings, whereby your old employer transfers your pension of 401(k) or 403(b) money directly to a new custodian. *Custodian-to-custodian transfers are not subject to this 20% withholding.* If you leave an employer with whom you have a retirement plan before age 59, make *sure* to have that employer transfer your retirement money directly to a **conduit IRA,** which you might set up with a new custodian, such as a no-load mutual fund family.

As of this writing, the IRS still allows 60-day rollovers of IRA money without withholding the 20% tax. But don't be surprised if early withdrawals from IRAs are Congress' next target.

Keeping Track of After-Tax Contributions

Earlier I said that you should use an IRA to its fullest ($2,000 per year), whether or not your contribution is tax-deductible. But if you do use after-tax dollars, be sure you don't pay taxes on that money twice. You see, if you contribute already-taxed dollars into your plan, you should be able to withdraw those dollars without paying any taxes when you retire. However, if you contribute pre-tax dollars, you will owe taxes on that money when you start making withdrawals. (And you'll owe taxes on your gains, no matter how you funded your plan.)

The important thing to remember here is to *keep track of which dollars are pre-tax and which are after tax.* Chances are pretty good that you may have *both* kinds within your IRA. Before 1986, all IRA contributions were tax-deductible. Also, you probably rolled over any pension plan you may have had with a previous employer into an IRA. But since 1986, most of us have *not* been eligible to deduct contributions, so these IRAs have been funded with after-tax dollars.

Again, the key, as with so many things in the mutual fund universe, is to *keep careful records.* Make sure you know what money you've already paid taxes on, and what you haven't. The easiest way to be sure is to keep your pre-tax IRA money in a different account from your after-tax IRA money.

For example, suppose you have an IRA that you've been funding with after-tax dollars and you also have money in a pension plan that you funded with pre-tax dollars. If you roll over the pension plan money into an IRA, roll it into a new IRA that is kept separate from your after-tax account. This will save you mounds of confusion and frustration come withdrawal time.

Retirement Saving Beyond an IRA

Individual retirement accounts are great as far as they go, but you can only save a maximum of $2,000 per year, regardless of your tax status. As we've seen, if you begin at age 40 and save the maximum amount each year, your money will grow to $157,119 (assuming an 8% annual return) by age 75. But will that be enough? According to

Figure 8-4, you'll probably need a lot more than that when you retire.

How Much Will You Need Once Inflation Takes Its Toll?

Inflation can erode your purchasing power over the years so that a comfortable income now becomes a fixed-income *trap* later on. Use Figure 8-4 to estimate just how much money you'll really need to maintain your current standard of living *after inflation.* Choose a rate of inflation you consider reasonable, say 6%. That means that if you earn $75,000 today, in five years you'd need an income of $75,000 × 1.34, or $100,500. Ten years from now, you'd need $75,000 × 1.79, or $134,250—almost *double* your current income.

401(k)s and 403 (b)s

So how can you save for retirement tax-free and have enough money to actually retire? This is where **401(k)s**—called 403(b)s in

---

Figure 8-4

Inflation Factor

Years from now	If annual rate of inflation is:							
	3%	4%	5%	6%	7%	8%	9%	10%
1	1.03	1.04	1.05	1.06	1.07	1.08	1.09	1.10
2	1.06	1.08	1.10	1.12	1.14	1.17	1.19	1.21
3	1.09	1.13	1.16	1.19	1.23	1.26	1.30	1.33
4	1.13	1.17	1.22	1.26	1.31	1.36	1.41	1.46
5	1.16	1.22	1.28	1.34	1.40	1.47	1.54	1.61
6	1.19	1.27	1.34	1.42	1.50	1.59	1.68	1.77
7	1.23	1.32	1.41	1.50	1.61	1.71	1.83	1.95
8	1.27	1.37	1.48	1.59	1.72	1.85	1.99	2.14
9	1.31	1.42	1.55	1.69	1.84	2.00	2.17	2.36
10	1.34	1.48	1.63	1.79	1.97	2.16	2.37	2.59
15	1.56	1.80	2.08	2.40	2.76	3.17	3.64	4.18
20	1.81	2.19	2.65	3.21	3.87	4.66	5.60	6.73
25	2.09	2.67	3.39	4.29	5.43	6.85	8.62	10.83
30	2.45	3.24	4.32	5.74	7.61	10.06	13.27	17.45

nonprofit companies—as well as tax-deferred annuities come into the picture. These plans also come under the classification of **qualified plans,** which means that the IRS allows you to grow your money tax-free within these plans. And you know how much I love tax-free growth!

Let's talk about 401(k)s first (this applies to 403(b)s as well). These plans, offered through your employer, allow you to put away pre-tax money (deducted from the gross pay on your paycheck so that your taxes are calculated on what's left) and let it grow tax-free until retirement. Some companies even match or contribute money to your 401(k). These plans allow you to put away more than the $2,000 IRA maximum.

In 1993, the 401(k) maximum was $8,994. The maximums are based on your annual income. You cannot set aside in your pension plan more than 15% of your gross pay.

A 401(k) plan usually offers participants a handful of different funds in which to invest. Sometimes these funds are recognizable from the mutual fund world, such as Fidelity Magellan. Others simply offer a stock fund, a government bond fund, a money market fund, and so on, managed by a trust company or bank. In most cases, you have the option of determining how your money is split among these funds, and you usually can change this allocation two or four times a year.

Again, unless you are five years or less from retirement, you want to follow a long-term approach with these plans, emphasizing stocks rather than bonds or money markets. Even when your choices are limited, a 401(k) is still a sensible way to save for retirement, especially if the plan has good performance—and especially if your employer is contributing money too. The opportunity to save with pre-tax dollars and let your money grow tax-free is irresistible.

Remember, if you leave an employer with whom you have a retirement plan, have your retirement money transferred directly to a conduit IRA.

Variable Annuities

Once you've maximized your opportunities for pre-tax retirement savings and contributed the full $2,000 per year to an IRA, suppose you want to save still more. Your next step should be to explore variable annuities.

Variable annuities are plans that offer tax-free growth, although they are funded with after-tax dollars. Unlike IRAs, they have no maximum annual contribution, and, like 401(k)s, they allow you to choose how your money is allocated among a handful of funds. Variable annuities are offered by three of my top no-load mutual fund families: Fidelity, Scudder, and Vanguard. Figure 8-5 gives you the vital statistics on these three plans. What I like best about them is their combination of low fees, solid performance, and seasoned management.

This Is a Long-Term Commitment

With all these qualified retirement plans, you must be willing to put the money away and not touch it for several years. These are long-term plans. Particularly with annuities, some plans themselves penalize you heavily when you withdraw money prematurely. But the IRS also encourages long-term planning. If you withdraw your money before age 59, you will be hit with a 10% penalty tax in addition to your regular current income taxes.

"Now, wait a minute, Jay," you may be saying, "current income taxes? I thought these were tax-free plans." Not exactly. These plans allow your money to grow tax-free, but you will have to pay taxes on any profits you withdraw. They are considered income, and you'll owe regular income tax. However, by growing your money tax-free, you will have saved considerably more in your retirement account. Also, once you retire, you may be in a significantly lower tax bracket than at the height of your earning power when you were saving these dollars.

Mutual Fund Strategies During Retirement

Which brings us to the whole point of saving for retirement--enjoying the money *in* retirement. At some point, your IRA and other retirement savings plans will become retirement income plans. You will begin taking money *out* and living on that income (along with

Figure 8–5

Top Three Variable Annuities

FIDELITY RETIREMENT RESERVE   800•544•2442

Minimum Investment	$2,500
Subsequent Investment	$250
A.M. Best Rating	A
Assets	$1 Billion
Annual Fee	• 1%
	• $30 annual maintenance fee for accounts under $25,000
Switching	• Unlimited
	• Automatic investment plan available
	• $100 minimum

Funds Available

Asset Manager
Investment Grade Bond
VIP Money Market
VIP High Income
VIP Equity Income
VIP Growth
VIP Overseas
VIP Index 500

SCUDDER HORIZON PLAN   800•225•2470

Minimum Investment	$2,500
Subsequent Investment	No Minimum
A.M. Best Rating	A
Assets	$373 Million
Annual Fee	• 1.45%
	• 2.25%for International
Switching	• Unlimited
	• Automatic investment plan available
	• $50 minimum

Funds Available

Money Market
Bond
Balanced
Capital Growth
International

VANGUARD VARIABLE ANNUITY   800•522•5555

Minimum Investment	$5,000
Subsequent Investment	$500
A.M. Best Rating	A+
Assets	$280 million
Annual Fee	• 1%
	• $25 annual maintenance fee
Switching	• Two round trip switches allowed per year
	• Switching over 51% of assets, 2 per yr.; under 50% unlimited

Funds Available

Money Market
High Grade Bond
Balanced
Equity Index
Equity Income
Growth

Social Security, of course). How should your strategy change once you retire?

Assuming you begin withdrawing money once you retire, you should switch to my Conservative strategy with your nest egg. At this point, you still want your money to grow (after all, you may live and enjoy retirement for 20–30 years!), but you also want to lower the short-term volatility and increase your safety.

As you can see in Figure 8-6, your nest egg can continue to grow *and* provide you with current income as well. For example, if you have $200,000 growing by 10% per year, you can withdraw 15% per year, and your nest egg will last for 11 years. And if you withdraw *less* than the growth rate of your plan (say only 9%), you'll preserve your nest egg to pass on to your heirs (more on this in a moment).

If your IRA is not already with a single fund family or discount broker, you want to consolidate at this point. Other than keeping your pre– and after–tax-funded IRAs separate, you don't need multiple plans. It will be a lot easier to withdraw money from a single place.

Now you want to start receiving that money you worked so hard

---

Figure 8-6

How Long Will Your Money Last?

		% Rate of Investment Return									
		5	6	7	8	9	10	11	12	13	14
% Rate of Annual Withdrawls	15	8	8	9	9	10	11	12	14	16	20
	14	9	9	10	11	11	13	14	17	21	
	13	9	10	11	12	13	15	17	22		
	12	11	11	12	14	16	18	23			
	11	12	13	14	16	19	25				
	10	14	15	17	20	26					
	9	16	18	22	28						
	8	20	23	30							
	7	25	33								
	6	36									

Number of Years Your Nest Egg Will Last

to earn and save. First, instruct your mutual funds to send you checks for dividends and distributions, instead of automatically reinvesting that money as they had been doing. If you find that this income is not enough, don't change your investment strategy. Instead, set up **an automatic withdrawal plan** with your mutual fund family. You can receive a regular monthly or quarterly check from your mutual fund that amounts to more than just the dividends.

For example, suppose you own a fund in your IRA that has a current yield of 5%. You can still withdraw more than 5% a year using an automatic withdrawal plan. If the fund's net asset value (NAV) is growing by 10% a year (in addition to the 5% yield), you can withdraw 15% per year and not even touch your principal. In fact, you can withdraw more than the annual growth of the fund. You will be chipping away at your nest egg, but that's what you saved it for, right? Figure 8-7 shows how you might use an automatic withdrawal plan, based on your current age and account size.

A Few Estate Planning Strategies to Consider

I mentioned a moment ago the possibility of preserving your nest egg and passing it on to your heirs. While many investors are simply worried about making sure their nest egg lasts for their lifetimes, some fortunate retirees are able to share their wealth with their friends and family after they've gone.

The consistent "money machine" you can create with a large portfolio of high-quality mutual funds can allow you to live off the profits and keep your principal intact or even growing over the years. If you are in such a position, your fortune also carries with it a cost: the challenge of setting up an estate plan to preserve your assets once you're gone.

I could write an entire chapter on estate planning; indeed, many books have been written on the subject. But in the context of this book's "safety-first mutual fund investing," let me simply suggest a few strategies you might wish to explore further.

First of all, anyone with any assets whatsoever (and if you're investing in mutual funds, you have assets!) *should have a will*. This might sound obvious, but the majority of Americans do *not* have

---

Figure 8-7

How You Might Use Mutual Fund Withdrawal Plans Based on Your Current Age

Present Age	**55**	**65**	**75**	**85**
Average Life Expectancy	24 Years	17 Years	11 Years	6 Years

	PRUDENT MUTUAL FUND CATEGORIES			
	Aggressive Long–Term Growth Funds	**Balanced and Flexible Funds**	**Conservative Bond Funds**	**Money Market Funds**
Historical Annual Returns	10% to 14%	8% to 12%	6% to 9%	3% to 8%
Maximum Recommended Annual Withdrawal	9%/Year	10%/Year	12%/Year	16%/Year
Maximum Recommended Monthly Withdrawal	0.75%/Month	0.83%/Month	0.83%/Month	1.33%/Month

What you could expect with a $100,000 portfolio using maximum withdrawal rates shown above:				
Assumed Portfolio Size	$100,000	$100,000	$100,000	$100,000
Annual Withdrawal	$9,000	$10,000	$12,000	$16,000
Monthly Withdrawal	$750	$833	$1,000	$1,333

What nest egg investment would you need at the above withdrawal rates to get $50,000 per year cash income?				
Portfolio Size	$555,555	$500,000	$416,666	$321,500
Annual Withdrawal	$50,000	$50,000	$50,000	$50,000
Monthly Withdrawal	$4,167	$4,167	$4,167	$4,167

wills. And, without a will, the court decides how your assets are divided up upon your death.

With only a will, however, your estate will have to go through **probate,** the legal process by which your creditors are paid off and your assets (including all your investments) are divided up per your will's instructions. Probate can be time-consuming for your heirs, and can cost approximately 5% or more of your total estate's value. Thus, many estate planning experts advise putting your investments and other *assets into a trust.*

There are different types of trusts; the most popular is probably something called a **revocable living trust.** This kind of trust allows maximum flexibility for controlling the assets within the trust during your lifetime and for changing the terms of the distribution of your assets, including abolishing the trust entirely (revoking) before you die. Assets within a trust do not go through probate when you die, because the "owner" of the assets is not the trust and the trust has not died. Since the trust is revocable, however, it does not shield your estate from federal estate taxes.

If you estimate that your estate will be worth less than $600,000 upon your death, you may not need to worry about federal estate taxes (at least under current laws), because you can pass on up to $600,000 to your heirs tax-free. (Of course, you can pass on an unlimited estate to your spouse, but to no one else.)

If your estate is likely to be worth more than $600,000 when you die, you may wish to explore some estate planning strategies that protect your assets both from probate and from federal estate taxes. Some popular strategies include an **irrevocable trust,** a **charitable lead trust,** and an **A/B trust** or credit shelter trust.

These are complicated and sophisticated strategies, but if your estate is large, they are certainly worth investigating. After all, you've worked this hard to accumulate your nest egg—why let the courts or the government take it away from your family?

Early Withdrawal Options

I do recommend that you let your money grow, untouched, for as long as possible. Even after you reach age 59, even after you pass 65, your money can continue to grow. In fact, you can wait until you're 70 before the IRS requires that you start withdrawing money from a qualified plan.

But what if you do want to retire early? What if you need to start withdrawing money *before* age 59? You still can do so, and avoid the 10% federal penalty tax, if you **annuitize.** That means withdrawing the money in regular, equal amounts for the rest of your life.

Now, the earlier you start, the less money you'll be allowed to take out each year (because your annual withdrawal amount is based on your life expectancy). So think this option through carefully before you start annuitizing. Once you start, you're committed to the schedule for the rest of your life or until the money is gone. A *tax attorney or accountant* can run some numbers for you and help you evaluate your options.

No matter how you choose to take your money out, you'll want to plan ahead, start early, and fully use the tax advantages still permitted by Uncle Sam. Tax-free growth before retirement can translate into a much bigger nest egg after retirement.

Summary of Chapter Eight

- Mutual funds are a great way to save and invest for retirement. You can use them in individual retirement accounts (IRAs) and Keoghs, as well as in many company retirement plans, such as 401(k)s and 403(b)s.

- Placing mutual funds in retirement plans allows you to take advantage of tax-free compounding, whereby your profits earn extra profits instead of being eaten up by taxes.

- My favorite fund families have excellent, cost-effective IRA plans.

- To transfer (or roll over) your retirement savings to a new custodian such as a no-load mutual fund company, you must take special care not to trigger a 20% withholding tax from the IRS. If you are rolling over money from a company pension plan, have your company roll over the money directly to the mutual fund company. By not taking direct possession of the funds, you avoid the tax.

- When you switch your IRA from one custodian to another, you can withdraw the money yourself and place it into a new account without triggering the 20% withholding, *as long as you roll over the money within 60 days.*

- You can also use some of my favorite fund families to set up a variable annuity, which combines tax-free growth in mutual funds with the protection of insurance to guarantee lifetime income.

- In general, you cannot withdraw money from your IRA or other retirement account until you are $59^1/2$. If you do, you face a 10% IRS penalty on top of your regular income taxes, which you must pay no matter when you withdraw your money. There are certain strategies (such as "annuitizing") that will allow you to avoid this 10% early withdrawal penalty, but they may restrict future withdrawal privileges.

- How much money will you need in retirement? The bad news: Inflation will make today's dollars buy less. The good news: You can still grow your nest egg in retirement. In fact, if you withdraw less per year than your account earns, you can protect your principal and pass it on to your heirs.

- Estate planning to provide for your family is a complicated subject and involves strategies from a simple will to a complex irrevocable trust. Avoiding probate can literally save your family a fortune; consult an estate planning specialist for advice on both.

Appendix 1

Letters to an Investor

A Letter to a 5-Year-Old
"Starting out in life."

A Letter to a 25-Year-Old
"Building a family."

A Letter to a 45-Year-Old
"Entering the high-income years."

A Letter to a 65-Year-Old
"Retirement time."

A Letter to an 85-Year-Old
"Late retirement years."

A Letter to a 5-Year-Old

Dear Master Billy Smith,

I'm writing you this letter because your Mom and Dad have told me that you are now in kindergarten. I'm proud of you. You are starting off a long life of learning, working, and investing so that you can enjoy the good things of life.

Did you know that in thirteen years you will be ready to enter college? Maybe you will go to Cornell University, a great college, like I did. But it costs a lot of money for college expenses, and just as somebody saved and invested for my college tuition, someone needs to start doing that for you—starting right now.

Ask your Mom and Dad or Grandad to start saving for your college education now. The earlier they start saving and investing, the better your college account will look when it is needed. Did you know that $10,000 invested in some good growth funds would be worth $43,630 (at 12% total return/year) or $107,000 (at 20% total return/year) after thirteen years!

Another possible way of starting a college fund is to invest $2,000 per year for thirteen years (that's a $26,000 investment) and at 12% total return per year, the college fund would be worth $62,785 after thirteen years! Note that I didn't allow for taxes in these calculations. Tell your Dad that a good accountant might give you some ways to minimize taxes during the investment process.

Billy, thirteen years, from now until college, is a good length of time for your Mom and Dad or Grandad to invest in some good growth stock funds such as T. Rowe Price International Stock and Fidelity Contrafund. Your college funds will ride out a number of economic cycles and in the end they will grow a lot. So, you see, as you grow, your college fund will grow also!

I'll write to you periodically, Billy, because I care about you and your future.

Your friend and admirer,
Jay Schabacker

A Letter to a 25-Year-Old

Dear Bill,

It's been good keeping in touch with you over the years. Congratulations on your recent marriage to a very fine lady—treat her well and she will treat you well for the rest of your lives. I also understand a lot has happened since you graduated from Cornell just three years ago. I'm proud of you that your first major career job is going so well and looks so promising.

I expect that you'll be thinking of buying a house for your family soon. Don't finance more than 80% of the purchase price of the house. You keep risks down this way—and get a better deal on your loan. On the other hand, as interest rates are historically low now, consider choosing the longest (30-year) mortgage available. This will lock in for the entirety of the loan the low mortgage rates we now have.

This is an exciting and challenging time for you and your wife. Starting a career and starting a family is expensive and requires some real budgeting discipline. Generally and quite often your family income exceeds your spending needs at this time in your life. Don't fall into the bad habit of overusing credit or credit cards. Remember, your credit rating is important and follows you wherever you go. I recommend (except for gasoline cards) you use only one or two credit cards (such as VISA) and pay your full bill each month! Why eat into your family finances by paying high-interest fees to the credit card companies? I urge you to keep a tight family budget, and in so doing, try to scrape together $2,000 per year to place in an IRA for your retirement. I know it's a shock to even mention retirement now when it is an event that is about 40 years in the future. But that's just the point—the earlier that you get started in saving and investing, the bigger your nest egg will be when you want to retire. This is because the power of compounding of investment returns can work wonders over 40 years!

For example, if you could invest $5,000 now, at age 25, in a great growth stock fund that grew at 10% total return per year over the next 40 years (tax deferred), that $5,000 would grow to $248,927 when you are age 65. If you can do a little better in your average annual investment return—say 12% per year—that $5,000 will grow to $521,085. Just look at what an added 2% per year can do for your nest egg! That's why I want you to pick out the best no-load mutual funds that you can find for the long term.

As you are building your family, it's very good to keep a cash reserve in your investment portfolio to allow you to pay for some unforeseen family needs. Yes, it's good to have some cash in money market funds there, but try not to disturb it if you don't have to. Other than that, your long-term time frame means you can invest rather aggressively. One way to break down your investment nest egg portfolio now would be as follows:

A small company stock fund	25%
A diversified stock fund	25
An international stock fund	30
A flexible bond fund	10
A money market cash fund	10
	100%

Now, Bill, I know you may not have $5,000 to sock away right now, but you certainly can come up with $300 to put in a fund like Lindner (for an IRA Lindner's initial investment need only be as high as $250). Did you know that if you got started now with $300 and then put $100 per month into the fund for 40 years that when you're ready to retire at age 65, your nest egg will be worth $524,000 at 10%/year return—or even better, $935,000 at 12%/year return—or even better, $1,666,000 at 14%/year return!

Bill, start early, do some family budgeting, and stick with a good investment program. If you do that, your whole family will be very glad you did.

Your friend,
Jay Schabacker

Life Cycle Spending and Earning Patterns

A 65-Year-Old at Retirement Time

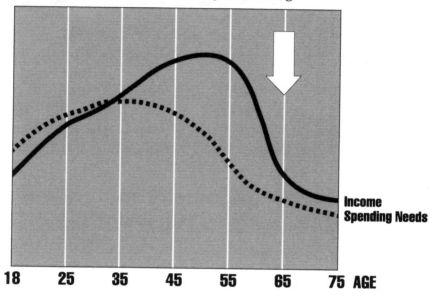

DOLLARS

"As your income falls, cut your spending but don't cut out your investing."

Income
Spending Needs

18   25   35   45   55   65   75 AGE

A Letter to a 45-Year-Old

Dear Bill,

It's good to hear that you and the family are doing fine. I'm glad at least one of your kids had the good sense to go to our old alma mater, Cornell University. Actually, as you know, the financing of your children through college is a big-ticket item, so it was real smart of you to set up a college investment fund to make sure the money was available when needed.

A tidbit on your housing and your home mortgage. If you haven't refinanced your house at lower rates as yet, it's a good idea to do it now—at our historically low interest rates. But, go for the 20 year (or less) mortgage. That means that your house will be paid off at age 65, just about your retirement time.

By the way, congratulations on the key promotion where you work. That brings me to the message of this letter. Now you are entering into your peak career earning years—but please don't let your lifestyle and spending move up to your annual earnings. You should be saving big-time now and investing a lot for you and your wife's retirement. I know you have maximized your pension opportunities and used all a 401(k) would allow you to; but here's a new idea—sock some savings into a tax-deferred variable annuity that uses no-load mutual funds. These mutual fund vehicles have all the advantages of a mutual fund plus tax-deferral—plus, you can put all that you want into it. The IRS has nothing to say about how much you put into it.

Bill, I want you to go over your budget again—with a sharp pencil—and put $2,500 in a variable annuity to get it started, and then keep paying into it at the rate of $500 per month. In 20 years, by the time you are 65, at 10% return per year, you will have $360,478; at 12% return you will have $456,446; at 14% return you will have $580,740; and at 20% return you will have $1,155,840.

In your variable annuity, or in your basic mutual fund portfolio for that matter, you might try to approximate an investment balance as follows:

U.S. equity funds	35%
International equity funds	30
Bond funds	20
Money market/cash funds	15
	100%

That 15% in money market funds is there just to accumulate some available cash to be used to scoop up some fund bargains if and when we get that market sell-off that I expect soon.

Just remember, Bill, with 20 years to retirement, you want to maximize all your tax-deferred investment plan options and choose the most reliable yet opportunistic funds available to you. Make your high-income years be high-investment years, and later on you will be experiencing a worry-free retirement.

Your friend,
Jay

Life Cycle Spending and Earning Patterns

A 45-Year-Old Entering the High-Earning Years

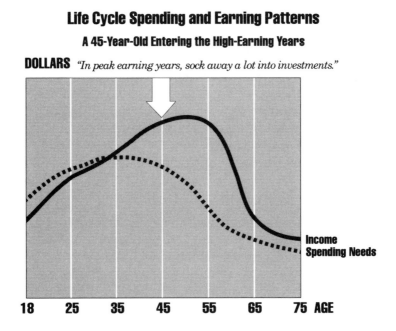

DOLLARS   *"In peak earning years, sock away a lot into investments."*

Income
Spending Needs

18   25   35   45   55   65   75 AGE

A Letter to a 65-Year-Old

Dear Bill,

Now that I know you have turned that magic age of 65, I'm very thankful that you have your health. I'm also glad things look good for you financially. You know my feelings well: Spiritual health is first in importance, physical health is second in importance, and financial health is third in importance. But, all are important!

Bill, I know from talking to scores of retired people that people above 65 years in age tend to get conservative—often too conservative—and load up on bonds—long-term bonds and bond funds and long-term municipal bonds and municipal bond funds. I caution you against that as the economic cycle we are entering (a growing economy) will not treat long-term bonds well in your portfolio. Rising interest rates could bring your bond's total return down to zero or below!

Don't forget about the use of great stock funds in your portfolio, because: (1) You're going to live at least another 15 to 20 years! You need to keep your nest egg growing ahead of inflation, and (2) I know you want to pass a good and ample inheritance on to others.

Here is the portfolio balance I would hold if I were you:

U.S. equity funds	25%
International equity funds	15
Bond funds (short-term)	30
Money market/cash funds	30
	100%

Bill, I'm not sure what your tax bracket is now, but if it is high, some of your bond fund allocation can be invested in short- and intermediate-term municipal bond funds.

And another thing, in case you need to get a good chunk of cash monthly or quarterly from your investments to live on, don't forget the use of automatic withdrawal plans to pull cash from your U.S. and international equity funds.

Bill, my parting comment I know you don't need—because you now have investing in your blood. But here is my comment, anyway—now that you are retired, as your income falls, cut your spending (so your income is always above your spending), and thereby you can continue your investing.

Your friend,
Jay

Life Cycle Spending and Earning Patterns

A 65-Year-Old at Retirement Time

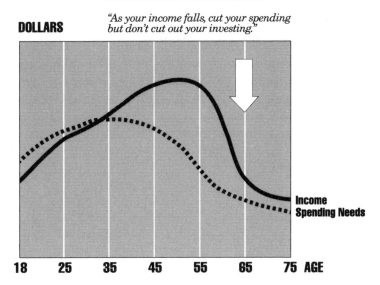

DOLLARS

"As your income falls, cut your spending but don't cut out your investing."

Income
Spending Needs

18   25   35   45   55   65   75 AGE

A Letter to an 85-Year-Old

Dear Bill,

My friend, I want to give you the good news that you don't have to worry about your investments. The good Lord has taken care of you this far; I'm sure He is not going to forsake you now. You know, the Bible says in Matthew 10:30 that the Lord knows even the number of hairs on your head (not much to count, I know).

But, having said that, I don't want you to be invested in the most risky stock mutual funds or risky long-term bond funds with any money that you may need to call on or use in the next 5 or 10 years. It's just not worth taking the risk; for over the next 5 years there is a good chance that stock and bond investments will not do well, and cash will be king. The 12-year-old bull market in financial investments that started in 1982 could soon come to an end. And, I don't want to see you or your nest egg get hurt.

In general, what I am saying is that a portfolio something like the following should now be your cup of tea:

Stock or equity funds	15%
Short-term bond funds	35
Money market/cash funds	50
	100%

As to daily living needs, don't forget to use the dividends from your money market funds and the dividends from your bond funds. If that's not enough, remember that you can use automatic withdrawal plans to pull more money out of your stock and bond funds—if you need it.

Well, Bill, sit back and enjoy your leisure—you deserve it! And pick a mild climate! My friend Pete Dickinson (who writes *Retirement Letter*) recommends relaxing spots like Prescott, Arizona; Mountain Home, Arkansas; McAllen, Texas; Tampa Bay, Florida; and Roswell, New Mexico.

I know decisions get tough these days, especially on finances. So, if you have some specific questions, call me at (301) 840-0301. You have helped a lot of people when you could. Now it's time for us to help you—and we're glad to!

Your friend,
Jay

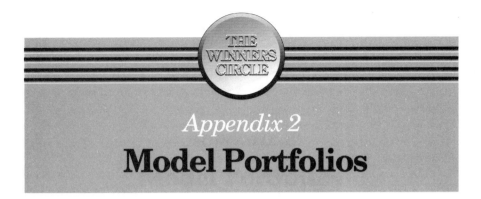

Appendix 2
Model Portfolios

Exhibit 1. The "Buy and Hold" Investor's Portfolio Asset Allocation.

Exhibit 2. Asset Allocation Using Back of the Envelope Technical Stock Market Forecaster: Lowest Risk Market.

Exhibit 3. Asset Allocation Using Back of the Envelope Technical Stock Market Forecaster: Highest Risk Market.

Exhibit 4. Portfolio Allocations Investing Per The Cycles: Phase I—Early Recovery.

Exhibit 5. Portfolio Allocations Investing Per The Cycles: Phase II—Late Recovery.

Exhibit 6. Portfolio Allocations Investing Per The Cycles: Phase III—Stagflation.

Exhibit 7. Portfolio Allocations Investing Per The Cycles: Phase IV—Recession.

EXHIBIT 1

The "Buy & Hold" Investor's Portfolio Asset Allocation
Example Portfolios

CONSERVATIVE INVESTOR

HYBRID/ALL–WEATHER STOCK FUNDS
Fidelity Puritan	15%
Vanguard Wellesley Income	15%

HIGH–QUALITY BOND FUNDS
Fidelity Government Securities Fund	20%
Vanguard Bond Index Fund	20%

CASH FUNDS
Fidelity Cash Reserves	15%
Vanguard MM Prime	15%
	100%

MODERATE RISK INVESTOR

HYBRID/ALL–WEATHER STOCK FUNDS
Evergreen Foundation Fund	15%
Fidelity Balanced	15%
Vanguard Wellington Fund	20%

HIGH–QUALITY BOND FUNDS
Fidelity Investment Grade Bond	15%
Vanguard Bond Index Fund	15%

CASH FUNDS
Fidelity Cash Reserves	10%
Vanguard MM Prime	10%
	100%

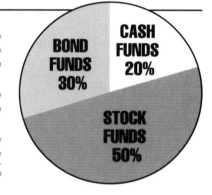

AGGRESSIVE INVESTOR

HYBRID/ALL–WEATHER STOCK FUNDS
CGM Mutual	20%
Fidelity Contrafund	20%
Nicholas Fund	20%
Neuberger Berman Partners Fund	10%

HIGH–QUALITY BOND FUNDS
Janus Flexible Income	20%

CASH FUNDS
Fidelity Cash Reserves	10%
	100%

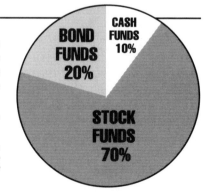

EXHIBIT 2

Asset Allocation Using Back of the Envelope Technical Stock Market Forecaster

Lowest Risk Market / "Bull Market"   Stock Forecaster Reading 40–50 Points

Example Portfolios

CONSERVATIVE INVESTOR

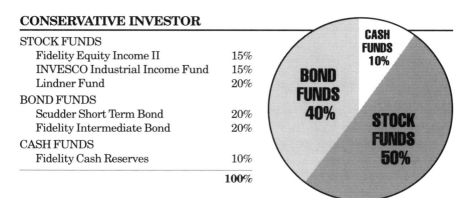

STOCK FUNDS	
Fidelity Equity Income II	15%
INVESCO Industrial Income Fund	15%
Lindner Fund	20%
BOND FUNDS	
Scudder Short Term Bond	20%
Fidelity Intermediate Bond	20%
CASH FUNDS	
Fidelity Cash Reserves	10%
	100%

MODERATE RISK INVESTOR

STOCK FUNDS	
Fidelity Contrafund	20%
Nicholas Fund	20%
T. Rowe Price Capital Appreciation	20%
T. Rowe Price International Stock	10%
BOND FUNDS	
Vanguard Bond Index	15%
Fidelity Intermediate Bond	15%
	100%

AGGRESSIVE INVESTOR

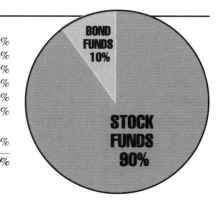

STOCK FUNDS	
Brandywine Fund	15%
Neuberger Berman Partners	15%
Strong Discovery	15%
Stein Roe Special	15%
T. Rowe Price International Stock	15%
Scudder International	15%
BOND FUNDS	
Vanguard F.I. High Yield	10%
	100%

EXHIBIT 3

Asset Allocation Using Back of the Envelope Technical Stock Market Forecaster

Highest Risk Market / "Bear Market"   Stock Forecaster Reading 10–19 Points

Example Portfolios

CONSERVATIVE INVESTOR

STOCK FUNDS	
Lindner Fund	10%
BOND FUNDS	
Scudder Short Term Bond	15%
Fidelity Intermediate Bond	15%
Vanguard Bond Index Fund	10%
CASH FUNDS	
Fidelity Cash Reserve	25%
Vanguard MM Prime	25%
	100%

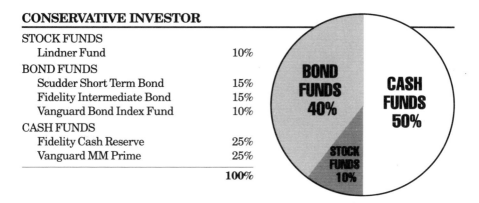

MODERATE RISK INVESTOR

STOCK FUNDS	
Fidelity Contrafund	15%
T. Rowe Price Capital Appreciation	15%
BOND FUNDS	
Vanguard F.I. Short Term Corporate	15%
Fidelity Intermediate Bond	15%
CASH FUNDS	
Fidelity Cash Reserve	20%
Vanguard MM Prime	20%
	100%

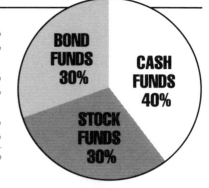

AGGRESSIVE INVESTOR

STOCK FUNDS	
Stein Roe Special	15%
Neuberger Berman Partners	15%
T. Rowe Price International Stock	10%
Scudder International	10%
BOND FUNDS	
Vanguard F.I. High Yield	20%
CASH FUNDS	
Vanguard MM Prime	30%
	100%

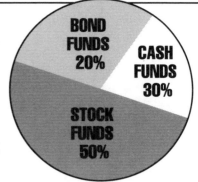

EXHIBIT 4

Portfolio Allocations Investing Per The Cycles
Phase I — Early Recovery

Favor: Stock Funds of Small Cap Growth Style

Example Portfolios

CONSERVATIVE INVESTOR

STOCK FUNDS	
Strong Discovery	20%
Columbia Special	15%
INVESCO Industrial Income	15%
BOND FUNDS	
Vanguard Bond Index Fund	20%
Fidelity Intermediate Bond	20%
CASH FUNDS	
Fidelity Cash Reserves	10%
	100%

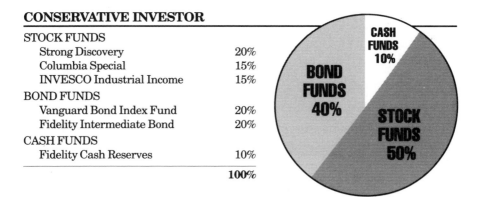

MODERATE RISK INVESTOR

STOCK FUNDS	
Strong Discovery	20%
Columbia Special	20%
Kaufmann Fund	20%
T. Rowe Price International Stock	10%
BOND FUNDS	
Fidelity Intermediate Bond	15%
Janus Flexible Income	10%
CASH FUNDS	
Fidelity Cash Reserves	5%
	100

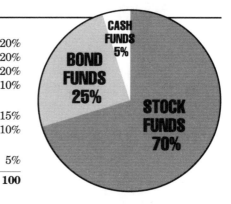

AGGRESSIVE INVESTOR

STOCK FUNDS	
Twentieth Century Ultra	15%
Strong Discovery	15%
Columbia Special	15%
Kaufmann Fund	15%
T. Rowe Price International Stock	15%
Scudder International	15%
BOND FUNDS	
Vanguard F.I. High Yield	10%
	100%

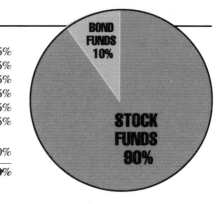

EXHIBIT 5

Portfolio Allocations Investing Per The Cycles
Phase II — Late Recovery
Favor: Stock Funds of Small Cap Value Style
Example Portfolios

CONSERVATIVE INVESTOR

STOCK FUNDS	
Mutual Beacon	15%
Lindner	15%
BOND FUNDS	
Vanguard F.I. Short Term Corporate	20%
CASH FUNDS	
Vanguard MM Prime	25%
Fidelity Cash Reserves	25%
	100%

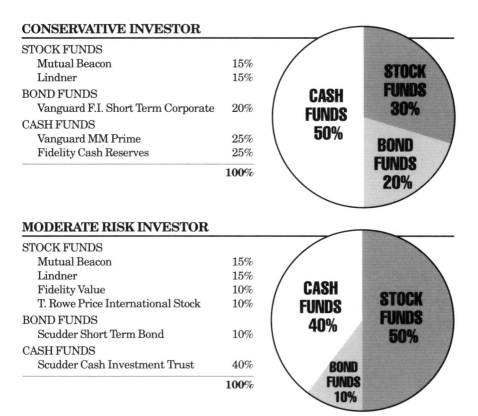

MODERATE RISK INVESTOR

STOCK FUNDS	
Mutual Beacon	15%
Lindner	15%
Fidelity Value	10%
T. Rowe Price International Stock	10%
BOND FUNDS	
Scudder Short Term Bond	10%
CASH FUNDS	
Scudder Cash Investment Trust	40%
	100%

AGGRESSIVE INVESTOR

STOCK FUNDS	
Lindner	15%
Mutual Beacon	15%
Fidelity Value	15%
Vanguard Specialized Gold	10%
Scudder International	15%
CASH FUNDS	
Scudder Cash Investment Trust	30%
	100%

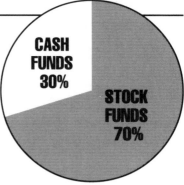

EXHIBIT 6

Portfolio Allocations Investing Per The Cycles
Phase III — Stagflation

Favor: Stock Funds of Large Cap Value Style

Example Portfolios

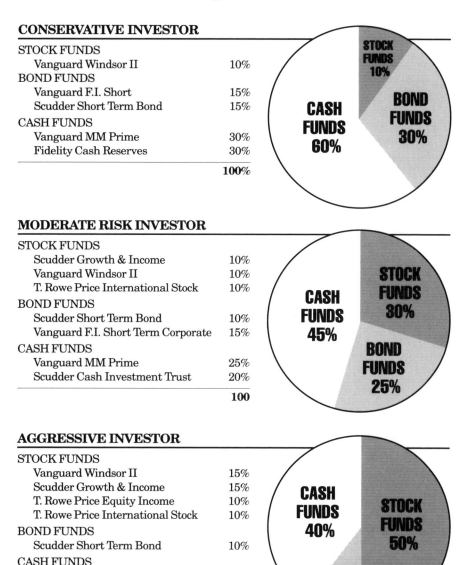

CONSERVATIVE INVESTOR

STOCK FUNDS	
Vanguard Windsor II	10%
BOND FUNDS	
Vanguard F.I. Short	15%
Scudder Short Term Bond	15%
CASH FUNDS	
Vanguard MM Prime	30%
Fidelity Cash Reserves	30%
	100%

MODERATE RISK INVESTOR

STOCK FUNDS	
Scudder Growth & Income	10%
Vanguard Windsor II	10%
T. Rowe Price International Stock	10%
BOND FUNDS	
Scudder Short Term Bond	10%
Vanguard F.I. Short Term Corporate	15%
CASH FUNDS	
Vanguard MM Prime	25%
Scudder Cash Investment Trust	20%
	100

AGGRESSIVE INVESTOR

STOCK FUNDS	
Vanguard Windsor II	15%
Scudder Growth & Income	15%
T. Rowe Price Equity Income	10%
T. Rowe Price International Stock	10%
BOND FUNDS	
Scudder Short Term Bond	10%
CASH FUNDS	
Vanguard MM Prime	20%
Scudder Cash Investment Trust	20%
	100

EXHIBIT 7

Portfolio Allocations Investing Per The Cycles
Phase IV—Recession

Favor: Stock Funds of Large Cap Growth Style
Example Portfolios

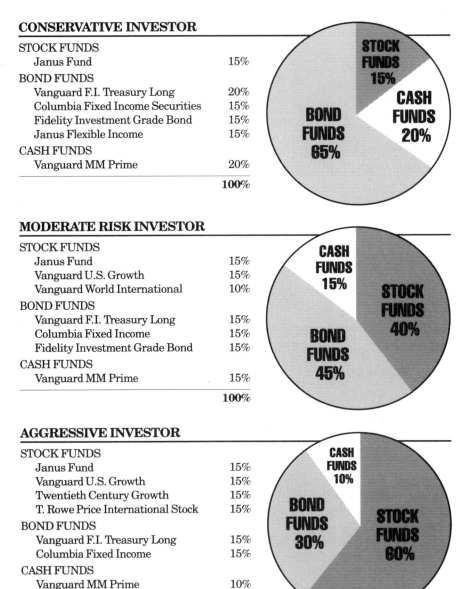

CONSERVATIVE INVESTOR

STOCK FUNDS	
Janus Fund	15%
BOND FUNDS	
Vanguard F.I. Treasury Long	20%
Columbia Fixed Income Securities	15%
Fidelity Investment Grade Bond	15%
Janus Flexible Income	15%
CASH FUNDS	
Vanguard MM Prime	20%
	100%

MODERATE RISK INVESTOR

STOCK FUNDS	
Janus Fund	15%
Vanguard U.S. Growth	15%
Vanguard World International	10%
BOND FUNDS	
Vanguard F.I. Treasury Long	15%
Columbia Fixed Income	15%
Fidelity Investment Grade Bond	15%
CASH FUNDS	
Vanguard MM Prime	15%
	100%

AGGRESSIVE INVESTOR

STOCK FUNDS	
Janus Fund	15%
Vanguard U.S. Growth	15%
Twentieth Century Growth	15%
T. Rowe Price International Stock	15%
BOND FUNDS	
Vanguard F.I. Treasury Long	15%
Columbia Fixed Income	15%
CASH FUNDS	
Vanguard MM Prime	10%
	100%

Appendix 3

Worksheets

Investor Risk Profile Scorecard.

Investor Activity Profile Scorecard.

Back of the Envelope Technical Forecaster.

Current Portfolio Worksheet.

Calculating Your Cost Basis.

Investor Risk Profile

SCORECARD

		Points
1.	Time Frame	
2.	Years to Retirement	
3.	Financial Cushion	
4.	Cash Flow	
5.	Special Circumstances	
6.	Need for Income	
7.	Investing Attitude	
8.	Long-Range Attitude	
9.	Primary Objective	
10.	Feeling Toward Risk	

YOUR TOTAL SCORE

What Your Score Means		
If your total score is:	**This is the amount of risk you should take:**	**And this is the type of investment plan you should follow:**
7–15	Low Risk	CONSERVATIVE
16–30	Medium Risk	MODERATE
31–38	High Risk	AGGRESSIVE

Your Activity Profile

SCORECARD

Add up your score for questions 1–5:

Question	1	
Question	2	
Question	3	
Question	4	
Question	5	

TOTAL A
for questions 1–5

Now add up your score for questions 6–10:

Question	6	
Question	7	
Question	8	
Question	9	
Question	10	

TOTAL B
for questions 6–10

What Your Score Means for Your Investing

IF your scores for both A and B are each below 8, you are probably best suited to a BUY AND HOLD investing approach. See Chapter 3.

IF at least one of your two scores is 8 or higher, and your "A" total is higher than "B," you are best suited for a periodic analysis of stock market risks, and to my ASSET ALLOCATION approach. See Chapter 3.

IF at least one of your two scores is 8 or higher, and your "B" total is higher than your "A," you are best suited for more involved fundamental economic analysis and to my MARKET TIMING investment approach. See Chapter 4.

IF your scores for A and B are both high (above 11), then investing is in your blood and you may try combining both asset allocation and market–timing strategies..

Your Forecaster Really Can Fit on the
Back of an Envelope
Technical Forecaster

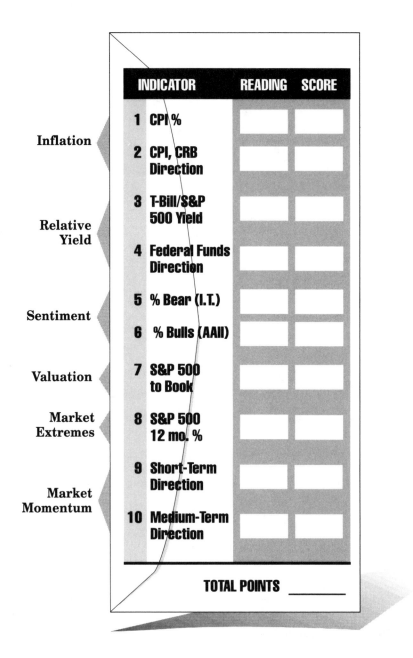

INDICATOR	READING	SCORE
1 CPI %		
2 CPI, CRB Direction		
3 T-Bill/S&P 500 Yield		
4 Federal Funds Direction		
5 % Bear (I.T.)		
6 % Bulls (AAII)		
7 S&P 500 to Book		
8 S&P 500 12 mo. %		
9 Short-Term Direction		
10 Medium-Term Direction		

Inflation

Relative Yield

Sentiment

Valuation

Market Extremes

Market Momentum

TOTAL POINTS _____

Current Portfolio Worksheet

Fund Name	Category	Amount Invested	% of Portfolio
		$	
		$	
		$	
		$	
		$	
		$	
		$	
		$	
		$	
		$	
		$	
		$	
		$	
		$	
		$	
		$	
		$	
		$	
		$	
		$	
		$	
TOTAL		**$**	**100%**

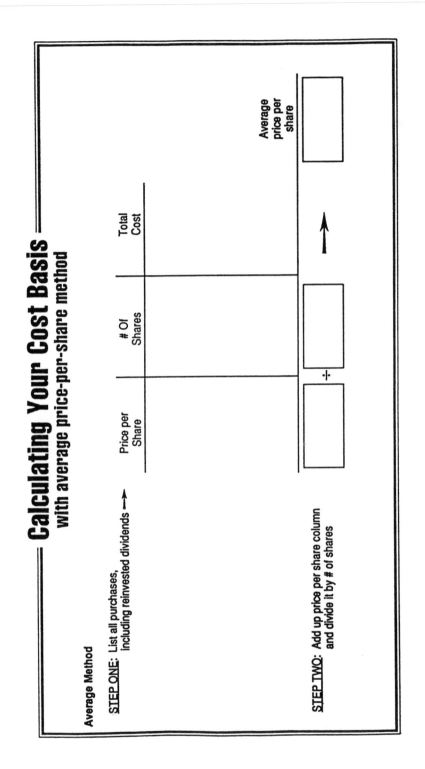

Appendix 4
Directory of Mutual Funds

Table 1. Fund Families.

Table 2. Individual Funds.

Introduction to the Directory

The following Directory of Mutual Funds has been prepared to help you contact the major mutual fund families and, more importantly, so that you can understand and compare the attributes of each mutual fund for which you have an interest.

As such, the Directory is divided into two parts in table form. Table 1 of the Directory is a listing of the names and phone numbers of the 242 major mutual fund families or groups as listed in our funds computer database. Table 2 of the Directory is a listing, in alphabetical order, of the 1,000 largest individual funds that we track in our funds database. You might say that this is the "Schabacker 1000." Money market funds are not included in this listing.

Here is a short explanation of the column headings in Table 2, describing the individual funds.

Fund Name—This should be self-explanatory. But, a few items should be noted:

*   Stands for a fund now closed to new investors
A   Usually denotes the fund utilizes a front-end load charge
B   Usually denotes the fund utilizes a back-end redemption fee
C   Usually denotes an institutional fund (for institutional investors)
L.P. This fund is legally organized as a limited partnership

Category (Cat.)—These are the major fund categories and their abbreviations:

AGGRO   Aggressive Growth
ASSET   Asset Allocation Funds
BAL   Balanced Funds
C-BD   Corporate Bonds
FLEX   Flexible
FLEXB   Flexible Bond
G&I   Growth & Income
GLSTK   Global Stock
GOLD   Gold Funds
GRO   Growth

HY-CB   High Yield Corporate Bonds
INTL   International
MUNI   Municipal Bonds
SECTOR   Sector Funds
US-BD   U.S. Government Bonds

Investment Style/Sector (Invest Style/Sector)—When appropriate, we have used this column to further define a mutual fund's objective and portfolio makeup, i.e., average maturity of a bond portfolio (short-term, long-term), style of a growth portfolio (large cap growth, etc.), and specialization of a sector fund (utilities, technology, etc.).

Quality Rating—This basic rating for every fund compares each fund to those others in its own category. The funds are analyzed by our computer for relative performance over a number of time periods and a few other factors, such as those shown on the remaining columns of the directory pages. "A+" for a fund is the highest (best) rating; "D" for a fund is the lowest (worst) rating.

Risk—Our computer calculates a risk rating for each fund (5 is riskiest, 3 is average, and 1 is lowest risk). This number really gauges the volatility of a fund. Conservative investors might not be comfortable with the high volatility of a "5" risk gold fund, for instance.

Reward-to-Risk Ratio (Rew/Risk)—The reward/risk calculation (also performed by our computer) divides the long-term performance (reward) of each fund above the return of a risk-free money market by the calculated risk or volatility of each fund. Since we want the performance to be high and the risk low, then the reward to risk ratio is best if it is high. A number 1 in the reward/risk column is "best," meaning the fund's reward/risk is high. The number 3 denotes average, and the number 5 denotes the lowest or poorest reward to risk history for the fund.

Just as a reminder, to keep things simple for you—for both the "Risk" column and the "Rew/Risk" column—the *lower* the number given, the better. That is to say, "1" is best and "5" is worst.

Also, as an added explanation, some might wonder why I have not included columns with percentage performance statistics for each fund. The reasons are numerous: (1) a lack of adequate space, (2) timeliness—you can get up-to-date performance from *Barron's,*

Morningstar, and *The Wall Street Journal,* and (3) the reward-to-risk (rew/risk) indication that I have calculated is the most useful number by which you can conveniently compare the funds.

Sales Charge (Sales Chg.)—Most of the funds that I favor have no number in this column because they are "no-load"—without any sales charge. Sometimes I will recommend using a low-load fund that has an initial sales charge of up to 3%. When a sales charge number has an "r" next to the number, this is an indication that that sales charge is not a front-end load but is *a back-end redemption fee* charged when you sell your fund.

5-Year Cost (5-yr. Cost)—This column was added to make your fund's comparison work more user-friendly or reader-friendly to you. Cutting through all the fund charges, including front-end load, expense ratios, 12b-1 marketing fees, and back-end loads, this column compares each fund to the norm as to how expensive it is to own.

Often this is not a major consideration. But, nevertheless, $$$ means the fund is more expensive in total fees than the average. $$ means the fund is about average. And $ (which is to be preferred) means that the fees charged by the fund are below average.

Bull/Bear—Both these columns indicate how a particular fund performs vs. the average common stock fund over a number of historical past periods—either bull markets or bear markets. A bond fund or a very conservative stock fund, such as Fidelity Utilities Income, would likely get a "Bull − /Bear + + +" designation, indicating the fund rises slower than the S&P 500 in a bull market (−) and, on the opposite end, falls much much less than the average stock fund in a bear market (+ + +). A very aggressive growth stock fund, which soars in a bull market and yet crashes in a bear market, gets the following designation: "Bull + + +/Bear − − −." One or more pluses (+) indicates the fund has done better than the S&P 500 over the bull markets or bear markets. One or more minuses (−) indicates the fund has done worse than the S&P 500 over the bull markets or bear markets. + + + is the highest rating and − − − is the lowest rating.

TABLE 1

FAMILY NAME	Phone	FAMILY NAME	Phone
AARP INVESTMENT PROGRAM	(800)253-2277	FIDUCIARY MGMT., INC.	(414)765-4124 (800)338-1579
ABT FUNDS	(800)553-7838	FIRST INVESTORS MGMT.	(800)221-3846
ADVEST ADVANTAGE GROUP	(203)525-1421 (800)243-8115	FIRST UNION FUNDS	(704)374-4343 (800)326-3241
AETNA MUTUAL FUNDS	(800)367-7732	FLAG INVESTORS GROUP	(410)727-1700 (800)767-3524
AIM MANAGEMENT GROUP	(800)998-4246	FLEX-FUNDS	(614)766-7000 (800)325-3539
ALGER FUNDS	(800)992-3863	FONTAINE ASSOCIATES	(410)385-1591 (800)247-1550
ALLIANCE CAPITAL MGMT. CORP.	(212)969-1000 (800)247-4154	FORTIS ADVISERS, INC.	(612)738-4000 (800)800-2638
AMERICAN CAPITAL	(713)993-0500 (800)421-5666	FORTRESS INVESTMENT GROUP	(412)288-1900 (800)245-5051
AMERICAN NATIONAL FUNDS GROUP	(800)392-9753 (800)231-4639	FORTY-FOUR MGMT. CO.	(212)248-8080
ANALYTIC INVESTMENT MGMT.	(714)833-0294	FOUNDERS ASSET MANAGEMENT	(303)394-4404 (800)525-2440
API TRUST FUNDS	(804)846-1361 (800)544-6060	FPA FUNDS	(310)473-0225 (800)982-4372
ARNHOLD AND S. BLEICHROEDER	(800)451-3623	FRANKLIN RESOURCES, INC.	(415)570-3000 (800)632-2180
ARNOLD INVESTMENT COUNSEL	(414)271-7870 (800)443-6544	FRIESS ASSOCIATES, INC.	(302)656-6200 (800)338-1579
BAIRD FUNDS	(414)765-3500 (800)792-2473	FUNDTRUST	(800)344-9033
BARON CAPITAL MANAGEMENT	(212)759-7700 (800)992-2766	G.T. CAPITAL MANAGEMENT	(415)392-6181 (800)824-1580
BARTLETT & CO.	(513)621-4612 (800)543-0863	GABELLI FUNDS, INC.	(914)921-5158 (800)331-7266
BAXTER FINANCIAL	(407)395-2155 (800)749-9933	GATEWAY INVESTMENT ADVISERS	(513)248-2700 (800)354-6339
BEACON HILL MANAGEMENT, INC.	(617)482-0795	GINTEL EQUITY MANAGEMENT	(203)622-6400 (800)243-5808
BENHAM CAPITAL MANAGEMENT	(800)472-3389	GIT INVESTMENT FUNDS	(703)528-3600 (800)336-3063
BERGER ASSOCIATES, INC.	(303)329-0200 (800)333-1001	GLOBAL ASSET MANAGEMENT	(212)888-4200
BLANCHARD GROUP	(212)779-7979 (800)922-7771	GRADISON FINANCIAL SERVICES	(800)869-5999
BOSTON COMPANY	(800)225-5267	GREAT WESTERN FINANCIAL SEC.	(213)488-2425 (800)222-5852
BRUCE FUND, INC.	(312)236-9160	GUARDIAN INVESTOR SERVICES	(212)598-8259 (800)221-3253
BULL & BEAR GROUP, INC.	(212)363-1100 (800)847-4200	HARBOR CAPITAL ADVISORS	(419)247-2477 (800)422-1050
BURNHAM ASSET MANAGEMENT	(800)874-3863	HARRIS ASSOCIATES L.P.	(312)621-0600 (800)476-9625
CALAMOS ASSET MGMT.	(800)323-9943	HEARTLAND GROUP	(800)432-7856
CALVERT GROUP	(301)951-4800 (800)368-2748	HERITAGE FUNDS	(813)573-3800 (800)421-4184
CAPITAL GROUP	(213)486-9200 (800)421-9900	HUNTINGTON FUNDS	(800)354-4111
CAPITAL GROWTH MANAGEMENT	(617)578-1333 (800)345-4048	IDEX GROUP	(813)585-6565 (800)624-4339
CAPSTONE GROUP	(800)262-6631	IDS FINANCIAL SERVICES	(612)372-3733 (800)328-8300
CENTERLAND KLEINWORT BENSON	(212)687-2515 (800)237-4218	INTERNATIONAL STRATEGIC & INV.	(212)446-5606 (800)955-7175
CENTURION FUNDS	(800)448-6984	INVESCO FUNDS GROUP, INC.	(800)525-8085
CENTURY SHARES TRUST	(617)482-3060 (800)321-1928	INVESTMENT ADVISERS, INC.	(612)376-2600 (800)945-3863
COHEN & STEERS CAPITAL MGMT.	(212)832-3232 (800)437-9912	INVESTMENT RESEARCH CORP.	(303)623-6137 (800)525-2406
COLONIAL MGMT. CO.	(617)426-3750 (800)426-3750	INVESTMENT SERIES TRUST	(412)288-1900 (800)245-5051
COLUMBIA MANAGEMENT COMPANY	(503)222-3600 (800)547-1037	INVESTORS RESEARCH CO.	(805)966-7792 (800)732-1733
COMMON SENSE TRUST	(404)381-1000 (800)544-5445	JANUS CAPITAL MANAGEMENT	(303)333-3863 (800)525-3713
COMMONWEALTH GROUP	(804)285-8211 (800)527-9500	JOHN HANCOCK ADVISORS	(800)225-5291
COMPOSITE GROUP OF FUNDS	(509)624-4101 (800)543-8072	JOHN NUVEEN & COMPANY	(312)917-7844 (800)621-7227
COPLEY FINANCIAL SERVICES	(508)674-8459	JONES & BABSON, INC.	(816)471-5200 (800)422-2766
CORNERSTONE CAPITAL CORP.	(800)628-4077	JP INVESTOR SERVICES, INC.	(919)691-3448 (800)458-4498
COWEN FUNDS, INC.	(212)495-6000 (800)221-5616	KAUFMANN FUND, INC.	(212)344-2661
CRAIG-HALLUM, INC.	(612)332-1212 (800)331-4923	KEMPER FINANCIAL SERVICES	(800)621-2414 (800)621-1048
DEAN WITTER REYNOLDS, INC.	(212)938-4553 (800)869-3863	KEY EQUITY MANAGEMENT	(410)823-5353 (800)366-3863
DELAWARE MGMT. CO.	(215)988-1333 (800)523-4640	KEYSTONE AMERICA GROUP	(617)621-6100 (800)343-2898
DIMENSIONAL FUND ADVISORS INC.	(310)395-8005	KEYSTONE MASSACHUSETTS INC.	(617)621-6100 (800)343-2898
DODGE & COX MGMT.	(415)981-1710	KIDDER PEABODY GROUP	(212)510-8101
DREMAN MUTUAL GROUP, INC.	(800)533-1608	LANDMARK FUNDS	(212)564-3456 (800)846-5300
DREYFUS CORPORATION	(800)782-6620	LAUREL MUTUAL FUNDS	(412)364-1746 (800)235-4331
EATON VANCE CORPORATION	(617)482-8260 (800)225-6265	LEGG MASON, INC.	(410)539-4000 (800)368-2558
ECLIPSE FINANCIAL SERVICES	(404)631-0414 (800)872-2710	LEPERCQ DE NEUFLIZE & CO.	(212)698-0700
ENTERPRISE GROUP	(404)396-8118 (800)432-4320	LEXINGTON MGMT.	(201)845-7300 (800)526-0057
EVERGREEN ASSET MGMT.	(914)694-2020 (800)235-0064	LIBERTY FAMILY	(412)288-1900 (800)245-5051
EXCEL ADVISORS	(619)485-9400 (800)783-3444	LIBERTY FINANCIAL TRUST	(617)722-6000 (800)542-3863
FBL INVESTMENT ADVISORY SERV.	(800)422-3175 (800)247-4170	LMH FUND, LTD.	(203)226-4768
FBP CONTRARIAN FUND	(800)525-3863	LOOMIS SAYLES & CO.	(617)482-2450 (800)633-3330
FEDERATED SECURITIES CORP.	(412)288-1900 (800)245-5051	LORD ABBETT & CO.	(212)848-1800 (800)223-4224
FENIMORE ASSET MANAGEMENT	(518)234-4393	MACKAY-SHIELDS MAINSTAY GROUP	(800)522-4202
FIDELITY ADVISOR GROUP	(617)523-1919 (800)522-7297	MACKENZIE GROUP OF FUNDS	(407)393-8900 (800)456-5111
FIDELITY MANAGEMENT & RESEARCH	(800)544-8888	MADISON INVESTMENT ADVISORS	(608)273-2020 (800)767-0300

FAMILY NAME	Phone	FAMILY NAME	Phone
MARKSTON INVESTMENT MANAGEMENT	(800)323-4726	RYBACK MANAGEMENT CORPORATION	(314)727-5305 (800)995-7777
MASS. FINANCIAL SERVICES	(617)954-5000 (800)343-2829	SACHS COMPANY	(502)636-5633 (800)262-9936
MATHERS & CO.	(708)295-7400 (800)962-3863	SAFECO GROUP	(206)545-5530 (800)426-6730
MERGER FUND	(800)343-8959 (914)241-3360	SAGAMORE FUNDS TRUST	(812)421-3213 (800)338-1579
MERRILL LYNCH ASSET MGMT.	(800)637-3863	SALOMON BROTHERS ASSET MGMT.	(212)747-7000 (800)725-6666
MERRIMAN INVESTMENT TRUST	(206)285-8877 (800)423-4893	SBSF FUNDS	(212)903-1200 (800)422-7273
METLIFE-STATE STREET	(617)348-2000 (800)882-0052	SCHIELD MANAGEMENT CO.	(303)985-9999 (800)275-2382
MIDWEST FUNDS	(513)629-2000 (800)543-8721	SCHWABFUNDS	(800)435-4000
MIM MUTUAL FUNDS	(216)642-3000 (800)233-1240	SCUDDER STEVENS & CLARK	(617)951-1828 (800)225-2470
MIMLIC FUNDS	(612)228-4833 (800)443-3677	SECURITY MGMT. CO.	(913)295-3127 (800)888-2461
MONETTA FINANCIAL SERVICES	(708)462-9800 (800)666-3882	SEI FINANCIAL SERVICES	(215)254-1000 (800)342-5734
MONITREND INVESTMENT MGMT.	(615)298-1000 (800)251-1970	SELECTED/VENTURE ADVISERS	(505)983-4335 (800)279-0279
MONTGOMERY ASSET MANAGEMENT	(415)627-2452 (800)428-1871	SELIGMAN GROUP	(212)850-1864 (800)221-7844
MUHLENKAMP & CO., INC.	(412)935-5520 (800)860-3863	SENTINEL ADVISORS, INC.	(802)229-3900 (800)233-4332
MUTUAL OF OMAHA FUND MGMT.	(402)397-8555 (800)228-9596	SENTRY EQUITY SERVICES	(715)346-6000 (800)533-7827
MUTUAL SERIES FUNDS	(800)553-3014	SIT MUTUAL FUND GROUP	(612)334-5888 (800)332-5580
NATIONAL INDUSTRIES FUND MGMT.	(303)220-8500 (800)367-7814	SKYLINE FUND	(312)670-6035 (800)458-5222
NATIONAL SECURITIES & RESEARCH	(203)253-2030 (800)243-1574	SMITH BARNEY FUNDS, INC.	(212)698-5349 (800)221-8806
NATIONWIDE FUNDS	(614)249-7855 (800)848-0920	SMITH BARNEY SHEARSON INC.	(212)720-9218
NEUBERGER & BERMAN MANAGEMENT	(212)476-8800 (800)877-9700	SMITH BREEDEN ASSOCIATES	(800)221-3138
NICHOLAS COMPANY, INC.	(414)272-6133	SOGEN SECURITIES, INC.	(212)399-1141 (800)334-2143
NOMURA	(212)208-9300 (800)833-0018	SOUND SHORE MANAGEMENT, INC.	(203)629-1980 (800)551-1980
NORTH AMERICAN SECURITIES	(800)872-8037	SOUTHEASTERN ASSET MANAGEMENT	(800)445-9469
NORTHEAST INVESTORS TRUST	(617)523-3588 (800)225-6704	STATE STREET RESEARCH & MGMT.	(617)348-2000 (800)882-0052
OHIO COMPANY	(800)282-9446 (800)848-7734	STEADMAN SECURITY CORP.	(202)223-1000 (800)424-8570
OLYMPIC TRUST	(213)362-8900 (800)346-7301	STEIN ROE & FARNHAM	(312)368-7800 (800)338-2550
OPPENHEIMER MGMT.	(800)525-7048	STRATTON FUNDS	(215)941-0255 (800)634-5726
OVERLAND EXPRESS FUNDS, INC.	(800)572-7797	STRONG/CORNELIUSON CAPITAL MGT	(414)359-1400 (800)368-3863
PACIFIC FINANCIAL RESEARCH	(213)278-4461 (800)776-5033	SUNAMERICA ASSET MANAGEMENT	(800)858-8850
PACIFIC HORIZON	(619)456-9196 (800)332-3863	T. ROWE PRICE ASSOCIATES	(410)547-2308 (800)638-5660
PACIFIC INVESTMENT MGMT. CO.	(800)927-4648	TEMPLETON GROUP	(813)823-8712 (800)237-0738
PACIFICA FUNDS	(800)845-8406	THE TORRAY CORPORATION	(301)493-4600
PAINE WEBBER, INC.	(212)713-2084 (800)647-1568	THIRD AVENUE VALUE FUND, INC.	(212)888-6685 (800)443-1021
PARNASSUS FINANCIAL MGMT.	(415)362-3505 (800)999-3505	THOMSON ADVISORY GROUP	(212)482-5894 (800)628-1237
PASADENA GROUP	(818)351-9686 (800)882-2855	THORNBURG FUNDS	(505)984-0200 (800)847-0200
PAX WORLD MGMT. CORP.	(603)431-8022 (800)767-1729	TNE GROUP OF FUNDS	(800)343-7104
PENN SQUARE MGMT. CORP.	(215)670-1031 (800)523-8440	TRANSAMERICA FUNDS	(800)472-3863
PERMANENT FUNDS	(512)453-7558 (800)531-5142	TRANSAMERICA SPECIAL FUNDS	(800)472-3863
PERRITT INVESTMENTS	(312)649-6940 (800)326-6941	TWENTIETH CENTURY INVESTORS	(816)531-5575 (800)345-2021
PHOENIX EQUITY PLANNING CORP.	(203)253-2030 (800)243-1574	U.S.T. MASTER FUNDS	(800)233-1136
PILGRIM MANAGEMENT	(213)551-0833 (800)331-1080	UNITED SERVICES ADVISORS, INC.	(512)696-1234 (800)873-8637
PILGRIM, BAXTER & ASSOCIATES	(215)254-2362 (800)809-8008	USAA INVESTMENT MGMT. CO.	(800)531-8000
PIONEER GROUP	(617)742-7825 (800)225-6292	VALUE LINE, INC.	(800)223-0818
PIPER JAFFRAY GROUP	(612)342-6000 (800)333-6000	VAN ECK SECURITIES CORP.	(212)687-5200 (800)221-2220
PORTICO FUNDS, INC.	(414)287-3808 (800)228-1024	VAN KAMPEN MERRITT	(800)225-2222
PRINCIPAL PRESERVATION	(414)334-5521 (800)826-4600	VANGUARD GROUP, INC.	(215)648-6000 (800)662-7447
PRINCOR MANAGEMENT CORPORATION	(515)247-5711 (800)247-4123	VECTOR INDEX ADVISORS, INC.	(800)445-2763
PRUDENT SPECULATOR GROUP	(213)778-7732 (800)444-4778	VISTA MUTUAL FUNDS	(800)348-4782
PRUDENTIAL MUTUAL FUND SVCS.	(908)417-7000 (800)648-7637	VOLUMETRIC FUND	(914)623-7637 (800)541-3863
PUTNAM MGMT. CO.	(617)292-1000 (800)354-5487	VOYAGEUR FUNDS	(800)247-1576 (800)553-2143
QUANTITATIVE ADVISORS, INC.	(617)259-1144 (800)331-1244	WADDELL AND REED	(913)236-2000 (800)366-5465
QUEST ADVISORY CORP.	(212)355-7311 (800)221-4268	WALL STREET MGMT.	(212)207-1660
QUEST FOR VALUE ADVISORS	(800)232-3863	WANGER ASSET MANAGEMENT, L.P.	(800)922-6769
REA-GRAHAM FUND, INC.	(310)208-2282 (800)433-1998	WARBURG, PINCUS COUNSELLORS	(800)888-6878
REICH & TANG	(212)370-1110 (800)221-3079	WAYNE HUMMER & CO.	(800)972-5566 (800)621-4477
REYNOLDS CAPITAL MANAGEMENT	(414)765-4124 (800)338-1579	WEISS, PECK & GREER	(212)908-9582 (800)223-3332
RIGHTIME ECONOMETRICS, INC.	(215)887-8111 (800)242-1421	WESTCHESTER CAPITAL MANAGEMENT	(914)241-3360 (800)343-8959
ROBERTSON, STEPHENS, & COMPANY	(415)781-9700 (800)766-3863	WESTCORE TRUST	(303)623-2577 (800)392-2673
ROCHESTER FUNDS	(716)383-1300 (800)955-3863	WILLIAM BLAIR & CO.	(312)853-2424 (800)742-7272
RODNEY SQUARE MANAGEMENT CORP.	(800)336-9970	WOOD STRUTHERS & WINTHROP	(212)504-4000 (800)521-3036
RUANE, CUNNIFF & CO., INC.	(212)245-4500	YACKTMAN ASSET MANAGEMENT CO.	(312)201-1200 (800)525-8258
RUSHMORE GROUP	(301)657-1500 (800)343-3355	ZWEIG/GLASER ADVISERS	(212)635-9800 (800)272-2700

TABLE 2

FUND NAME	Category	Invest Style/Sector	Quality Rating	Risk	Rew/ Risk	Sales Chg.	5-yr. Cost	Bull	Bear
AARP CAPITAL GROWTH FUND	GRO	GROWTH	B-	4	4		$	++	-
AARP GNMA AND U.S. TREASURY FUND	US-BD		B+	1	1		$	- - -	++
AARP GROWTH AND INCOME	Gz&I	VALUE	A	3	3		$	-	++
AARP HIGH QUALITY BOND FUND	FLEXB		A-	2	2		$$	- - -	++
AARP INSURED TAX FREE BOND FUND	MUNI		A	3	3		$	- - -	++
ABT UTILITY INCOME FUND	SECTR	UTILITIES	B-	3	3	4.75	$$	-	+
ACORN FUND*	AGGRO	SMALL CAP GROWTH	A	4	2	2.00r	$	++	-
ACORN INTERNATIONAL	INTL		B+	4	2	2.00r	$		
ADVANTAGE GOVERNMENT SECURITIES	US-BD		A	3	2	4.00r	$$	- - -	++
ADVANTAGE HIGH YIELD BOND	HY-CB		A-	3	2	4.00r	$$	+	+
AIM AGGRESSIVE GROWTH--A	AGGRO	SMALL CAP GROWTH	B	5	3	5.50	$$	+	
AIM CHARTER--A	G&I	LARGE CAP	B+	3	3	5.50	$$	-	- -
AIM CONSTELLATION GROWTH--A	AGGRO	GROWTH	B+	5	3	5.50	$$	+++	- - -
AIM GOVERNMENT SECURITIES--A	US-BD		B	1	3	4.75	$$	- - -	+++
AIM GROWTH--A	GRO	LARGE CAP GROWTH	C	4	4	5.50	$$	+-	-
AIM HIGH YIELD--A	HY-CB		A	3	2	4.75	$$$	-	+++
AIM INCOME--A	FLEXB		A-	2	3	4.75	$$	- -	+++
AIM MUNICIPAL BOND--A	MUNI		B-	2	4	4.75	$$	- -	+++
AIM SUMMIT	GRO	LARGE CAP	B-	4	4	8.50	$	+-	- -
AIM UTILITIES--A	SECTR	UTILITIES	B-	3	3	5.50	$$	- -	++
AIM VALUE--A	GRO	MID CAP	B+	4	3	5.50	$$	-	+-
AIM WEINGARTEN EQUITY	AGGRO	LARGE CAP GROWTH	C+	4	4	5.50	$$	++	- -
ALGER SMALL CAPITALIZATION	AGGRO	SMALL CAP GROWTH	B	5	3	5.00r	$$	+++	-
ALLIANCE BALANCED SHARES	BAL	LARGE CAP	C+	3	2	4.25	$$	-	++
ALLIANCE BOND--CORPORATE--A	C-BD		A+	3	2	4.25	$$$	- -	+++
ALLIANCE BOND--U.S. GOVERNMENT--A	US-BD		B	2	3	4.25	$$	- - -	++
ALLIANCE FUND--A	GRO	LARGE CAP GROWTH	B-	4	3	4.25	$$	+	- -
ALLIANCE GROWTH AND INCOME--A	G&I	LARGE CAP	B-	3	4	4.25	$$	+-	+
ALLIANCE INTERNATIONAL--A	INTL		C	5	4	4.25	$$$	+-	+-
ALLIANCE MORTGAGE SECURITIES INCOME--A	US-BD		B+	2	2	4.25	$$	- -	+++
ALLIANCE MULTI-MARKET INCOME & GROWTH	FLEX		D	2	4	1.00	$$		
ALLIANCE MUNI. INCOME--INSURED--A	MUNI		B+	2	3	4.25	$$	- -	++
ALLIANCE MUNI. INCOME--NATIONAL--A	MUNI		A-	2	3	4.25	$$	- -	++
ALLIANCE QUASAR ASSOCIATES--A	AGGRO	SMALL CAP	C-	5	4	4.25	$$	+++	- - -
ALLIANCE SHORT-TERM MULTI-MARKET--A	GLBND	SHORT-TERM	C+	2	4	4.25	$$	- - -	- - -
ALLIANCE TECHNOLOGY	SECTR	TECHNOLOGY	C+	5	3	4.25	$$$	+++	- - -
ALLIANCE WORLD INCOME TRUST	GLBND	SHORT-TERM	C-	1	5		$$		
AMCAP FUND	GRO	LARGE CAP	B-	3	4	5.75	$$	+-	+
AMERICAN BALANCED FUND	BAL	LARGE CAP VALUE	B-	2	3	5.75	$$	-	+
AMERICAN CAPITAL COMSTOCK--A	GRO	LARGE CAP	C+	3	4	5.75	$$	-	+
AMERICAN CAPITAL CORPORATE BOND--A	C-BD		B	2	3	4.75	$$	- -	+++
AMERICAN CAPITAL EMERGING GROWTH--A	AGGRO	GROWTH	B+	4	3	5.75	$$	+-	+
AMERICAN CAPITAL ENTERPRISE--A	GRO	GROWTH	B-	4	3	5.75	$$	+	- -
AMERICAN CAPITAL EQUITY INCOME--A	FLEX	LARGE CAP	B-	3	3	5.75	$$	-	++
AMERICAN CAPITAL GOVERNMENT SEC.--A	US-BD		A-	2	2	4.75	$$	- - -	++
AMERICAN CAPITAL GROWTH AND INCOME	G&I	LARGE CAP	B-	3	4	5.75	$$	-	+
AMERICAN CAPITAL HARBOR--A	G&I	CONVERTIBLE	B-	3	4	5.75	$$	-	+
AMERICAN CAPITAL HIGH YIELD INVEST.	HY-CB		B-	3	3	4.75	$$	-	++
AMERICAN CAPITAL MUNICIPAL BOND	MUNI		B-	3	3	4.75	$$	- -	+++
AMERICAN CAPITAL PACE--A	GRO	LARGE CAP GROWTH	C+	3	4	5.75	$$	-	+
AMERICAN CAPITAL TAX-EXEMPT HY	MUNI	HIGH YIELD	B-	1	3	4.75	$$	- - -	++
AMERICAN HIGH INCOME TRUST	HY-CB		A-	3	2	4.75	$$	-	+
AMERICAN LEADERS	G&I	LARGE CAP VALUE	B+	3	3	4.50	$$	-	+
AMERICAN MUTUAL FUND	G&I	LARGE CAP VALUE	B	3	3	5.75	$$	-	+
AMERICAN NATIONAL GROWTH	GRO	LARGE CAP GROWTH	D	4	4	5.75	$$	+	-
AMERICAN NATIONAL INCOME	G&I	LARGE CAP	C	3	4	5.75	$$$	-	++
ANALYTIC OPTIONED EQUITY FUND	G&I	LARGE CAP VALUE	C+	2	3		$	-	++
BABSON BOND TRUST--LONG	C-BD	LONG-TERM	B+	2	1		$$	- -	+++
BABSON ENTERPRISE FUND*	AGGRO	SMALL CAP VALUE	B-	4	3		$	+	-
BABSON GROWTH FUND	GRO	LARGE CAP VALUE	C+	3	3		$	+-	-
BARTLETT BASIC VALUE	G&I	VALUE	C+	3	3		$	-	+

*Fund closed to new investors

FUND NAME	Category	InvestStyle/Sector	Quality Rating	Risk	Rew/ Risk	Sales Chg.	5-yr. Cost	Bull	Bear
BARTLETT FIXED INCOME	US-BD		B+	1	2		$$	---	++
BENHAM ADJUSTABLE RATE GOVERNMENT	US-BD	ADJUSTABLE RATE	B+	1	2		$		
BENHAM EUROPEAN GOVERNMENT BOND	GLBND		C	4	5		$		
BENHAM GNMA INCOME	US-BD	GOV'T MORTGAGE	A	1	1		$	---	+++
BENHAM GOLD EQUITIES INDEX FUND	GOLD	INDEX	B-	5	4		$	---	+-
BENHAM INCOME AND GROWTH FUND	G&I	LARGE CAP	B+	3	3		$		
BENHAM TARGET MATURITIES--2000	US-BD	INTERMEDIATE	A	3	2		$	---	+++
BENHAM TARGET MATURITIES--2005	US-BD	INTERMEDIATE	A	3	2		$	--	++
BENHAM TARGET MATURITIES--2015	US-BD	LONG-TERM	A	4	2		$	--	++
BENHAM TREASURY NOTE FUND	US-BD		B+	1	1		$	---	+++
BERGER ONE HUNDRED AND ONE FUND	G&I	GROWTH	B+	4	3		$$$	-	+
BERGER ONE HUNDRED FUND	AGGRO	GROWTH	B+	5	2		$$	++	---
BLANCHARD GLOBAL GROWTH	ASSET	LARGE CAP	C+	3	4		$$$	-	+
BLANCHARD SHORT TERM GLOBAL INCOME	GLBND	SHORT-TERM	B-	1	3		$$		
BOND FUND OF AMERICA	C-BD		A	2	2	4.75	$$	--	+++
BOSTON CO. CAPITAL APPRECIATION	GRO	LARGE CAP VALUE	B-	4	3		$	+-	+-
BRANDYWINE FUND	AGGRO	GROWTH	A-	4	3		$	++	-
BURNHAM FUND	G&I	LARGE CAP VALUE	B-	3	3	3.00	$$	-	+
CALVERT ARIEL GROWTH*	GRO	SMALL CAP VALUE	C	4	4	4.75	$$	+++	-
CALVERT SOCIAL INV. MANAGED GROWTH	G&I	MID CAP	C+	3	3	4.75	$$	-	+
CALVERT TAX-FREE--LTD. TERM	MUNI	SHORT-TERM	C	1	3	2.00	$$	---	+++
CAPITAL INCOME BUILDER	FLEX	LARGE CAP VALUE	B	3	3	5.75	$$	-	+
CAPITAL WORLD BOND	GLBND		B-	3	3	4.75	$$$	---	+++
CAPSTONE GOVERNMENT INCOME FUND	US-BD		C-	2	4		$$	---	++
CAPSTONE U.S. TREND FUND	GRO	LARGE CAP	C-	3	4	4.75	$$	+-	--
CARDINAL FUND	GRO	LARGE CAP	C+	3	4	6.00	$$	+-	+
CENTURY SHARES TRUST	SECTR	INSURANCE	A-	4	2		$	+	+
CGM MUTUAL	BAL	MID CAP	A+	3	2		$	+-	+
CLIPPER FUND	GRO	LARGE CAP VALUE	B-	3	3		$	+-	+
COHEN & STEERS REALTY SHARES	SECTR	REAL ESTATE	B+	4	3		$		
COLONIAL FEDERAL SECURITIES--A	US-BD		A-	2	2	4.75	$$$	---	++
COLONIAL FUND--A	G&I	VALUE	B	3	3	5.75	$$	-	+
COLONIAL GROWTH SHARES--A	GRO	VALUE	B-	4	4	5.75	$$	+	-
COLONIAL HIGH YIELD SECURITIES--A	HY-CB		A-	3	2	4.75	$$$	-	++
COLONIAL INCOME FUND--A	FLEXB		B-	2	3	4.75	$$$	--	+++
COLONIAL STRATEGIC INCOME FUND--A	FLEXB		B-	3	3	4.75	$$$	-	+
COLONIAL TAX-EXEMPT FUND--A	MUNI		C+	1	3	4.75	$$	---	++
COLONIAL TAX-EXEMPT INSURED FUND--A	MUNI		B-	2	3	4.75	$$	---	++
COLONIAL U.S. GOVERNMENT TRUST--A	US-BD		B-	1	3	4.75	$$$	---	+++
COLUMBIA BALANCED FUND	BAL	LARGE CAP	A-	3	2		$		
COLUMBIA COMMON STOCK FUND	G&I	LARGE CAP	B+	3	3		$		
COLUMBIA FIXED INCOME SECURITIES	FLEXB		A	2	1		$	--	+++
COLUMBIA GROWTH	GRO	GROWTH	B+	4	3		$	+	-
COLUMBIA MUNICIPAL BOND	MUNI		B-	2	3		$	--	++
COLUMBIA SPECIAL	AGGRO	SMALL CAP GROWTH	B+	5	3		$	+++	--
COMMON SENSE GOVERNMENT	US-BD		A-	2	2	6.75	$$$	--	++
COMMON SENSE GROWTH	GRO	LARGE CAP	B-	3	3	8.50	$$$	+	+-
COMMON SENSE GROWTH & INCOME	G&I	LARGE CAP	B-	3	4	8.50	$$$	-	+
COMPOSITE BOND & STOCK FUND	FLEX	LARGE CAP VALUE	C+	3	3	4.50	$$	-	+
COMPOSITE GROWTH	G&I	LARGE CAP VALUE	C	3	3	4.50	$$	-	+
COMPOSITE INCOME FUND	C-BD		B-	3	3	4.00	$$	--	+++
COMPOSITE NORTHWEST 50	GRO	MID CAP	C	4	4	4.50	$$	+++	-
COMPOSITE TAX-EXEMPT BOND	MUNI		B-	2	3	4.00	$$	--	+++
COMPOSITE U.S. GOVERNMENT	US-BD		B+	1	2	4.00	$$	--	+++
DEAN WITTER AMERICAN VALUED SEC.	GRO	LARGE CAP GROWTH	A-	4	2	5.00r	$$	-	-
DEAN WITTER CONVERTIBLE SECURITIES	FLEX	CONVERTIBLE	C+	3	3	5.00r	$$	-	+-
DEAN WITTER DEVELOPING GROWTH	AGGRO	GROWTH	C	5	3	5.00r	$$	-	---
DEAN WITTER DIVIDEND GROWTH	G&I	LARGE CAP	B+	3	2	5.00r	$$	-	+
DEAN WITTER EQUITY INCOME	G&I	LARGE CAP	C-	3	4	5.00r	$$	-	+
DEAN WITTER HIGH YIELD SECURITIES	HY-CB		C+	4	3	5.50	$$	-	++
DEAN WITTER NATURAL RESOURCES	SECTR	NAT. RESOURCES	C-	3	4	5.00r	$$	-	--
DEAN WITTER TAX-EXEMPT SECURITIES	MUNI		B+	2	3	4.00	$$	--	+++
DEAN WITTER U.S. GOVERNMENT SEC.	US-BD		B	1	1	5.00r	$$	---	++

▨ = *Schabacker 100*

FUND NAME	Category	InvestStyle/Sector	Quality Rating	Risk	Rew/ Risk	Sales Chg.	5-yr. Cost	Bull	Bear
DEAN WITTER WORLD WIDE INVESTMENT	GLSTK		C+	3	4	5.00r	$$$	-	+
DELAWARE GROUP DECATUR SERIES I	G&I	LARGE CAP VALUE	B-	3	4	8.50	$$	-	+
DELAWARE GROUP DECATUR SERIES II	G&I	LARGE CAP VALUE	B-	3	3	5.75	$$	-	+
DELAWARE GROUP DELAWARE FUND	BAL	MID CAP	B-	3	3	5.75	$$	+-	+
DELAWARE GROUP DELCAP FUND	GRO	SMALL CAP GROWTH	B-	4	4	5.75	$$	+++	-
DELAWARE GROUP DELCHESTER FUND	HY-CB		B	3	3	4.75	$$	-	++
DELAWARE GROUP TAX-FREE--INSURED	MUNI		C+	2	3	4.75	$$	---	++
DELAWARE GROUP TAX-FREE--USA SERIES	MUNI		B	3	3	4.75	$$	--	++
DELAWARE GROUP TREAS. RES. INTERMEDIATE	US-BD	INTERMEDIATE	B-	1	2	3.00	$$	---	+++
DELAWARE GROUP TREND FUND	AGGRO	SMALL CAP GROWTH	B+	5	3	5.75	$$	+++	- -
DELAWARE GROUP U.S. GOVERNMENT FUND	US-BD		B	1	3	4.75	$$$	---	+++
DFA CONTINENTAL SMALL COMPANY	INTL	EUROPE	C	4	4	1.50	$	--	+
DFA FIVE-YEAR GOVERNMENT	US-BD		A-	2	2		$	---	+++
DFA GLOBAL BOND	GLBND		B	2	3		$		
DFA JAPANESE SMALL COMPANY	INTL	PACIFIC BASIN	B-	5	4	1.00	$	-	+
DFA ONE-YEAR FIXED INCOME	C-BD	SHORT-TERM	B-	1	2		$	---	++
DFA U.S. 9-10 SMALL COMPANY	AGGRO	SMALL CAP VALUE	C+	4	3		$	+	-
DFA UNITED KINGDOM SMALL COMPANY	INTL	EUROPE	C	5	5	1.50	$	--	+
DODGE & COX BALANCED FUND	BAL	LARGE CAP VALUE	A+	3	2		$	-	+
DODGE & COX INCOME	FLEXB		A	2	2		$	--	+++
DODGE & COX STOCK FUND	G&I	LARGE CAP VALUE	A	3	2		$	+	+
DREYFUS 100% U.S. TREAS. INTERM., L.P.	US-BD	INTERMEDIATE	A+	2	2		$	---	+++
DREYFUS 100% U.S. TREAS. LONG TERM, L.P.	US-BD	LONG-TERM	A+	3	2		$$	--	++
DREYFUS A BONDS PLUS	C-BD	HIGH GRADE	A+	2	2		$	--	+++
DREYFUS APPRECIATION FUND	GRO	LARGE CAP GROWTH	C+	3	4		$	+-	+
DREYFUS CAPITAL GROWTH FUND	GRO	LARGE CAP	B-	3	3	3.00	$$	-	+
DREYFUS CAPITAL VALUE--A	FLEX	GROWTH	C	3	5	4.50	$$	--	+++
DREYFUS FUND	G&I	LARGE CAP	C+	3	4		$	-	+
DREYFUS GNMA	US-BD	GOV'T MORTGAGE	B+	1	1		$	---	++
DREYFUS GROWTH OPPORTUNITY	GRO	LARGE CAP GROWTH	C	4	4		$	-	- -
DREYFUS INSURED MUNICIPAL	MUNI		A-	2	3		$	---	++
DREYFUS INTERMEDIATE MUNICIPAL	MUNI	INTERMEDIATE	B	2	2		$	---	++
DREYFUS MUNICIPAL BOND FUND	MUNI		A-	2	2		$	--	+++
DREYFUS NEW LEADERS	AGGRO	SMALL CAP	B-	3	2	1.00r	$$	+	-
DREYFUS PEOPLES INDEX FUND	G&I	LARGE CAP	B-	3	3	1.00r	$	+-	+-
DREYFUS SHORT-INTERM. GOVERNMENT	US-BD	SHORT-TERM	B+	1	1		$	---	+++
DREYFUS SHORT-INTERM. MUNICIPAL	MUNI	SHORT-TERM	B-	1	2		$	---	++
DREYFUS STRATEGIC INCOME	C-BD		A	2	2	3.00	$$$	--	++
DREYFUS STRATEGIC INVESTING--A	GRO	GROWTH	B+	3	3	4.50	$$	-	+
DREYFUS STRATEGIC WORLD INVESTING	GLSTK		B-	3	4	3.00	$$	-	++
DREYFUS THIRD CENTURY FUND	GRO	GROWTH	B-	4	3		$	-	-
EATON VANCE GOV'T OBLIGATION	US-BD		A-	1	2	4.75	$$$	---	+++
EATON VANCE GROWTH FUND	GRO	LARGE CAP GROWTH	C+	4	4	4.75	$$	+-	+-
EATON VANCE INCOME FUND OF BOSTON	HY-CB		B+	3	2	4.75	$$	-	++
EATON VANCE INVESTORS FUND	G&I	LARGE CAP VALUE	C+	2	3	4.75	$$	-	+
EATON VANCE MARATHON HIGH INCOME	HY-CB		C+	3	2	6.00r	$$$	--	+
EATON VANCE MARATHON NATIONAL MUNICIPAL	MUNI		B-	3	3	6.00r	$$$	--	++
EATON VANCE MUNICIPAL BOND FUND	MUNI		A	2	3	4.75	$$	--	+++
EATON VANCE SHORT TERM GLOBAL INCOME	GLBND	SHORT-TERM	D	2	5	3.00r	$$		
EATON VANCE STOCK FUND	G&I	LARGE CAP GROWTH	C+	3	4	4.75	$$	-	+
EATON VANCE TOTAL RETURN TRUST	G&I	LARGE CAP VALUE	A	3	3	4.75	$$	-	++
ECLIPSE EQUITY	GRO	SMALL CAP VALUE	B+	4	3		$	-	+
ENTERPRISE CAPITAL APPRECIATION	GRO	LARGE CAP GROWTH	B	4	3	4.75	$$	+	+-
ENTERPRISE GOVERNMENT SECURITIES	US-BD		B+	1	2	4.75	$$$	---	+++
EUROPACIFIC GROWTH	INTL		B	3	4	5.75	$$	-	+
EVERGREEN FOUNDATION FUND	FLEX	VALUE	A	3	2		$$	+-	+
EVERGREEN FUND	AGGRO	MID CAP	C	4	4		$	+	-
EVERGREEN LIMITED MARKET FUND	AGGRO	SMALL CAP	B	4	3		$$	++	+
EVERGREEN TOTAL RETURN FUND	G&I	VALUE	B	3	3		$	-	++
F.A.M. VALUE*	G&I	SMALL CAP VALUE	A-	4	3		$$	++	+-
FEDERATED ARMS FUND	US-BD	ADJUSTABLE RATE	B	2	2		$	---	++
FEDERATED GNMA TRUST	US-BD	GOV'T MORTGAGE	A	1	1		$	--	+++
FEDERATED GROWTH	GRO	MID CAP	B-	4	4		$	++	+-

▨ = *Schabacker 100*   **Fund closed to new investors*

FUND NAME	Category	InvestStyle/Sector	Quality Rating	Risk	Rew/ Risk	Sales Chg.	5-yr. Cost	Bull	Bear
FEDERATED INCOME TRUST	US-BD		B+	1	2		$	--	+++
FEDERATED INTERMEDIATE GOV'T. TRUST	US-BD	INTERMEDIATE	B+	1	2		$	--	+++
FEDERATED SHORT-TERM MUNICIPAL	MUNI	SHORT-TERM	C	1	4		$	---	+++
FEDERATED STOCK & BOND FUND	FLEX	LARGE CAP VALUE	B-	2	3		$	-	++
FIDELITY ADVIS. GROWTH OPPORTUNITIES	AGGRO	MID CAP	C+	4	3	4.75	$$	+++	-
FIDELITY ADVIS. HIGH INCOME MUNICIPAL	MUNI	HIGH YIELD	A	2	2	4.75	$$	--	+++
FIDELITY ADVIS. HIGH YIELD	HY-CB		A	3	2	4.75	$$	-	++
FIDELITY ADVIS. INCOME AND GROWTH	FLEX	SMALL CAP VALUE	A-	3	2	4.75	$$	+-	+
FIDELITY ADVIS. SHORT FIXED INCOME	FLEXB	SHORT-TERM	B-	1	2	1.50	$$	---	++
FIDELITY ADVIS. STRATEGIC OPPORTUNITIES	GRO	LARGE CAP VALUE	B+	3	3	4.75	$$	-	+
FIDELITY AGGRESSIVE TAX-FREE	MUNI	HIGH YIELD	A	2	2	1.00r	$	---	++
FIDELITY ASSET MANAGER	ASSET	MID CAP	A	3	2		$	-	+
FIDELITY ASSET MANAGER--GROWTH	ASSET	MID CAP	A+	3	1		$$		
FIDELITY BALANCED	BAL	VALUE	A+	3	1		$	-	+
FIDELITY BLUE CHIP GROWTH	GRO	LARGE CAP GROWTH	A	3	2	3.00	$$	++	+
FIDELITY CANADA	INTL	CANADA	B	4	4		$$	+-	+
FIDELITY CAPITAL AND INCOME	HY-CB		A+	3	2	1.50r	$	-	+++
FIDELITY CAPITAL APPRECIATION	GRO	SMALL CAP VALUE	B	3	3	3.00	$	++	+-
FIDELITY CONTRAFUND	GRO	VALUE	A	4	1	3.00	$$	+	-
FIDELITY CONVERTIBLE	G&I	CONVERTIBLE	A	3	2		$	+-	+
FIDELITY DESTINY I	GRO	LARGE CAP VALUE	A	3	3	8.50	$	++	+
FIDELITY DESTINY II	GRO	LARGE CAP VALUE	B+	3	3	8.50	$	+++	-
FIDELITY DISCIPLINED EQUITY	GRO	VALUE	B+	3	3		$	++	+
FIDELITY DIVERSIFIED INTERNATIONAL	INTL		C+	4	4		$$		
FIDELITY EMERGING GROWTH	AGGRO	GROWTH	A-	4	2	3.00	$$		
FIDELITY EMERGING MARKETS	INTL		B-	3	4	1.50r	$$$		
FIDELITY EQUITY INCOME I	G&I	VALUE	A-	3	3	2.00	$	-	+
FIDELITY EQUITY INCOME II	G&I	VALUE	A	3	1		$	++	
FIDELITY EUROPE	INTL	EUROPE	C+	4	4	3.00	$	--	+
FIDELITY FUND	G&I	VALUE	A-	3	2		$	+-	+
FIDELITY GLOBAL BOND	GLBND		A-	2	3		$$	---	+++
FIDELITY GNMA PORTFOLIO	US-BD	GOV'T MORTGAGE	A-	1	1		$	---	+++
FIDELITY GOVERNMENT SECURITIES FUND	US-BD		A	2	1		$	--	+++
FIDELITY GROWTH & INCOME	G&I	VALUE	A-	3	2	3.00	$	+	+
FIDELITY GROWTH COMPANY	AGGRO	GROWTH	A-	4	3	3.00	$$	++	--
FIDELITY HIGH YIELD MUNICIPALS	MUNI	HIGH YIELD	A	3	2		$	--	+++
FIDELITY INSURED TAX-FREE	MUNI		A-	2	3		$	---	++
FIDELITY INT'L GROWTH & INCOME	GLSTK		B	4	4		$$	--	+
FIDELITY INTERMEDIATE BOND	C-BD	INTERMEDIATE	B+	2	2		$	--	+++
FIDELITY INVESTMENT GRADE BOND	FLEXB		A	2	1		$	--	+++
FIDELITY LIMITED TERM MUNICIPALS	MUNI	INTERMEDIATE	B	2	2		$	--	+++
FIDELITY LOW-PRICED STOCK	AGGRO	SMALL CAP VALUE	B+	4	2	3.00	$	+++	+
FIDELITY MAGELLAN FUND	GRO	VALUE	A	4	2	3.00	$$	+++	+
FIDELITY MARKET INDEX FUND	G&I	LARGE CAP	B-	3	3	0.50r	$$	+-	+-
FIDELITY MORTGAGE SECURITIES	US-BD		B+	1	2		$	---	+++
FIDELITY MUNICIPAL BOND FUND	MUNI		A-	2	2		$	--	+++
FIDELITY OVER-THE-COUNTER	GRO	SMALL CAP	B+	4	3	3.00	$$	++	+-
FIDELITY OVERSEAS FUND	INTL		C+	4	5	3.00	$$	--	+
FIDELITY PACIFIC BASIN	INTL	PACIFIC BASIN	B-	4	4	3.00	$$	---	+
FIDELITY PURITAN FUND	FLEX	VALUE	A+	3	2		$	-	++
FIDELITY REAL ESTATE	SECTR	REAL ESTATE	B	4	3		$	+-	+
FIDELITY RETIREMENT GROWTH	AGGRO	MID CAP	B+	4	2		$	+	-
FIDELITY SELECT-AMERICAN GOLD	GOLD		B+	5	3	3.00	$$	--	+
FIDELITY SELECT-AUTOMOTIVE	SECTR	SMOKESTACK IND.	B	4	3	3.00	$$	+	-
FIDELITY SELECT-BIOTECHNOLOGY	SECTR	HEALTH CARE	B-	5	4	3.00	$$	++	+
FIDELITY SELECT-BROKERAGE & INVEST.	SECTR	FINANCIAL	B	5	3	3.00	$$$	+	--
FIDELITY SELECT-DEVELOPING COMMUN.	SECTR	TECHNOLOGY	B+	4	2	3.00	$$	++	--
FIDELITY SELECT-ELECTRONICS	SECTR	TECHNOLOGY	B	5	5	3.00	$$	+	--
FIDELITY SELECT-ENERGY	SECTR	ENERGY	C+	4	4	3.00	$$	-	+
FIDELITY SELECT-ENERGY SERVICE	SECTR	ENERGY	C+	5	4	3.00	$$	-	+-
FIDELITY SELECT-FINANCIAL SERVICES	SECTR	FINANCIAL	B+	5	3	3.00	$$	+++	+-
FIDELITY SELECT-FOOD & AGRICULTURE	SECTR	SERVICES	B	3	3	3.00	$$	+	+
FIDELITY SELECT-HEALTH CARE	SECTR	HEALTH CARE	C+	5	3	3.00	$$	+++	--

▨ = *Schabacker 100*

FUND NAME	Category	Invest.Style/Sector	Quality Rating	Risk	Rew/ Risk	Sales Chg.	5-yr. Cost	Bull	Bear
FIDELITY SELECT-HOME FINANCE	SECTR	FINANCIAL	A-	5	3	3.00	$$	+++	-
FIDELITY SELECT-LEISURE	SECTR	SERVICES	B	4	3	3.00	$$	+++	-
FIDELITY SELECT-PREC. METALS & MINERALS	GOLD		B	5	4	3.00	$$	-	--
FIDELITY SELECT-REGIONAL BANKS	SECTR	FINANCIAL	B+	5	3	3.00	$$	++	-
FIDELITY SELECT-SOFTWARE & COMPUTER	SECTR	TECHNOLOGY	B+	5	3	3.00	$$	++	-
FIDELITY SELECT-TECHNOLOGY	SECTR	TECHNOLOGY	B-	4	3	3.00	$$	++	---
FIDELITY SELECT-TELECOMMUNICATIONS	SECTR	TELECOM.	A-	4	2	3.00	$$	+	+
FIDELITY SELECT-UTILITIES	SECTR	UTILITIES	A-	3	2	3.00	$$	-	+++
FIDELITY SHORT-TERM BOND	C-BD	SHORT-TERM	B	1	2		$	---	++
FIDELITY SHORT-TERM WORLD INCOME	GLBND	SHORT-TERM	B-	2	4		$$		
FIDELITY SPARTAN GOVERNMENT INCOME	US-BD		A	1	1		$	--	+++
FIDELITY SPARTAN LONG-TERM GOV'T	US-BD	LONG-TERM	A+	2	1		$	--	+++
FIDELITY SPARTAN LTD. MATURITY GOV'T	US-BD	SHORT-TERM	B+	1	1		$	---	+++
FIDELITY SPARTAN MUNICIPAL INCOME	MUNI		A-	3	3	0.50r	$	--	++
FIDELITY SPARTAN SHORT-INTERM. MUNI	MUNI	SHORT-TERM	B-	1	2		$	---	++
FIDELITY STOCK SELECTOR	GRO	VALUE	B+	3	3		$	+++	
FIDELITY TREND FUND	GRO	MID CAP	A-	4	3		$	+	-
FIDELITY UTILITIES INCOME	SECTR	UTILITIES	A-	3	2		$	--	+++
FIDELITY VALUE	GRO	SMALL CAP VALUE	B+	4	3		$	+	-
FIDELITY WORLDWIDE	GLSTK		B+	3	4		$$	-	+
FIRST EAGLE FUND OF AMERICA	GRO	SMALL CAP VALUE	B+	4	3	1.00r	$$	-	+-
FIRST INVESTORS FUND FOR INCOME	HY-CB		C	3	3	6.25	$$$	--	++
FIRST INVESTORS GLOBAL	GLSTK		C-	4	4	6.25	$$$	-	-
FIRST INVESTORS GOVERNMENT	US-BD		C+	1	3	6.25	$$$	---	+++
FIRST INVESTORS HIGH YIELD FUND	HY-CB		C+	3	3	6.25	$$$	--	+
FIRST INVESTORS INSURED TAX EXEMPT	MUNI		C	2	4	6.25	$$$	--	+++
FIRST UNION VALUE--B	GRO	LARGE CAP VALUE	B-	3	3	4.00	$$	-	+
FLAG INVESTORS TELEPHONE INCOME--A	SECTR	TELECOM.	B+	3	3	4.50	$$	-	+
FLAG INVESTORS TOTAL RET. US TREAS.--A	US-BD		A	3	3	4.50	$$	--	++
FORTIS ADVANTAGE--ASSET ALLOCATION	ASSET	GROWTH	B-	3	3	4.50	$$	-	+
FORTIS ADVANTAGE--GOV'T TOTAL RETURN	US-BD		B-	2	3	4.50	$$$	---	+++
FORTIS CAPITAL FUND	GRO	LARGE CAP GROWTH	B-	4	4	4.75	$$	+	-
FORTIS GROWTH FUND	AGGRO	GROWTH	B	5	3	4.75	$$	++	--
FORTIS U.S. GOVERNMENT SECURITIES	US-BD		B+	1	3	4.50	$$	--	+++
FORTRESS BOND FUND	HY-CB		A-	3	3	1.00	$$	+	+
FORTRESS GOVERNMENT INCOME SEC.	US-BD		B	1	2	1.00	$$	---	+++
FORTRESS MUNICIPAL INCOME	MUNI		B	2	2	1.00	$$	--	++
FORTRESS UTILITY	SECTR	UTILITIES	B	3	2	1.00	$	-	++
FOUNDERS BLUE CHIP	G&I	LARGE CAP	B+	4	3		$	+-	+
FOUNDERS DISCOVERY	AGGRO	SMALL CAP GROWTH	B	5	3		$$	+++	+
FOUNDERS FRONTIER	AGGRO	SMALL CAP GROWTH	B+	4	3		$$	+++	+
FOUNDERS GROWTH	GRO	LARGE CAP GROWTH	A	4	3		$$	+	-
FOUNDERS SPECIAL	AGGRO	GROWTH	B	4	3		$	++	---
FPA CAPITAL FUND	AGGRO	SMALL CAP VALUE	B-	4	3	6.50	$$	++	--
FPA NEW INCOME	US-BD		A+	2	2	4.50	$$	--	++
FPA PARAMOUNT*	G&I	SMALL CAP VALUE	B+	3	3	6.50	$$	-	++
FRANKLIN ADJUSTABLE U.S. GOVERNMENT	US-BD	ADJUSTABLE RATE	C	1	4	2.25	$$	---	+++
FRANKLIN AGE HIGH INCOME FUND	HY-CB		B-	3	3	4.00	$$	-	++
FRANKLIN ALABAMA TAX-FREE INCOME	MUNI	SINGLE STATE	B-	2	3	4.00	$$	--	++
FRANKLIN ARIZONA TAX-FREE INCOME	MUNI	SINGLE STATE	B-	2	3	4.00	$$	--	++
FRANKLIN CALIFORNIA TAX-FREE INCOME	MUNI	SINGLE STATE	C+	2	4	4.00	$$	--	+++
FRANKLIN COLORADO TAX-FREE INCOME	MUNI	SINGLE STATE	B+	2	3	4.00	$$	--	++
FRANKLIN CONNECTICUT TAX-FREE INCOME	MUNI	SINGLE STATE	B	3	3	4.00	$$	---	++
FRANKLIN EQUITY FUND	GRO	VALUE	C-	4	4	4.00	$$	+	-
FRANKLIN FEDERAL TAX-FREE INCOME	MUNI		B-	2	3	4.00	$$	--	++
FRANKLIN FLORIDA TAX-FREE INCOME	MUNI	SINGLE STATE	B-	2	3	4.00	$$	--	++
FRANKLIN GEORGIA TAX-FREE INCOME	MUNI	SINGLE STATE	B-	2	3	4.00	$$	--	++
FRANKLIN GLOBAL GOVERNMENT INCOME	GLBND		B-	3	4	4.00	$$	---	+++
FRANKLIN GOLD FUND	GOLD		B-	5	4	4.00	$$	-	---
FRANKLIN GROWTH SERIES	GRO	MID CAP	C+	3	4	4.00	$$	+-	+-
FRANKLIN HIGH YIELD TAX-FREE INCOME	MUNI	HIGH YIELD	B	2	3	4.00	$$	---	++
FRANKLIN INCOME SERIES	FLEX	SMALL CAP	A-	3	2	4.00	$	-	++
FRANKLIN INSURED TAX-FREE INCOME	MUNI		B-	2	3	4.00	$$	---	++

▨ = *Schabacker 100*

FUND NAME	Category	InvestStyle/Sector	Quality Rating	Risk	Rew/ Risk	Sales Chg.	5-yr. Cost	Bull	Bear
FRANKLIN LOUISIANA TAX-FREE INCOME	MUNI	SINGLE STATE	B-	2	3	4.00	$$	--	++
FRANKLIN MANAGED RISING DIVIDENDS	G&I	VALUE	C	3	4	4.00	$$	+	+
FRANKLIN MARYLAND TAX-FREE INCOME	MUNI	SINGLE STATE	B-	3	3	4.00	$$	---	++
FRANKLIN MASS. INSURED TAX-FREE INCOME	MUNI	SINGLE STATE	B-	2	3	4.00	$$	---	++
FRANKLIN MICHIGAN INSURED TAX-FREE	MUNI	SINGLE STATE	B-	2	3	4.00	$$	---	++
FRANKLIN MINNESOTA INSURED TAX-FREE	MUNI	SINGLE STATE	B-	2	3	4.00	$$	---	++
FRANKLIN MISSOURI TAX-FREE INCOME	MUNI	SINGLE STATE	B	2	3	4.00	$$	--	++
FRANKLIN NEW JERSEY TAX-FREE INCOME	MUNI	SINGLE STATE	B-	2	3	4.00	$$	---	++
FRANKLIN NEW YORK TAX-FREE INCOME	MUNI	SINGLE STATE	B	2	3	4.00	$$	--	+++
FRANKLIN NORTH CAROLINA TAX-FREE INCOME	MUNI	SINGLE STATE	B	2	3	4.00	$$	--	++
FRANKLIN OHIO INSURED TAX-FREE INCOME	MUNI	SINGLE STATE	B	2	3	4.00	$$	---	++
FRANKLIN OREGON TAX-FREE INCOME	MUNI	SINGLE STATE	B-	2	3	4.00	$$	--	++
FRANKLIN PENNSYLVANIA TAX-FREE INCOME	MUNI	SINGLE STATE	B	2	3	4.00	$$	--	++
FRANKLIN PUERTO RICO TAX-FREE INCOME	MUNI	SINGLE STATE	B-	2	3	4.00	$$	---	++
FRANKLIN SHORT-INTERM. U.S. GOV'T	US-BD	SHORT-TERM	B	1	3	2.25	$$	---	+++
FRANKLIN TEXAS TAX-FREE INCOME	MUNI	SINGLE STATE	B-	2	3	4.00	$$	--	++
FRANKLIN U.S. GOV'T SERIES	US-BD		B	1	3	4.00	$$	--	+++
FRANKLIN UTILITIES SERIES	SECTR	UTILITIES	B	3	3	4.00	$$	-	+++
FRANKLIN VIRGINIA TAX-FREE INCOME	MUNI	SINGLE STATE	B-	2	3	4.00	$$	--	++
FT INTERNATIONAL	INTL		C	4	5	4.50	$$	-	+
FUND FOR U.S. GOV'T SECURITIES	US-BD		B-	1	3	4.50	$$	--	+++
FUNDAMENTAL INVESTORS FUND	G&I	LARGE CAP VALUE	A-	3	3	5.75	$$	+	+
G.T. AMERICA GROWTH	AGGRO	SMALL CAP	C	5	4	4.75	$$	+	-
G.T. EUROPE GROWTH	INTL	EUROPE	C	4	5	4.75	$$$	-	+
G.T. GLOBAL GOVERNMENT INCOME--A	GLBND		B	3	3	4.75	$$$	---	+++
G.T. GLOBAL GROWTH & INCOME--A	GLSTK		C+	3	3	4.75	$$$	--	
G.T. GLOBAL HEALTH CARE	SECTR	HEALTH CARE	C	5	5	4.75	$$$	++	+
G.T. GLOBAL STRATEGIC INCOME--A	GLBND		A	3	3	4.75	$$$	---	+++
G.T. GLOBAL TELECOMMUNICATIONS FUND	SECTR	TELECOM.	B	4	3	4.75	$$$		
G.T. INTERNATIONAL GROWTH	INTL		B-	4	5	4.75	$$$	-	+
G.T. JAPAN GROWTH	INTL	PACIFIC BASIN	C	5	4	4.75	$$$	-	+
G.T. LATIN AMERICA GROWTH	INTL		C	5	5	4.75	$$$		
G.T. PACIFIC GROWTH FUND	INTL	PACIFIC BASIN	B+	4	4	4.75	$$$	-	+
G.T. WORLDWIDE GROWTH	GLSTK		B+	3	4	4.75	$$$	-	+
GABELLI ASSET FUND	GRO	MID CAP	B+	3	3		$	+-	+
GABELLI CONVERTIBLE SECURITIES	FLEX	CONVERTIBLE	A-	2	1	4.50	$$	--	++
GABELLI GROWTH	GRO	GROWTH	B+	4	4		$$	++	+
GABELLI VALUE	GRO	VALUE	B	4	3	5.50	$$	+-	+-
GATEWAY INDEX PLUS	G&I	LARGE CAP	C+	2	3		$	-	+
GINTEL FUND	AGGRO	MID CAP	C+	4	3		$$	+-	+-
GRADISON-MCDONALD ESTABLISHED VALUE	GRO	VALUE	B+	3	3		$$	-	+
GRADISON-MCDONALD GOVERNMENT INCOME	US-BD		B+	1	2	2.00	$$	--	+++
GROWTH FUND OF AMERICA	GRO	LARGE CAP	B	4	4	5.75	$$	+	-
GUARDIAN PARK AVENUE FUND	GRO	VALUE	A	3	3	4.50	$$	+	+
HANCOCK (JOHN) FREEDOM GLOBAL INCOME--B	GLBND		C	3	4	4.00r	$$$	---	+++
HANCOCK (JOHN) FREEDOM REGIONAL BANK--B	SECTR	FINANCIAL	B+	4	2	4.00r	$$	+	-
HANCOCK (JOHN) GROWTH	GRO	GROWTH	B-	4	4	5.00	$$	+	--
HANCOCK (JOHN) LIMITED TERM GOV'T--A	US-BD		C+	1	4	3.00	$$$	--	+++
HANCOCK (JOHN) MANAGED TAX-EXEMPT--B	MUNI		B	3	3	4.00r	$$	--	++
HANCOCK (JOHN) SOVEREIGN ACHIEVERS--B	GRO	MID CAP	C	3	4	4.00r	$$	+-	+-
HANCOCK (JOHN) SOVEREIGN BOND	C-BD		B+	2	3	4.50	$$$	--	+++
HANCOCK (JOHN) SOVEREIGN GOV'T INC.--B	US-BD		B+	2	2	4.00r	$$	---	+++
HANCOCK (JOHN) SOVEREIGN INVESTORS	G&I	LARGE CAP	B-	3	3	5.00	$$	--	++
HANCOCK (JOHN) SPECIAL EQUITIES*	AGGRO	SMALL CAP GROWTH	B+	5	3	5.00	$$$	++	-
HANCOCK (JOHN) STRATEGIC INCOME	HY-CB		C	3	3	4.50	$$$	-	+
HANCOCK (JOHN) TAX-EXEMPT INCOME	MUNI		B-	2	4	4.50	$$$	--	+++
HARBOR BOND	FLEXB		A+	2	1		$	--	+++
HARBOR CAPITAL APPRECIATION	AGGRO	LARGE CAP GROWTH	B-	4	3		$	+++	-
HARBOR GROWTH	GRO	SMALL CAP	B-	4	4		$	+++	--
HARBOR INTERNATIONAL	INTL		B+	4	4		$	--	+
HARTWELL EMERGING GROWTH	AGGRO	SMALL CAP GROWTH	B	5	3	5.75	$$	+++	---
HEARTLAND VALUE	GRO	SMALL CAP VALUE	B+	4	3	3.00r	$$	+	-
IAI BOND	FLEXB		A	3	2		$$	--	+++

▨ = *Schabacker 100*

FUND NAME	Category	Invest.Style/Sector	Quality Rating	Risk	Rew/ Risk	Sales Chg.	5-yr. Cost	Bull	Bear
IAI EMERGING GROWTH	AGGRO	SMALL CAP GROWTH	B	5	3				
IAI GROWTH & INCOME	G&I	LARGE CAP GROWTH	B-	3	3		$	-	+
IAI REGIONAL	GRO	MID CAP	B+	3	3		$	+	+-
IAI RESERVE	C-BD	SHORT-TERM	B-	1	3		$	---	++
IDEX FUND	GRO	LARGE CAP GROWTH	B	4	4	8.50	$$$	++	+
IDEX FUND 3*	AGGRO	LARGE CAP GROWTH	B-	4	3	8.50	$$$	++	+
IDEX II	GRO	LARGE CAP GROWTH	B	4	3	5.50	$$	++	+
IDS BLUE CHIP ADVANTAGE	G&I	LARGE CAP	B-	3	4	5.00	$$	+-	+
IDS BOND	C-BD		A	2	2	5.00	$$	-	+++
IDS DISCOVERY	AGGRO	GROWTH	C	4	3	5.00	$$	+	---
IDS DIVERSIFIED EQUITY INCOME	G&I	VALUE	A-	3	1	5.00	$$	-	
IDS EQUITY PLUS	G&I	GROWTH	B+	3	3	5.00	$$	+-	-
IDS EXTRA INCOME	HY-CB		B+	3	2	5.00	$$	-	+
IDS FEDERAL INCOME	US-BD		B	1	2	5.00	$$	---	+++
IDS GLOBAL BOND	GLBND		A-	3	2	5.00	$$$	---	+++
IDS GLOBAL GROWTH	GLSTK		C+	4	5	5.00	$$	---	+
IDS GROWTH	AGGRO	LARGE CAP GROWTH	C+	5	3	5.00	$$	++	--
IDS HIGH YIELD TAX-EXEMPT	MUNI	HIGH YIELD	B-	2	4	5.00	$$	--	+++
IDS INSURED TAX-EXEMPT	MUNI		B-	2	4	5.00	$$	---	++
IDS INTERNATIONAL	GLSTK		C	4	4	5.00	$$	-	+
IDS MANAGED RETIREMENT	FLEX	LARGE CAP GROWTH	B+	3	3	5.00	$$	+-	+
IDS MUTUAL FUND	BAL	VALUE	B+	3	3	5.00	$$	-	++
IDS NEW DIMENSIONS	GRO	LARGE CAP GROWTH	B+	4	3	5.00	$$	+	-
IDS PROGRESSIVE	GRO	SMALL CAP VALUE	C	3	4	5.00	$$	-	+
IDS SELECTIVE	C-BD		A-	2	3	5.00	$$	--	+++
IDS STOCK	G&I	LARGE CAP	B	3	3	5.00	$$	-	+
IDS STRATEGY-AGGRESSIVE EQUITIES	AGGRO	GROWTH	C	4	3	5.00r	$$	+	-
IDS STRATEGY-EQUITY PORTFOLIO	G&I	MID CAP	B	3	2	5.00r	$$	-	+
IDS STRATEGY-INCOME PORTFOLIO	C-BD		B	3	2	5.00r	$$$	--	++
IDS STRATEGY-SHORT TERM INCOME	C-BD	SHORT-TERM	C	2	4	5.00r	$$$	---	+++
IDS STRATEGY-WORLDWIDE GROWTH	GLSTK		C-	4	4	5.00r	$$$	--	+
IDS TAX-EXEMPT BOND	MUNI		C+	2	4	5.00	$$	--	+++
IDS UTILITIES INCOME	SECTR	UTILITIES	B	3	2	5.00	$$	--	++
INCOME FUND OF AMERICA	FLEX	LARGE CAP VALUE	B+	3	3	5.75	$$	-	+++
INTERMEDIATE BOND FUND OF AMERICA	FLEXB	INTERMEDIATE	B-	2	3	4.75	$$	---	+++
INTERNATIONAL INVESTORS	GOLD		B	5	4	5.75	$$$	--	--
INVESCO DYNAMICS FUND	AGGRO	GROWTH	B	4	3		$	+	--
INVESCO EMERGING GROWTH	AGGRO	SMALL CAP GROWTH	B+	5	3				
INVESCO EUROPEAN FUND	INTL	EUROPE	C+	4	4		$$	--	+
INVESCO GROWTH FUND	GRO	LARGE CAP GROWTH	B	4	3		$	-	-
INVESCO HIGH YIELD	HY-CB		B+	3	2		$$	-	++
INVESCO INDUSTRIAL INCOME FUND	G&I	MID CAP	A+	3	2		$	+-	+
INVESCO INTERNATIONAL GROWTH	INTL		C	4	5		$$		
INVESCO PACIFIC BASIN FUND	INTL	PACIFIC BASIN	B-	4	4		$$	-	+
INVESCO SELECT INCOME	FLEXB		B	2	2		$$	--	+++
INVESCO STRATEGIC--FINANCIAL SERVICES	SECTR	FINANCIAL	A-	4	2		$	++	+-
INVESCO STRATEGIC--GOLD	GOLD		B-	5	3		$$	---	+-
INVESCO STRATEGIC--HEALTH SCIENCES	SECTR	HEALTH CARE	B	5	4		$	+++	+
INVESCO STRATEGIC--LEISURE	SECTR	SERVICES	A-	4	2		$$	+++	-
INVESCO STRATEGIC--TECHNOLOGY	SECTR	TECHNOLOGY	A-	4	3		$	++	--
INVESCO STRATEGIC--UTILITIES	SECTR	UTILITIES	A-	3	2		$	-	+
INVESCO TAX-FREE LONG-TERM BOND	MUNI		A	3	3		$$	--	+++
INVESCO TOTAL RETURN	FLEX	LARGE CAP VALUE	B-	2	3		$		
INVESTMENT CO. OF AMERICA	G&I	LARGE CAP	B+	3	3	5.75	$$	+-	+
ISI TOTAL RETURN US TREASURY FUND	US-BD		A	3	3	4.45	$$	--	++
IVY GROWTH FUND	GRO	LARGE CAP	B-	3	3	5.75	$$	-	+
IVY INTERNATIONAL	INTL		B-	4	4	5.75	$$$	-	+
JANUS FLEXIBLE INCOME	FLEXB	HIGH YIELD	A-	3	2		$$	--	++
JANUS FUND	GRO	LARGE CAP GROWTH	A	4	2		$	+-	+
JANUS GROWTH & INCOME	G&I	LARGE CAP GROWTH	B-	4	4		$$		
JANUS TWENTY*	AGGRO	LARGE CAP GROWTH	B+	4	3		$	+	+
JANUS VENTURE*	GRO	SMALL CAP	A	3	3		$	+-	+
JANUS WORLDWIDE	GLSTK		B-	4	4		$$		

▢ = *Schabacker 100*   *Fund closed to new investors*

FUND NAME	Category	InvestStyle/Sector	Quality Rating	Risk	Rew/ Risk	Sales Chg.	5-yr. Cost	Bull	Bear
JAPAN FUND	INTL	PACIFIC BASIN	B-	5	4		$$	---	++
KAUFMANN FUND	AGGRO	SMALL CAP GROWTH	B	5	3	0.20r	$$$	+++	--
KEMPER ADJUSTABLE RATE U.S. GOVERNMENT	US-BD	ADJUSTABLE RATE	B-	1	3	3.50	$$	--	+++
KEMPER BLUE CHIP	G&I	LARGE CAP GROWTH	B-	3	4	5.75	$$$	--	+
KEMPER DIVERSIFIED INCOME	HY-CB		B+	3	3	4.50	$$$	-	+
KEMPER GLOBAL INCOME FUND	GLBND		B	2	4	4.50	$$$	---	+++
KEMPER GROWTH	GRO	LARGE CAP GROWTH	B	4	3	5.75	$$	+	-
KEMPER HIGH YIELD	HY-CB		A-	3	3	4.50	$$	-	+++
KEMPER INC. & CAPITAL PRESERVATION	C-BD		B	2	3	4.50	$$	--	+++
KEMPER INTERNATIONAL	GLSTK		B-	4	5	5.75	$$	-	+
KEMPER INVEST. PORT-DIVERSIFIED INC.	HY-CB		B	3	3	3.00r	$$$	-	+
KEMPER INVEST. PORT-GOVERNMENT	US-BD		C+	2	3	3.00r	$$$	---	++
KEMPER INVEST. PORT-GROWTH	GRO	LARGE CAP GROWTH	B	4	3	3.00r	$$	-	+
KEMPER INVEST. PORT-HIGH YIELD	HY-CB		B-	3	3	3.00r	$$$	-	+
KEMPER INVEST. PORT-SHORT INTERM. GOV'T	US-BD	SHORT-TERM	B-	1	3	3.00r	$$$	---	+++
KEMPER INVEST. PORT-SHORT TERM GLOBAL	GLBND	SHORT-TERM	D	3	5	3.00r	$$$		
KEMPER INVEST. PORT-TOTAL RETURN	FLEX	GROWTH	B+	3	3	3.00r	$$	-	+
KEMPER MUNICIPAL BOND	MUNI		A	2	3	4.50	$$	--	+++
KEMPER RETIREMENT FUND I*	BAL	LARGE CAP GROWTH	B	3	3	5.00		-	+
KEMPER RETIREMENT FUND II*	BAL	LARGE CAP GROWTH	B+	3	2	5.00		-	+
KEMPER SHORT TERM GLOBAL INCOME	GLBND	SHORT-TERM	C-	3	5	3.50	$$	---	
KEMPER SMALL CAPITALIZATION STOCK	AGGRO	GROWTH	B-	4	4	5.75	$$	+	--
KEMPER TECHNOLOGY FUND	SECTR	TECHNOLOGY	C+	4	4	5.75	$$	-	--
KEMPER TOTAL RETURN	BAL	GROWTH	B+	3	4	5.75	$$	-	+-
KEMPER U.S. GOVERNMENT SECURITIES	US-BD		B+	2	3	4.50	$$	--	+++
KEYSTONE B-1	C-BD		C+	2	3	4.00r	$$$	--	+++
KEYSTONE B-2	C-BD		C+	3	2	4.00r	$$	--	++
KEYSTONE B-4	HY-CB		B-	4	3	4.00r	$$$	--	++
KEYSTONE INTERNATIONAL FUND	GLSTK		D	4	4	4.00r	$$$	-	-
KEYSTONE K-1	FLEX	LARGE CAP VALUE	C+	3	3	4.00r	$$	-	+
KEYSTONE K-2	GRO	LARGE CAP GROWTH	B-	4	3	4.00r	$$	+-	--
KEYSTONE PRECIOUS METALS HOLDINGS	GOLD		B-	5	3	4.00r	$$$	-	---
KEYSTONE S-1	G&I	LARGE CAP	C-	3	4	4.00r	$$	-	-
KEYSTONE S-3	GRO	GROWTH	C	4	3	4.00r	$$	+	--
KEYSTONE S-4	AGGRO	SMALL CAP GROWTH	B	5	3	4.00r	$$	+++	---
KEYSTONE TAX-EXEMPT	MUNI		C+	2	3	4.00r	$$	---	++
KEYSTONE TAX-FREE*	MUNI		C+	2	3	4.00r	$$	--	+++
KIDDER PEABODY EQUITY INCOME--A	G&I	LARGE CAP GROWTH	C+	3	4	5.75	$$	-	+
LANDMARK BALANCED	BAL	LARGE CAP GROWTH	B-	3	3	3.50	$$	-	+
LANDMARK EQUITY	GRO	GROWTH	C+	4	3	3.50	$$	-	-
LEGG MASON SPECIAL INVESTMENT TRUST	GRO	SMALL CAP	A-	4	3		$$	++	+-
LEGG MASON TOTAL RETURN TRUST	G&I	LARGE CAP	B-	3	3		$$	-	+-
LEGG MASON U.S. GOVERNMENT INTERM.	US-BD	INTERMEDIATE	B	1	2		$	--	+++
LEGG MASON VALUE TRUST	GRO	LARGE CAP	C+	4	3		$$	+	+
LEXINGTON CORPORATE LEADERS TRUST	GRO	LARGE CAP VALUE	A-	3	3		$	-	+
LEXINGTON GLOBAL	GLSTK		B	4	4		$$	-	+
LEXINGTON GNMA INCOME	US-BD	GOV'T MORTGAGE	B+	2	2		$$	--	+++
LEXINGTON GOLDFUND	GOLD		C+	5	4		$$	--	--
LEXINGTON GROWTH & INCOME	G&I	LARGE CAP	C+	3	3		$$	-	-
LIBERTY FINANCIAL TAX-FREE BOND	MUNI		B+	3	3	4.50	$$	---	+++
LIBERTY FINANCIAL U.S. GOVERNMENT	US-BD		B+	1	1	4.50	$$	---	+++
LIBERTY HIGH INCOME BOND	HY-CB		B+	3	2	4.50	$$	-	+++
LIBERTY MUNICIPAL SECURITIES	MUNI		B-	2	3	4.50	$$	--	++
LIBERTY UTILITY--A	SECTR	UTILITIES	B+	3	2	4.50	$$	--	++
LINDNER DIVIDEND	FLEX	VALUE	A	2	1	2.00r	$	-	+++
LINDNER FUND	GRO	SMALL CAP VALUE	A-	3	2	2.00r	$	-	+++
LOOMIS SAYLES MUNICIPAL BOND	MUNI		B+	3	2		$		
LORD ABBETT AFFILIATED FUND	G&I	LARGE CAP VALUE	B-	3	3	5.75	$$	-	+
LORD ABBETT BOND-DEBENTURE FUND	HY-CB		B	3	3	4.75	$$	-	++
LORD ABBETT DEVELOPING GROWTH FUND	AGGRO	SMALL CAP GROWTH	D	4	5	5.75	$$	+	---
LORD ABBETT GLOBAL INCOME	GLBND		B-	3	3	4.75	$$$	---	+++
LORD ABBETT TAX-FREE INCOME--NAT'L	MUNI		B+	2	3	4.75	$$	--	++
LORD ABBETT U.S. GOV'T SECURITIES	US-BD		B+	2	3	4.75	$$	--	+++

▢ = *Schabacker 100*   *Fund closed to new investors*

FUND NAME	Category	InvestStyle/Sector	Quality Rating	Risk	Rew/ Risk	Sales Chg.	5-yr. Cost	Bull	Bear
LORD ABBETT VALUE APPRECIATION	GRO	VALUE	C+	3	3	5.75	$$	+-	-
MACKENZIE FIXED INCOME	C-BD		B+	2	3	4.75	$$$	--	++
MAINSTAY CAPITAL APPRECIATION	GRO	GROWTH	A-	4	2	5.00r	$$	+-	+
MAINSTAY GOVERNMENT FUND	US-BD		C+	2	3	5.00r	$$	---	++
MAINSTAY HY CORPORATE BOND	HY-CB		B	3	2	5.00r	$$$	-	+
MAINSTAY TAX-FREE BOND	MUNI		C+	2	3	5.00r	$$	---	++
MAINSTAY TOTAL RETURN	FLEX	GROWTH	B+	3	3	5.00r	$$	-	+
MAINSTAY VALUE	G&I	VALUE	A-	4	3	5.00r	$$	-	+
MERGER FUND	GRO	SMALL CAP	B-	3	4		$$$	-	+
MATHERS FUND	GRO	SMALL CAP	C+	3	3		$	-	+-
MERRILL LYNCH BALANCED--I & R--B	BAL	LARGE CAP	C+	3	3	4.00r	$$	-	+
MERRILL LYNCH BASIC VALUE--A	GRO	LARGE CAP VALUE	B	3	3	6.50	$$	+-	+
MERRILL LYNCH CAPITAL--A	G&I	LARGE CAP VALUE	B	3	3	6.50	$$	-	+
MERRILL LYNCH CORP.--HIGH INCOME--A	HY-CB		A	3	2	4.00	$$	-	++
MERRILL LYNCH CORP.--HIGH QLTY--A	C-BD	HIGH GRADE	A-	2	2	4.00	$$	--	+++
MERRILL LYNCH CORP.--INTERM.--A	C-BD	INTERMEDIATE	B+	2	2	2.00	$$	--	+++
MERRILL LYNCH DEVELOPING CAPITAL MARKETS	INTL		C+	4	5	6.50	$$	-	+
MERRILL LYNCH EUROFUND--B	INTL	EUROPE	C	4	4	4.00r	$$	--	+
MERRILL LYNCH FEDERAL SECURITIES--A	US-BD		B+	1	2	4.00	$$	---	+++
MERRILL LYNCH FEDERAL SECURITIES--B	US-BD	GOV'T MORTGAGE	B	1	1	4.00r	$$	---	+++
MERRILL LYNCH FUND FOR TOMORROW--B	GRO	LARGE CAP GROWTH	C	3	4	4.00r	$$	+-	+
MERRILL LYNCH GLOBAL ALLOCATION--A	ASSET	ASSET ALLOCATION	B+	3	2	6.50	$$	-	++
MERRILL LYNCH GLOBAL ALLOCATION--B	ASSET	ASSET ALLOCATION	B	3	2	4.00r	$$	-	++
MERRILL LYNCH GLOBAL BD--I & R--B	GLBND		A-	2	2	4.00r	$$	---	+++
MERRILL LYNCH GROWTH-INV. & RET.--B	GRO	GROWTH	B+	5	3	4.00r	$$	+++	+-
MERRILL LYNCH INTERNATIONAL--A	GLSTK		B-	3	4	6.50	$$	-	+
MERRILL LYNCH MUNI.--INSURED--A	MUNI		B+	2	3	4.00	$$	--	+++
MERRILL LYNCH MUNI.--LTD. MAT.--A	MUNI	SHORT-TERM	C	1	4	0.75	$	---	+++
MERRILL LYNCH MUNI.--NATIONAL--A	MUNI		A-	2	3	4.00	$$	--	+++
MERRILL LYNCH MUNICIPAL INCOME--B	MUNI		B-	2	3	2.00r	$$	---	++
MERRILL LYNCH NATURAL RESOURCES--B	SECTR	NAT. RESOURCES	D	4	5	4.00r	$$	-	+
MERRILL LYNCH PACIFIC--A	INTL	PACIFIC BASIN	A-	4	4	6.50	$$	+	+++
MERRILL LYNCH PHOENIX--A	GRO	SMALL CAP	B+	3	3	6.50	$$	+	+
MERRILL LYNCH STRATEGIC DIVIDEND--B	G&I	LARGE CAP VALUE	C	3	3	4.00r	$$	-	+
METLIFE-STATE STREET CAP. APPREC.	AGGRO	GROWTH	B+	5	3	4.50	$$	++	-
METLIFE-STATE STREET GOV'T SEC.--A	US-BD		B+	2	3	4.50	$$$	---	++
METLIFE-STATE STREET HIGH INCOME--A	HY-CB		B+	3	2	4.50	$$$	-	+
METLIFE-STATE STREET TAX-EXEMPT NAT'L--A	MUNI		B	2	3	4.50	$$$	---	++
MFS BOND FUND	C-BD		B	2	4	4.75	$$	--	+++
MFS CAPITAL GROWTH--B	GRO	LARGE CAP	C+	3	3	4.00r	$$$	+	+
MFS EMERGING GROWTH--B	AGGRO	SMALL CAP GROWTH	B	4	3	4.00r	$$$	+++	--
MFS GOVERNMENT LIMITED MATURITY--A	US-BD	SHORT-TERM	B-	2	2	2.50	$$$	---	+++
MFS GOVERNMENT MORTGAGE FUND--A	US-BD		B-	2	3	4.75	$$$	---	++
MFS GOVERNMENT SECURITIES FUND	US-BD		B	2	3	4.75	$$$	--	++
MFS GROWTH OPPORTUNITIES--A	GRO	LARGE CAP	C+	3	4	5.75	$$	+	---
MFS HIGH INCOME FUND--A	HY-CB		B-	3	3	4.75	$$	-	++
MFS MANAGED SECTORS FUND--B	AGGRO	GROWTH	C	5	3	4.00r	$$$	+	-
MFS MASS. INVESTORS GROWTH FUND	AGGRO	GROWTH	C+	5	4	5.75	$$	+	--
MFS MASS. INVESTORS TRUST FUND	G&I	LARGE CAP	B-	3	3	5.75	$$	-	+-
MFS MUNICIPAL BOND FUND	MUNI		A-	3	4	4.75	$$	--	++
MFS MUNICIPAL HIGH INCOME--A	MUNI	HIGH YIELD	B-	2	3	4.75	$$	---	++
MFS MUNICIPAL INCOME--B	MUNI		C+	2	3	4.00r	$$$	--	++
MFS RESEARCH FUND	GRO	GROWTH	B-	4	3	5.75	$$	+-	--
MFS TOTAL RETURN FUND--A	FLEX	LARGE CAP	B+	3	3	4.75	$$	-	+
MFS VALUE FUND--A	AGGRO	SMALL CAP VALUE	C+	4	3	5.75	$$	+-	--
MFS WORLD EQUITY FUND--B	GLSTK		C	3	4	4.00r	$$$	--	+
MFS WORLD GOVERNMENTS FUND--A	GLBND		A-	3	4	4.75	$$$	--	+++
MONETTA FUND*	GRO	SMALL CAP	B	4	3		$$	+	+-
MONTGOMERY EMERGING MARKETS	INTL		B-	3	4		$$		
MUTUAL BEACON	GRO	SMALL CAP VALUE	B+	3	2		$	-	+
MUTUAL OF OMAHA AMERICA FUND	US-BD		A-	2	2	4.75	$$$	---	+++
MUTUAL OF OMAHA GROWTH FUND	AGGRO	SMALL CAP GROWTH	C+	5	4	4.75	$$	+	--
MUTUAL OF OMAHA INCOME FUND	FLEX	LARGE CAP	C+	2	4	4.75	$$	-	+++

▢ = *Schabacker 100*   *Fund closed to new investors*

FUND NAME	Category	InvestStyle/Sector	Quality Rating	Risk	Rew/ Risk	Sales Chg.	5-yr. Cost	Bull	Bear
MUTUAL OF OMAHA TAX-FREE INCOME	MUNI		B+	3	4	4.75	$$	--	+++
MUTUAL QUALIFIED*	GRO	VALUE	A	3	2		$	-	+++
MUTUAL SHARES*	GRO	VALUE	A-	3	2		$	-	++
NAT'L SECURITIES BOND	HY-CB		B-	4	3	4.75	$$$	-	++
NAT'L SECURITIES FEDERAL SECURITIES	US-BD		B	2	3	4.75	$$	---	++
NAT'L SECURITIES INCOME & GROWTH--A	FLEX	LARGE CAP	B+	3	3	5.75	$$	-	++
NAT'L SECURITIES STOCK	GRO	MID CAP	C+	4	3	5.75	$$	-	+
NAT'L SECURITIES TAX-EXEMPT BOND	MUNI		B-	2	4	4.75	$$	--	+++
NAT'L SECURITIES TOTAL RETURN	G&I	LARGE CAP	B-	3	3	5.75	$$	-	+
NAT'L SECURITIES WORLDWIDE OPPORT.	GLSTK		D	3	5	5.75	$$$	+	---
NATIONWIDE BOND FUND	C-BD		B	2	4	4.50	$$$	--	+++
NATIONWIDE FUND	G&I	LARGE CAP	B-	3	4	4.50	$$	+-	+
NATIONWIDE GROWTH FUND	GRO	LARGE CAP	B-	3	4	4.50	$$	+	+
NATIONWIDE TAX-FREE	MUNI		B+	2	3	5.00r	$$	---	++
NEUBERGER BERMAN GENESIS FUND	AGGRO	SMALL CAP VALUE	C+	4	4		$$	+++	--
NEUBERGER BERMAN GUARDIAN MUTUAL	G&I	LARGE CAP VALUE	A	3	2		$	+	+-
NEUBERGER BERMAN LIMITED MATURITY BOND	FLEXB	SHORT-TERM	B	1	1		$	---	+++
NEUBERGER BERMAN MANHATTAN FUND	AGGRO	GROWTH	B+	4	2		$	+	+-
NEUBERGER BERMAN PARTNERS FUND	GRO	VALUE	A-	3	2		$	-	+
NEUBERGER BERMAN SELECTED SECTORS	GRO	LARGE CAP	A-	3	2		$	-	+-
NEUBERGER BERMAN ULTRA SHORT BOND	C-BD	SHORT-TERM	C+	1	3		$	---	++
NEW ECONOMY	GRO	LARGE CAP GROWTH	A-	4	3	5.75	$$	+	+-
NEW PERSPECTIVE	GLSTK		B	3	4	5.75	$$	-	+
NEW YORK VENTURE FUND	AGGRO	LARGE CAP VALUE	A-	4	3	4.75	$$	+	+-
NEWPORT TIGER FUND	INTL	PACIFIC BASIN	B	5	3	5.00	$$$	-	+
NICHOLAS FUND	GRO	MID CAP	B+	3	3		$	+	+
NICHOLAS II	GRO	SMALL CAP VALUE	B-	4	3		$	+	+-
NICHOLAS INCOME FUND	HY-CB		B-	2	2		$	--	+++
NICHOLAS LIMITED EDITION*	GRO	SMALL CAP	A-	4	2		$	+++	+
NORTH AMERICAN U.S. GOVERNMENT	US-BD		B-	2	3	4.00	$$$	--	++
NORTHEAST INVESTORS TRUST	HY-CB		A-	3	2		$	--	+++
NUVEEN INSURED MUNICIPAL BOND FUND	MUNI		A	3	3	4.75	$$	--	++
NUVEEN MUNICIPAL BOND FUND	MUNI		B-	2	3	4.75	$$	--	+++
OAKMARK FUND	GRO	SMALL CAP VALUE	A+	4	1		$$		
OAKMARK INTERNATIONAL	INTL		B+	4	3		$$		
OLYMPIC TRUST EQUITY INCOME	G&I	LARGE CAP VALUE	B-	4	3		$	-	+
OPPENHEIMER ASSET ALLOCATION	ASSET	MID CAP	C+	3	3	5.75	$$	-	+
OPPENHEIMER DISCOVERY	AGGRO	SMALL CAP GROWTH	B	5	3	5.75	$$	++	+-
OPPENHEIMER EQUITY INCOME	G&I	LARGE CAP VALUE	B-	3	4	5.75	$$	-	+
OPPENHEIMER FUND	GRO	MID CAP	D	3	4	5.75	$$	+-	---
OPPENHEIMER GLOBAL BIO-TECH*	SECTR	HEALTH CARE	C+	5	4	5.75	$$	+++	+
OPPENHEIMER GLOBAL--A	GLSTK		C+	4	4	5.75	$$$	+-	+
OPPENHEIMER GOLD & SPECIAL MINERALS	GOLD		C+	5	4	5.75	$$	--	+
OPPENHEIMER GOVERNMENT SECURITIES--A	US-BD		B+	1	2	4.75	$$	---	+++
OPPENHEIMER HIGH YIELD FUND	HY-CB		B	3	3	4.75	$$	-	++
OPPENHEIMER MORTGAGE INCOME--A	US-BD	GOV'T MORTGAGE	B-	2	3	4.75	$$$	---	+++
OPPENHEIMER SPECIAL FUND	GRO	GROWTH	C	4	4	5.75	$$	-	-
OPPENHEIMER STRATEGIC INCOME--A	FLEXB	HIGH YIELD	A-	2	2	4.75	$$$	--	++
OPPENHEIMER TARGET FUND	GRO	GROWTH	C-	4	4	5.75	$$	++	---
OPPENHEIMER TAX-FREE BOND FUND--A	MUNI		B+	2	4	4.75	$$	--	+++
OPPENHEIMER TIME FUND	AGGRO	GROWTH	C+	4	4	5.75	$$	+	--
OPPENHEIMER TOTAL RETURN--A	G&I	GROWTH	B	3	3	5.75	$$	+-	--
OPPENHEIMER U.S. GOVERNMENT TRUST	US-BD		B	2	3	4.75	$$$	---	++
OVERLAND EXPRESS VARIABLE RATE GOV'T	US-BD	ADJUSTABLE RATE	C+	1	3	3.00	$$		
PACIFIC HORIZON AGGRESSIVE GROWTH	AGGRO	GROWTH	B	5	3	4.50	$$	++	-
PACIFIC HORIZON CAPITAL INCOME	FLEX	CONVERTIBLE	A	3	2	4.50	$	+-	+-
PACIFIC HORIZON U.S. GOV'T SECURITIES	US-BD		B+	1	2	4.50	$$	--	++
PACIFICA ASSET PRESERVATION FUND	C-BD	SHORT-TERM	B-	1	3		$	---	+++
PACIFICA BALANCED FUND	BAL	MID CAP	A-	3	2	4.50	$$	-	+
PACIFICA EQUITY VALUE	GRO	LARGE CAP VALUE	B	3	3	4.50	$$	+-	+-
PACIFICA GOVERNMENT INCOME FUND	US-BD		B+	1	2	4.50	$$	--	+
PAINE WEBBER ASSET ALLOCATION--B	FLEX	LARGE CAP GROWTH	C	3	3	5.00r	$$	--	++
PAINE WEBBER ATLAS GLOBAL GROWTH--A	GLSTK		C	3	5	4.50	$$	+-	+

▓ = *Schabacker 100*   *Fund closed to new investors*

FUND NAME	Category	Invest.Style/Sector	Quality Rating	Risk	Rew/ Risk	Sales Chg.	5-yr. Cost	Bull	Bear
PAINE WEBBER DIVIDEND GROWTH--A	G&I	LARGE CAP	C	3	4	4.50	$$	-	+
PAINE WEBBER GLOBAL INCOME--B	GLBND		B-	3	3	5.00r	$$$	---	+++
PAINE WEBBER GROWTH--A	GRO	GROWTH	B+	4	4	4.50	$$	+	+-
PAINE WEBBER HIGH INCOME--A	HY-CB		A-	3	2	4.00	$$	-	+
PAINE WEBBER INVESTMENT GRADE--A	C-BD	HIGH GRADE	A	2	2	4.00	$$	---	++
PAINE WEBBER NATIONAL TAX-FREE--A	MUNI		B-	2	4	4.00	$$	---	++
PAINE WEBBER U.S. GOVERNMENT--A	US-BD		B	1	3	4.00	$$	---	+++
PASADENA GROWTH	AGGRO	LARGE CAP GROWTH	C-	5	4	5.50	$$$	+++	-
PASADENA NIFTY FIFTY FUND	AGGRO	LARGE CAP GROWTH	D	4	5	5.50	$$$		
PAX WORLD	BAL	MID CAP	C	3	3		$	-	+
PENN SQUARE MUTUAL FUND	G&I	LARGE CAP	B-	3	3	4.75	$$	-	+
PENNSYLVANIA MUTUAL FUND*	GRO	SMALL CAP VALUE	B	3	2	1.00r	$	+	+
PHILADELPHIA FUND	G&I	MID CAP	C	3	3		$$	-	-
PHOENIX BALANCED FUND SERIES	BAL	LARGE CAP GROWTH	B+	3	3	4.75	$$	-	++
PHOENIX CONVERTIBLE FUND	G&I	CONVERTIBLE	C+	2	3	4.75	$$	-	+
PHOENIX GROWTH FUND SERIES	GRO	LARGE CAP	B-	3	3	4.75	$$	-	++
PHOENIX HIGH YIELD FUND SERIES	HY-CB		A-	3	2	4.75	$$$	-	++
PHOENIX STOCK FUND SERIES	GRO	LARGE CAP GROWTH	C+	3	4	4.75	$$	+	+
PILGRIM MAGNACAP FUND	GRO	LARGE CAP	C+	3	4	5.00	$$	+-	+
PIMCO LOW DURATION FUND	FLEXB	SHORT-TERM	B+	1	1		$	---	+++
PIMCO TOTAL RETURN FUND	FLEXB	SHORT-TERM	A+	2	1		$	--	++
PIONEER BOND FUND	FLEXB		B	1	3	4.50	$$	--	+++
PIONEER CAPITAL GROWTH FUND	GRO	SMALL CAP VALUE	B	5	3	5.75	$$$	+++	
PIONEER EQUITY INCOME FUND	G&I	VALUE	A-	3	1	5.75	$$$	-	
PIONEER FUND	G&I	VALUE	C	3	4	5.75	$$	+-	-
PIONEER II FUND	G&I	VALUE	C+	3	4	5.75	$$	+-	-
PIONEER THREE FUND	G&I	SMALL CAP VALUE	B	4	3	5.75	$$	+	+-
PIONEER U.S. GOVERNMENT TRUST	US-BD		A-	1	2	4.50	$$	---	+++
PIPER JAFFRAY GOVERNMENT INCOME	US-BD		B+	2	3	4.00	$$	---	+++
PIPER JAFFRAY INSTITUTIONAL GOV'T INC.	US-BD		A+	2	1	1.50	$	--	++
PIPER JAFFRAY VALUE	GRO	LARGE CAP	B	4	3	4.00	$$	++	+
PORTICO BOND IMMDEX	FLEXB	INDEX	A-	2	2	0.25	$	--	+++
PORTICO GROWTH AND INCOME	G&I	LARGE CAP VALUE	B-	3	4		$	-	+
PORTICO SHORT TERM BOND MARKET	FLEXB	SHORT-TERM	B+	1	2	0.25	$	---	+++
PORTICO SPECIAL GROWTH	AGGRO	SMALL CAP	B-	4	4		$	+++	+
PRINCOR CAPITAL ACCUMULATION	G&I	LARGE CAP VALUE	C+	3	3	5.00	$$	+	+
PRINCOR GOVERNMENT SEC. INCOME	US-BD		A-	2	3	5.00	$$	---	+++
PRINCOR TAX-EXEMPT BOND	MUNI		B	3	3	5.00	$$	---	++
PRUDENTIAL EQUITY INCOME--B	G&I	VALUE	B	3	2	5.00r	$$	-	+
PRUDENTIAL EQUITY--B	GRO	LARGE CAP VALUE	B+	3	3	5.00r	$$	+	+
PRUDENTIAL GLOBAL--B	GLSTK		C+	3	4	5.00r	$$	-	+
PRUDENTIAL GNMA--B	US-BD	GOV'T MORTGAGE	C+	1	2	5.00r	$$	---	+++
PRUDENTIAL GOVERNMENT INTERMEDIATE	US-BD	INTERMEDIATE	B+	1	2		$	--	+++
PRUDENTIAL GOVERNMENT PLUS--B	US-BD		B-	2	2	5.00r	$$	---	++
PRUDENTIAL GROWTH OPPORTUNITY--B	GRO	SMALL CAP VALUE	B-	4	3	5.00r	$$	+	---
PRUDENTIAL GROWTH--B	GRO	MID CAP	C-	3	4	5.00r	$$	-	-
PRUDENTIAL HIGH YIELD--B	HY-CB		B-	3	2	5.00r	$$	-	+++
PRUDENTIAL INCOMEVERTIBLE--B	G&I	CONVERTIBLE	B-	3	3	5.00r	$$	-	+
PRUDENTIAL NATIONAL MUNICIPAL--B	MUNI		B+	2	3	5.00r	$$	--	+++
PRUDENTIAL UTILITY--B	SECTR	UTILITIES	B+	4	2	5.00r	$$	-	+++
PUTNAM (GEORGE) FUND OF BOSTON--A	BAL	LARGE CAP VALUE	B-	3	4	5.75	$$	-	+
PUTNAM AMERICAN GOVERNMENT INCOME	US-BD		C+	2	4	4.75	$$	---	++
PUTNAM CONVERTIBLE INCOME & GROWTH	G&I	CONVERTIBLE	B	3	3	5.75	$$	-	+
PUTNAM ENERGY RESOURCES FUND	SECTR	ENERGY	C-	3	4	5.75	$$	-	--
PUTNAM FUND FOR GROWTH & INCOME--A	G&I	LARGE CAP GROWTH	B+	3	3	5.75	$$	-	+
PUTNAM GLOBAL GOVERNMENTAL INCOME	GLBND		A-	3	2	4.75	$$$	---	+++
PUTNAM GLOBAL GROWTH--A	GLSTK		B-	4	4	5.75	$$	+-	+
PUTNAM HEALTH SCIENCES TRUST FUND	SECTR	HEALTH CARE	C	5	4	5.75	$$	+	--
PUTNAM HIGH YIELD	HY-CB		B+	3	3	4.75	$$	-	++
PUTNAM INCOME FUND	C-BD		B+	2	3	4.75	$$	--	+++
PUTNAM INVESTORS FUND	GRO	LARGE CAP GROWTH	B	4	4	5.75	$$	+	-
PUTNAM MANAGED INCOME TRUST	G&I	LARGE CAP	B-	3	3	5.75	$$	-	+
PUTNAM OTC EMERGING GROWTH	AGGRO	SMALL CAP GROWTH	B-	5	3	5.75	$$	++	--

Fund closed to new investors

FUND NAME	Category	Invest.Style/Sector	Quality Rating	Risk	Rew/ Risk	Sales Chg.	5-yr. Cost	Bull	Bear
PUTNAM TAX-EXEMPT INCOME FUND	MUNI		A-	3	4	4.75	$$	--	+++
PUTNAM U.S. GOVERNMENT--A	US-BD		B-	1	3	4.75	$$	---	+++
PUTNAM VISTA FUND--A	AGGRO	MID CAP	B-	4	3	5.75	$$	+	-
PUTNAM VOYAGER FUND--A	AGGRO	GROWTH	B	4	3	5.75	$$	++	--
QUEST FOR VALUE FUND	GRO	VALUE	B-	3	3	5.50	$$$	+-	++
QUEST FOR VALUE GLOBAL EQUITY	GLSTK		C+	3	3	5.50	$$$	---	
QUEST FOR VALUE NATIONAL TAX-EXEMPT	MUNI		B	3	3	4.75		---	
QUEST FOR VALUE OPPORTUNITY	FLEX	MID CAP	C+	3	3	5.50	$$$	++	+-
QUEST FOR VALUE SMALL CAPITALIZATION	AGGRO	SMALL CAP	C+	4	3	5.50	$$$	+++	-
QUEST FOR VALUE U.S. GOVERNMENT INCOME	US-BD		B	1	2	4.75	$$$	--	+++
REICH & TANG EQUITY	GRO	VALUE	B	3	3		$	+-	+
RIGHTIME BLUE CHIP	GRO	LARGE CAP	C	3	4	4.75	$$$	-	++
RIGHTIME FUND	GRO	LARGE CAP GROWTH	C+	3	4		$$	-	+
ROBERTSON STEPHENS EMERGING GROWTH	AGGRO	SMALL CAP GROWTH	B-	5	4		$$	+++	-
ROYCE EQUITY INCOME	G&I		B+	3	2	1.00r	$	++	-
ROYCE VALUE SERIES	GRO	SMALL CAP VALUE	C+	3	3	1.00r	$$	-	+
RUSHMORE AMERICAN GAS INDEX	SECTR	UTILITIES	B+	4	3		$	---	++
SAFECO EQUITY	G&I	MID CAP	A	4	2		$	+	-
SAFECO GROWTH	AGGRO	SMALL CAP GROWTH	C+	4	4		$	++	--
SAFECO INCOME	G&I	LARGE CAP VALUE	B	3	3		$	-	+
SAFECO MUNICIPAL BOND	MUNI		A+	3	2		$	--	+++
SALOMON BROTHERS CAPITAL	GRO	MID CAP	B	4	4		$$	+	+
SALOMON BROTHERS INVESTORS	G&I	LARGE CAP	B	3	3		$$	-	+
SALOMON BROTHERS OPPORTUNITY	GRO	VALUE	B	3	3		$	+	+
SAM VALUE TRUST	GRO	MID CAP	A-	4	2			+++	+-
SBSF FUND	GRO	LARGE CAP	A-	3	2			-	+
SCHWAB 1000 FUND	GRO	LARGE CAP	B-	3	3	0.50r	$		
SCUDDER CAPITAL GROWTH FUND	AGGRO	GROWTH	B-	4	3		$	++	-
SCUDDER DEVELOPMENT FUND	AGGRO	SMALL CAP GROWTH	B-	4	3		$	+	--
SCUDDER GLOBAL	GLSTK		A-	3	3		$$	-	+
SCUDDER GNMA	US-BD	GOV'T MORTGAGE	A-	1	1		$$	---	+++
SCUDDER GOLD	GOLD		C+	5	4		$$	---	+
SCUDDER GROWTH & INCOME FUND	G&I	LARGE CAP VALUE	A-	3	3		$	-	+
SCUDDER HIGH YIELD TAX FREE	MUNI	HIGH YIELD	A+	3	2		$$	--	++
SCUDDER INCOME FUND	FLEXB		A	2	2		$$	--	+++
SCUDDER INTERNATIONAL BOND	GLBND		A+	3	2		$$	---	+++
SCUDDER INTERNATIONAL FUND	INTL		B+	4	4		$	-	+
SCUDDER MANAGED MUNICIPAL BONDS	MUNI		A	3	2		$	--	+++
SCUDDER MEDIUM TERM TAX-FREE	MUNI	INTERMEDIATE	B-	2	3			--	+++
SCUDDER SHORT TERM BOND	C-BD	SHORT-TERM	B+	1	1		$	--	+++
SCUDDER SHORT-TERM GLOBAL INCOME	GLBND	SHORT-TERM	B+	1	2		$$		
SECURITY EQUITY FUND	GRO	LARGE CAP	B	4	4	5.75	$$	+	--
SECURITY INCOME--CORPORATE BOND	C-BD		B+	2	3	4.75	$$	--	+++
SEI BOND FUND	FLEXB		A	3	2		$	--	++
SEI CAPITAL APPRECIATION--A	GRO	LARGE CAP	B+	3	3		$	+-	+
SEI EQUITY INCOME	FLEX	LARGE CAP VALUE	B+	3	3		$	+	+-
SEI GNMA FUND--A	US-BD	GOV'T MORTGAGE	A-	1	1		$	--	+++
SEI INTERMEDIATE TERM GOVERNMENT--A	US-BD	INTERMEDIATE	B+	1	2		$	---	+++
SEI INTERMEDIATE TERM MUNICIPAL	MUNI	INTERMEDIATE	B	1	3		$	---	+++
SEI INTERNATIONAL FUND--A	INTL		C+	4	5		$	---	+
SEI LIMITED VOLATILITY BOND	C-BD		B+	2	2		$	---	++
SEI S&P 500 INDEX	G&I	LARGE CAP	A-	3	3		$	+	+
SEI SHORT TERM GOVERNMENT--A	US-BD	SHORT-TERM	B	1	2		$	---	+++
SEI VALUE FUND	G&I	LARGE CAP	C	3	4		$	+	+-
SELECTED AMERICAN SHARES	GRO	LARGE CAP	B+	4	3		$	+	++
SELIGMAN CALIFORNIA TAX-EXEMPT QUALITY	MUNI	SINGLE STATE	B+	3	3	4.75	$$	---	++
SELIGMAN CAPITAL--A	AGGRO	GROWTH	B-	4	3	4.75	$$	++	---
SELIGMAN COMMON STOCK FUND--A	G&I	LARGE CAP	B	3	3	4.75	$$	+-	+-
SELIGMAN GROWTH FUND--A	GRO	GROWTH	C+	4	4	4.75	$$	+	--
SELIGMAN INCOME--A	FLEX	LARGE CAP VALUE	B	3	3	4.75	$$	-	++
SELIGMAN TAX-EXEMPT MASSACHUSETTS	MUNI	SINGLE STATE	B	2	3	4.75	$$	--	++
SELIGMAN TAX-EXEMPT MICHIGAN	MUNI	SINGLE STATE	B+	2	3	4.75	$$	--	++
SELIGMAN TAX-EXEMPT MINNESOTA	MUNI	SINGLE STATE	B-	2	4	4.75	$$	--	++

▨ = *Schabacker 100*

FUND NAME	Category	InvestStyle/Sector	Quality Rating	Risk	Rew/ Risk	Sales Chg.	5-yr. Cost	Bull	Bear
SELIGMAN TAX-EXEMPT NATIONAL	MUNI		B+	3	3	4.75	$$	--	++
SELIGMAN TAX-EXEMPT NEW YORK	MUNI	SINGLE STATE	A-	3	3	4.75	$$	--	++
SELIGMAN TAX-EXEMPT OHIO	MUNI	SINGLE STATE	B	2	3	4.75	$$	--	++
SELIGMAN TAX-EXEMPT SOUTH CAROLINA	MUNI	SINGLE STATE	B	2	3	4.75	$$	--	++
SENTINEL BALANCED	BAL	LARGE CAP	C+	3	4	5.00	$$	-	++
SENTINEL COMMON STOCK	G&I	LARGE CAP	B	3	4	5.00	$$	-	++
SENTINEL GOVERNMENT SECURITIES	US-BD		B+	2	3	5.00	$$	---	+++
SENTINEL TAX-FREE INCOME FUND	MUNI		B-	3	3	5.00	$$	---	
SEQUOIA FUND*	GRO	LARGE CAP	A	3	2		$	-	+++
SIERRA TRUST CORPORATE INCOME	C-BD		A-	2	2	4.50	$$	-	
SIERRA TRUST EMERGING GROWTH	AGGRO	SMALL CAP GROWTH	B-	4	3	4.50	$$$	+	
SIERRA TRUST GROWTH AND INCOME	G&I	LARGE CAP	C	3	4	4.50	$$	+	+-
SIERRA TRUST NATIONAL MUNICIPAL	MUNI	LONG-TERM	B+	3	3	4.50	$$	--	
SIERRA TRUST U.S. GOVERNMENT SECURITIES	US-BD		B+	1	2	4.50	$$	--	+++
SIT "NEW BEGINNING" GROWTH	AGGRO	GROWTH	B-	4	3		$	+++	--
SIT "NEW BEGINNING" TAX-FREE INCOME	MUNI		B	2	3		$	---	+++
SKYLINE SPECIAL EQUITIES*	AGGRO	SMALL CAP	A	4	2		$$	+++	-
SMITH BARNEY EQUITY FUND--A	GRO	LARGE CAP	C+	3	3	4.50	$$	-	-
SMITH BARNEY INCOME & GROWTH PORT.--A	G&I	LARGE CAP VALUE	B	3	3	4.50	$$	-	+
SMITH BARNEY INTERNATIONAL EQUITY--A	INTL		B+	4	4	4.50	$$	-	+
SMITH BARNEY SHEARSON AGGR. GROWTH--A	AGGRO	GROWTH	C+	5	4	5.00	$$	++	-
SMITH BARNEY SHEARSON APPREC. FUND--A	GRO	LARGE CAP	B-	3	3	5.00	$$	+-	+
SMITH BARNEY SHEARSON DIRECT. VALUE--B	GRO	VALUE	C-	3	4	5.00r	$$	-	+-
SMITH BARNEY SHEARSON FUNDAMTL. VALUE--A	GRO	GROWTH	B	3	3	5.00	$$	-	+
SMITH BARNEY SHEARSON GOV'T. SEC.--B	US-BD		A-	2	2	4.50r	$$	--	++
SMITH BARNEY SHEARSON GRO. & OPPORT.--B	GRO	VALUE	C	4	3	5.00r	$$	-	+-
SMITH BARNEY SHEARSON HIGH INCOME--B	HY-CB		B	3	2	4.50r	$$	--	+
SMITH BARNEY SHEARSON INVES. GR. BOND--B	C-BD		A	3	2	4.50r	$$	--	+++
SMITH BARNEY SHEARSON MANAGED GOV'T.--A	US-BD		B	2	3	4.50	$$	---	++
SMITH BARNEY SHEARSON MANAGED MUNI--A	MUNI		A-	3	4	4.50	$$	--	+++
SMITH BARNEY SHEARSON PREM. TOT. RET.--B	G&I	LARGE CAP VALUE	B	3	3	5.00r	$$	-	+
SMITH BARNEY SHEARSON SECTOR ANALYSIS--B	AGGRO	LARGE CAP	C-	3	4	5.00r	$$	-	+
SMITH BARNEY SHEARSON SPEC. EQUITIES--B	GRO	GROWTH	C+	5	3	5.00r	$$	-	---
SMITH BARNEY SHEARSON STRAT. INVEST.--B	FLEX	LARGE CAP VALUE	B-	3	3	5.00r	$$	-	+
SMITH BARNEY SHEARSON TAX-EXEMPT INC.--B	MUNI		B-	2	2	4.50r	$$	---	++
SMITH BARNEY SHEARSON UTILITIES FUND--B	SECTR	UTILITIES	B-	3	2	5.00r	$$	--	++
SMITH BARNEY U.S. GOV'T SEC.--A	US-BD		B+	1	2	4.00	$$	---	+++
SOGEN INTERNATIONAL	GLSTK		A-	3	3	3.75	$$	-	++
STATE STREET RESEARCH GOV'T INCOME--A	US-BD		A-	2	2	4.50	$$	--	++
STATE STREET RESEARCH INVEST. TRUST--C	GRO	LARGE CAP	B	3	3		$$	+-	-
STEIN ROE CAPITAL OPPORTUNITIES	AGGRO	GROWTH	C+	5	4		$$	++	---
STEIN ROE HIGH YIELD MUNICIPALS	MUNI	HIGH YIELD	B-	2	3		$	--	++
STEIN ROE INTERMEDIATE BONDS	FLEXB	INTERMEDIATE	B	2	2		$	--	++
STEIN ROE INTERMEDIATE MUNICIPALS	MUNI	INTERMEDIATE	B	2	2		$	---	++
STEIN ROE MANAGED MUNICIPALS	MUNI		A-	2	2		$	--	+++
STEIN ROE PRIME EQUITIES	GRO	GROWTH	A-	3	3		$	-	+
STEIN ROE SPECIAL FUND	AGGRO	MID CAP	B+	4	2		$	++	-
STEIN ROE STOCK	GRO	LARGE CAP GROWTH	C+	4	3		$	+-	---
STEIN ROE TOTAL RETURN	FLEX	LARGE CAP	B	3	2		$	-	+
STRATTON MONTHLY DIVIDEND SHARES	SECTR	UTILITIES	B+	3	2		$	-	++
STRONG ADVANTAGE	C-BD	SHORT-TERM	A-	1	1		$$	---	+++
STRONG COMMON STOCK*	GRO	SMALL CAP	A-	4	3		$$	++	+
STRONG DISCOVERY	AGGRO	SMALL CAP GROWTH	B+	4	3		$$	++	+
STRONG GOVERNMENT SECURITIES	US-BD		A+	2	1		$$	--	+++
STRONG INCOME FUND	FLEXB		B+	3	3		$$	---	++
STRONG INVESTMENT	BAL	GROWTH	B-	2	3		$	--	+++
STRONG MUNICIPAL BOND	MUNI		B+	3	3		$$	---	++
STRONG OPPORTUNITY FUND	GRO	MID CAP	B+	3	3		$$	-	+
STRONG SHORT-TERM BOND	C-BD	SHORT-TERM	B	2	2		$$	---	+++
STRONG TOTAL RETURN	G&I	GROWTH	B+	3	3		$	-	++
SUNAMERICA BALANCED ASSETS--B	BAL	LARGE CAP VALUE	B	3	2	5.00r	$$	-	+
SUNAMERICA FEDERAL SECURITIES--B	US-BD		C+	2	2	5.00r	$$$	--	+++
SUNAMERICA TAX-EXEMPT INSURED--A	MUNI		C	1	4	4.75	$$$	---	++

▭ = *Schabacker 100*   *Fund closed to new investors*

FUND NAME	Category	Invest.Style/Sector	Quality Rating	Risk	Rew/ Risk	Sales Chg.	5-yr. Cost	Bull	Bear
SUNAMERICA U.S. GOV'T SECURITIES--B	US-BD		C+	1	2	5.00r	$$$	---	++
T. ROWE PRICE ADJUSTABLE RATE U.S. GOV'T	US-BD		C-	1	5		$		
T. ROWE PRICE BALANCED FUND	BAL	LARGE CAP	B	2	3		$		
T. ROWE PRICE CAPITAL APPRECIATION	GRO	VALUE	B	3	2		$	-	+
T. ROWE PRICE EQUITY INCOME FUND	G&I	LARGE CAP VALUE	B-	3	3		$	-	+
T. ROWE PRICE EUROPEAN STOCK FUND	INTL	EUROPE	C	4	5		$$	---	+
T. ROWE PRICE GNMA	US-BD	GOV'T MORTGAGE	A-	1	1		$	---	++
T. ROWE PRICE GROWTH & INCOME FUND	G&I	LARGE CAP	B	3	3		$	+-	+-
T. ROWE PRICE GROWTH STOCK FUND	GRO	LARGE CAP	C+	4	3		$	+-	--
T. ROWE PRICE HIGH YIELD	HY-CB		B+	3	2	1.00r	$$	--	+
T. ROWE PRICE INTERNATIONAL BOND	GLBND		A-	3	3		$$	---	+++
T. ROWE PRICE INTERNATIONAL DISCOVERY	INTL	SMALL CAP	B-	4	5		$$	---	+
T. ROWE PRICE INTERNATIONAL STOCK	INTL		B+	4	4		$	-	+
T. ROWE PRICE JAPAN FUND	INTL		B+	5	3		$		
T. ROWE PRICE MARYLAND TAX-FREE FUND	MUNI	SINGLE STATE	A-	2	2		$	---	++
T. ROWE PRICE NEW AMERICA GROWTH	AGGRO	GROWTH	B	5	3		$	++	-
T. ROWE PRICE NEW ASIA FUND	INTL	PACIFIC BASIN	B-	4	4		$$	-	
T. ROWE PRICE NEW ERA FUND	GRO	LARGE CAP GROWTH	C	3	3		$	-	-
T. ROWE PRICE NEW HORIZONS FUND	AGGRO	SMALL CAP GROWTH	C+	4	3		$	++	---
T. ROWE PRICE NEW INCOME FUND	FLEXB		B	2	2		$	--	+++
T. ROWE PRICE OTC SECURITIES	GRO	SMALL CAP	B-	4	4		$$	+	-
T. ROWE PRICE SCIENCE/TECHNOLOGY	SECTR	TECHNOLOGY	A-	4	2		$	+++	--
T. ROWE PRICE SHORT-TERM BOND	C-BD	SHORT-TERM	B+	1	1		$	---	+++
T. ROWE PRICE SMALL CAP VALUE*	GRO	SMALL CAP VALUE	B+	4	3		$	++	-
T. ROWE PRICE SPECTRUM GROWTH FUND	GRO	LARGE CAP	B+	3	3		$	+	
T. ROWE PRICE SPECTRUM INCOME FUND	FLEXB	FUND OF FUNDS	A-	1	1		$	--	
T. ROWE PRICE TAX-FREE HIGH YIELD	MUNI	HIGH YIELD	A	2	2		$	---	++
T. ROWE PRICE TAX-FREE INCOME	MUNI		B+	2	3		$	--	+++
T. ROWE PRICE TAX-FREE SHORT INTER.	MUNI	SHORT-TERM	B-	1	3		$	---	++
T. ROWE PRICE U.S. TREASURY--INTERM.	US-BD	INTERMEDIATE	A-	2	3		$	---	+++
TAX-EXEMPT BOND FUND OF AMERICA	MUNI		B-	2	4	4.75	$$	--	+++
TEMPLETON FOREIGN FUND	INTL	VALUE	B-	3	4	5.75	$$	-	+
TEMPLETON GLOBAL OPPORTUNITIES	GLSTK	VALUE	B-	3	4	5.75	$$$	-	+-
TEMPLETON GROWTH	GLSTK	VALUE	B	3	4	5.75	$$	-	+
TEMPLETON INCOME	GLBND		B-	3	4	4.50	$$$	---	+++
TEMPLETON SMALLER COMPANIES GROWTH	GLSTK	SMALL CAP VALUE	C+	3	4	5.75	$$	+	+-
TEMPLETON WORLD	GLSTK	VALUE	B-	3	4	5.75	$$	-	+
THIRD AVENUE VALUE	GRO	SMALL CAP VALUE	A-	4	1	5.75	$$$	+++	
THOMSON GROWTH--B	GRO	LARGE CAP GROWTH	B	3	3	1.00r	$$	+-	+
THOMSON INCOME--B	FLEXB		C+	2	3	1.00r	$$	--	++
THOMSON INTERNATIONAL--B	GLSTK		B-	4	4	1.00r	$$	-	+
THOMSON OPPORTUNITY--B*	AGGRO	SMALL CAP GROWTH	A	5	2	1.00r	$$	+	+-
THOMSON U.S. GOVERNMENT FUND--B	US-BD		B-	2	3	1.00r	$$	---	++
THORNBURG LIMITED TERM MUNICIPAL	MUNI	SHORT-TERM	C+	1	3	2.50	$$	---	++
THORNBURG LIMITED TERM U.S. GOV'T	US-BD	SHORT-TERM	B	1	2	2.50	$$	---	+++
TNE BALANCED FUND--A	BAL	LARGE CAP VALUE	C+	3	4	5.75	$$$	-	+
TNE BOND INCOME--A	FLEXB		B-	2	3	4.50	$$	--	+++
TNE GOVERNMENT SECURITIES--A	US-BD		B-	3	3	4.50	$$$	---	+++
TNE GROWTH FUND--A*	GRO	GROWTH	B	4	4	6.50	$$	++	+-
TNE GROWTH OPPORTUNITY PORTFOLIO--A	G&I	LARGE CAP	C	3	3	5.75	$$	-	--
TNE TAX-EXEMPT INCOME--A	MUNI		B	2	4	4.50	$$	--	+++
TNE VALUE FUND--A	GRO	LARGE CAP	C+	3	4	5.75	$$	+-	+
TRANSAMERICA GOVERNMENT SECURITIES	US-BD		B	2	3	4.75	$$$	--	++
TRANSAMERICA GROWTH AND INCOME--A	G&I	VALUE	C+	3	3	5.75	$$	-	+
TRANSAMERICA INVEST. QUALITY BOND	FLEXB		B-	2	3	4.75	$$$	--	+++
TRANSAMERICA SPECIAL--EMERGING GROWTH-B	AGGRO	SMALL CAP GROWTH	B-	4	2	5.00r	$$$	++	--
TRANSAMERICA SPECIAL--HY TAX FREE	MUNI	HIGH YIELD	B-	2	2	5.00r	$$$	--	++
TWENTIETH CENTURY BALANCED	BAL	LARGE CAP GROWTH	C+	3	4		$	-	+
TWENTIETH CENTURY GROWTH	AGGRO	LARGE CAP GROWTH	B-	5	3		$	++	---
TWENTIETH CENTURY HERITAGE INV.	GRO	MID CAP	A	4	3		$	+	+-
TWENTIETH CENTURY INTERNATIONAL EQUITY	INTL		C+	3	4				
TWENTIETH CENTURY LONG-TERM BOND	US-BD	LONG-TERM	A	2	2		$$	--	++
TWENTIETH CENTURY SELECT FUND	GRO	LARGE CAP GROWTH	B+	3	3		$	+	-

▨ = *Schabacker 100*

FUND NAME	Category	InvestStyle/Sector	Quality Rating	Risk	Rew/Risk	Sales Chg.	5-yr. Cost	Bull	Bear
TWENTIETH CENTURY TAX-EXEMPT--INT.	MUNI	INTERMEDIATE	B-	1	3		$	---	++
TWENTIETH CENTURY U.S. GOVERNMENT	US-BD	SHORT-TERM	B-	1	3		$$	---	+++
TWENTIETH CENTURY ULTRA	AGGRO	SMALL CAP GROWTH	A	5	3		$	+++	---
TWENTIETH CENTURY VISTA	AGGRO	GROWTH	B-	5	3		$	++	--
U.S. GOVERNMENT SECURITIES	US-BD		A-	2	2	4.75	$$	---	+++
U.S.T. MASTER TAX-EXEMPT INTERM.	MUNI	INTERMEDIATE	C+	2	3	4.50	$$	---	++
U.S.T. MASTER--EQUITY	GRO	MID CAP	B	4	3	4.50	$$	+-	-
U.S.T. MASTER--MANAGED INCOME	FLEXB		A	3	2	4.50	$$	--	+++
UMB BOND	US-BD		B+	1	2		$	--	+++
UMB STOCK	G&I	LARGE CAP	B-	3	3		$	-	+
UNITED ACCUMULATIVE	GRO	VALUE	B-	3	4	5.75	$$	+-	+
UNITED BOND FUND	FLEXB		B+	2	4	5.75	$$$	--	+++
UNITED CONTINENTAL INCOME FUND	BAL	VALUE	B	3	4	5.75	$$	-	+
UNITED GOVERNMENT SECURITIES FUND	US-BD		B+	2	3	4.25	$$	--	++
UNITED HIGH INCOME	HY-CB		C+	3	3	5.75	$$$	-	++
UNITED HIGH INCOME II	HY-CB		B-	3	2	5.75	$$$	--	++
UNITED INCOME FUND	G&I	LARGE CAP	A-	3	4	5.75	$$	+	+
UNITED INTERNATIONAL GROWTH	GLSTK		C+	4	5	5.75	$$$	-	+
UNITED MUNICIPAL BOND FUND	MUNI		A	3	3	4.25	$$	--	+++
UNITED MUNICIPAL HIGH INCOME	MUNI	HIGH YIELD	A	2	2	4.25	$$	---	++
UNITED NEW CONCEPTS FUND	GRO	SMALL CAP GROWTH	B	4	3	5.75	$$$	+-	+-
UNITED RETIREMENT SHARES	GRO	LARGE CAP	C+	3	4	5.75	$$	-	+
UNITED SCIENCE AND ENERGY	AGGRO	GROWTH	C-	4	4	5.75	$$	+-	-
UNITED VANGUARD	AGGRO	GROWTH	C	4	5	5.75	$$	+-	+-
US GOLD SHARES	GOLD	SOUTH AFRICAN	C-	5	5		$$	--	---
US WORLD GOLD	GOLD		B	5	4		$$	--	+-
USAA AGGRESSIVE GROWTH	AGGRO	SMALL CAP GROWTH	C	4	4		$	++	---
USAA BALANCED	BAL	LARGE CAP VALUE	B	3	3		$	--	++
USAA CORNERSTONE FUND	ASSET	MID CAP	B+	3	3		$	-	+
USAA GNMA TRUST	US-BD	GOV'T MORTGAGE	A-	1	1		$	--	+++
USAA GOLD FUND	GOLD		C+	5	4		$$	-	+
USAA GROWTH FUND	GRO	LARGE CAP	B-	3	3		$	-	--
USAA INCOME FUND	FLEXB		A+	2	1		$	--	+++
USAA INCOME STOCK	G&I	LARGE CAP VALUE	A	3	2		$	-	+
USAA TAX-EXEMPT--INTERMEDIATE	MUNI	INTERMEDIATE	B	2	2		$	---	+++
USAA TAX-EXEMPT--LONG TERM	MUNI	LONG-TERM	A	3	2		$	--	+++
USAA TAX-EXEMPT--SHORT TERM	MUNI	SHORT-TERM	C+	1	3		$	---	+++
VALUE LINE FUND	GRO	GROWTH	A-	4	3		$	+-	--
VALUE LINE INCOME FUND	FLEX	MID CAP	B	3	2		$	-	+
VALUE LINE LEVERAGED GROWTH	AGGRO	GROWTH	B-	4	3		$	+	-
VALUE LINE SPECIAL SITUATIONS FUND	AGGRO	SMALL CAP	C-	4	4		$	+	---
VALUE LINE TAX-EXEMPT HIGH YIELD	MUNI	HIGH YIELD	B	2	3		$	--	++
VALUE LINE U.S. GOV'T SEC.	US-BD		A+	2	2		$	--	+++
VAN ECK GOLD/RESOURCES	GOLD		B-	5	4	5.75	$$$	-	+
VAN ECK WORLD INCOME	GLBND		C+	3	4	4.75	$$$	---	+++
VAN KAMPEN MERRITT HIGH YIELD--A	HY-CB		B-	3	2	4.65	$$$	-	+
VAN KAMPEN MERRITT INSURED TAX-FREE	MUNI		B-	2	4	4.65	$$	---	++
VAN KAMPEN MERRITT MUNICIPAL INCOME	MUNI		B-	3	3	4.65	$$	--	
VAN KAMPEN MERRITT SHORT-TERM GLOBAL--A	GLBND	SHORT-TERM	C-	1	5	3.00	$$	---	
VAN KAMPEN MERRITT TAX-FREE HIGH	MUNI	HIGH YIELD	C	2	5	4.65	$$$	---	++
VAN KAMPEN MERRITT U.S. GOV'T FUND	US-BD		A-	1	2	4.65	$$	--	+++
VANGUARD ASSET ALLOCATION	ASSET	LARGE CAP	B+	3	3		$	-	+
VANGUARD BALANCED INDEX	BAL	LARGE CAP	B+	3	3		$		
VANGUARD BOND INDEX FUND	FLEXB	INDEX	A-	1	1		$$	--	+++
VANGUARD CALIFORNIA INSURED LONG-TERM	MUNI	SINGLE STATE	A	3	3		$	---	++
VANGUARD CONVERTIBLE SECURITIES	G&I	CONVERTIBLE	A-	3	2		$	-	+
VANGUARD EQUITY INCOME	G&I	LARGE CAP VALUE	B	3	3		$	+-	-
VANGUARD EXPLORER	AGGRO	SMALL CAP	C	4	3		$	+	--
VANGUARD FIXED INCOME-GNMA	US-BD	GOV'T MORTGAGE	A	2	1		$	--	+++
VANGUARD FIXED INCOME-HIGH YIELD	HY-CB		A-	3	2	1.00r	$	--	+++
VANGUARD FIXED INCOME-LONG CORP.	C-BD	HIGH GRADE	A+	3	2		$	--	+++
VANGUARD FIXED INCOME-SHORT CORP.	C-BD	SHORT-TERM	B	1	1		$	--	+++
VANGUARD FIXED INCOME-SHORT FEDERAL	US-BD	SHORT-TERM	B+	1	1		$	---	+++

▢ = *Schabacker 100*

FUND NAME	Category	InvestStyle/Sector	Quality Rating	Risk	Rew/ Risk	Sales Chg.	5-yr. Cost	Bull	Bear
VANGUARD FIXED INCOME-TREASURY INTERM.	US-BD	INTERMEDIATE	A	2	2		$		
VANGUARD FIXED INCOME-TREASURY LONG	US-BD	LONG-TERM	A+	3	2		$	---	++
VANGUARD FIXED INCOME-TREASURY SHORT	US-BD	SHORT-TERM	B+	1	2		$		
VANGUARD FLORIDA INSURED TAX-FREE	MUNI	SINGLE STATE	B+	2	3		$		
VANGUARD INDEX 500 TRUST	G&I	LARGE CAP	A-	3	2		$	+-	+
VANGUARD INDEX EXTENDED MARKET	GRO	MID CAP	B	4	3	1.00	$	++	-
VANGUARD INDEX TOTAL STOCK MARKET	G&I	LARGE CAP	B-	3	3	0.25	$		
VANGUARD INDEX VALUE PORTFOLIO	GRO	LARGE CAP VALUE	B+	3	3		$		
VANGUARD INT'L EQUITY INDEX-EUROPEAN	INTL	EUROPE	C-	4	5	1.00	$$	---	
VANGUARD INT'L EQUITY INDEX-PACIFIC	INTL	PACIFIC BASIN	B+	5	3	1.00	$$	---	
VANGUARD INTERNATIONAL GROWTH	INTL		B-	4	4		$	-	+
VANGUARD MORGAN GROWTH	GRO	LARGE CAP	B-	3	3		$	+	-
VANGUARD MUNI BOND-HIGH YIELD	MUNI	HIGH YIELD	A+	3	2		$	--	+++
VANGUARD MUNI BOND-INSURED LONG TERM	MUNI	LONG-TERM	A	3	3		$	---	++
VANGUARD MUNI BOND-INTERMEDIATE	MUNI	INTERMEDIATE	B+	2	2		$	--	+++
VANGUARD MUNI BOND-LIMITED TERM	MUNI	SHORT-TERM	B-	1	2		$	---	++
VANGUARD MUNI BOND-LONG TERM	MUNI	LONG-TERM	A	3	2		$	--	+++
VANGUARD MUNI BOND-SHORT TERM	MUNI	SHORT-TERM	C	1	4		$	---	+++
VANGUARD NEW JERSEY INSURED LONG-TERM	MUNI	SINGLE STATE	A	3	3		$	--	+++
VANGUARD NEW YORK INSURED TAX-FREE	MUNI	SINGLE STATE	A	3	2		$	---	++
VANGUARD OHIO INSURED LONG-TERM	MUNI	SINGLE STATE	B+	3	3		$	--	
VANGUARD PA INSURED LONG-TERM	MUNI	SINGLE STATE	A+	2	2		$	---	++
VANGUARD PREFERRED STOCK	FLEX	MID CAP	B+	2	1		$	-	++
VANGUARD PRIMECAP	GRO	MID CAP	B	4	3		$	+	-
VANGUARD QUANTITATIVE PORTFOLIO	GRO	LARGE CAP VALUE	B+	3	3		$	+	+
VANGUARD SMALL CAPITALIZATION STOCK	AGGRO	SMALL CAP	C	4	3	1.00	$	++	---
VANGUARD SPECIALIZED--ENERGY	SECTR	ENERGY	B	5	3	1.00r	$	-	+
VANGUARD SPECIALIZED--GOLD	GOLD		B+	5	3	1.00r	$	--	+
VANGUARD SPECIALIZED--HEALTH	SECTR	HEALTH CARE	B	4	3	1.00r	$	++	+
VANGUARD SPECIALIZED--UTILITIES INCOME	SECTR	UTILITIES	A-	3	2		$		
VANGUARD STAR FUND	BAL	LARGE CAP VALUE	B+	3	2		$	-	+
VANGUARD TRUSTEES'--INTL PORTFOLIO	INTL		B	4	4		$	-	+
VANGUARD TRUSTEES'--U.S. PORTFOLIO	GRO	VALUE	B	3	3		$	+-	+
VANGUARD U.S. GROWTH	GRO	LARGE CAP VALUE	B	4	4		$	+-	+
VANGUARD WELLESLEY INCOME FUND	BAL	LARGE CAP VALUE	A	3	1		$	-	+++
VANGUARD WELLINGTON FUND	BAL	LARGE CAP VALUE	A-	3	2		$	-	+
VANGUARD WINDSOR II	G&I	LARGE CAP VALUE	A-	3	3		$	+	+
VANGUARD WINDSOR*	G&I	LARGE CAP VALUE	A-	4	3		$	+	+
VENTURE MUNI PLUS	MUNI	HIGH YIELD	C+	1	2	4.00r	$$$	---	++
VISTA CAPITAL GROWTH	AGGRO	SMALL CAP	B+	4	3	4.75	$$	+++	-
VISTA GROWTH AND INCOME	G&I	VALUE	B+	4	3	4.75	$$	+++	+-
VISTA U.S. GOVERNMENT INCOME	US-BD		A-	2	3	4.50	$	--	+++
VONTOBEL EUROPACIFIC FUND	INTL		B-	3	5		$$$	--	+
VOYAGEUR U.S. GOVERNMENT SECURITIES	US-BD		A	2	2	4.75	$$	--	+++
WARBURG PINCUS CAPITAL APPRECIATION	GRO	GROWTH	B	4	3		$	+	+
WARBURG PINCUS EMERGING GROWTH	AGGRO	SMALL CAP GROWTH	B+	4	3		$	++	-
WARBURG PINCUS INTERM. MATURITY GOV'T	US-BD	INTERMEDIATE	B+	2	3		$	---	+++
WARBURG PINCUS INTERNATIONAL EQUITY	GLSTK		B	4	4		$$	-	+
WASHINGTON MUTUAL INVESTORS	G&I	LARGE CAP VALUE	A-	3	3	5.75	$$	+-	+
WAYNE HUMMER GROWTH TRUST	G&I	MID CAP	B	3	3		$	-	+
WESTCORE BASIC VALUE	GRO	LARGE CAP VALUE	C	3	4	4.50	$$	++	-
WESTCORE INTERMEDIATE-TERM BOND	C-BD	INTERMEDIATE	B+	2	2	4.50	$$	--	++
WESTCORE MIDCO GROWTH	AGGRO	GROWTH	B+	4	3	4.50	$$	+++	+-
WILLIAM BLAIR GROWTH SHARES	GRO	GROWTH	B+	4	3		$	+-	-
WILLIAM BLAIR INCOME SHARES	C-BD		B+	2	2		$	--	
WPG GOVERNMENT SECURITIES	US-BD		A+	1	1		$	---	+++
WPG GROWTH FUND	AGGRO	SMALL CAP GROWTH	B-	4	3		$	+	-
WPG TUDOR FUND	AGGRO	SMALL CAP GROWTH	B-	4	3		$	++	-
YACKTMAN FUND	GRO		C-	3	5		$		

▭ = *Schabacker 100*

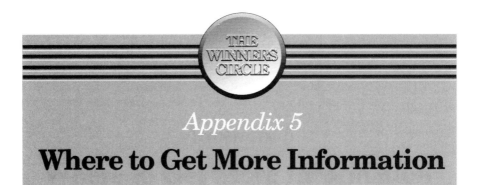

Appendix 5

Where to Get More Information

Business and Financial Weekly

Barron's
200 Burnett Road
Chicopee, MA 01020
1-800-221-1940

Daily Financial Newspapers

Investor's Business Daily
12655 Beatrice Street
Los Angeles, CA 90066
1-800-831-2525

The Wall Street Journal
200 Burnett Road
Chicopee, MA 01020
1-800-221-1940

Funds Rating Services

Morningstar, Inc.
53 West Jackson Boulevard
Chicago, IL 60604
1-800-876-5005

The Value Line Mutual Fund Survey
711 3rd Avenue
New York, NY 10017-4064
1-800-284-7607

Managed Accounts Services

Schabacker Investment Management
15245 Shady Grove Road, Suite 100
Rockville, MD 20850
1-800-346-0138

Monthly Investment Newsletter

Mutual Fund Investing
Phillips Publishing International
7811 Montrose Road
Potomac, MD 20854
1-800-777-5005

Glossary

12b-1 fee

Fee charged by some funds and named after the 1980 Securities and Exchange Commission rule that permits them. Such fees pay for distribution costs such as advertising or for commissions paid to brokers. The fund's prospectus details 12b-1 charges, if applicable.

401(k)

A qualified employee benefit plan where employee contributions are made on a pretax basis. Both employer and employee contributions compound tax-free until withdrawn. Mutual funds are among the investment options offered.

403(b) plan

This tax-deferred retirement plan is for employees of public school systems and certain charitable and nonprofit organizations. Like 401(k) plans, 403(b) plans offer mutual funds as investment options.

A-B trust

Language in a will or trust that gives a surviving spouse full use of the family's accumulated wealth, while minimizing the federal estate tax due upon the deaths of both spouses. By using an A-B trust, a married couple can save 37% to 55% of every dollar in the estate above $600,000. As much as $235,000 can be saved by a married couple if the estate is $1.2 million. Also called a credit shelter or by-pass trust.

account

Used in such terms as mutual fund account or open account. It denotes an investor's business arrangement or record of his investments, together with reinvestments or distributions and/or withdrawals and charges; an open account is open to further investment. Example: mutual fund account.

accumulation plan

A voluntary or contractual plan for the acquisition of mutual fund shares.

administrative expenses

The fund expenses paid directly by the fund.

advisor

The organization employed by a mutual fund to give professional advice on the fund's investments and asset management practices (also called investment advisor).

advisory fee

The fee paid by the fund to the investment advisor for managing the fund.

aggressive growth fund

A mutual fund that seeks maximum capital appreciation through the use of investment techniques involving greater than ordinary risk, including such techniques as borrowing money in order to provide leverage, short selling, hedging, and options and warrants.

all-weather fund

A fund that long-term investors can hold safely throughout a complete economic and market cycle. The fund does not specialize in its investment style in any one type of economically sensitive investments. This fund is the best for the inactive buy and hold investor.

alpha

A statistical measure representing the difference between the actual and expected performance of a fund given its characteristic volatility. A positive alpha is often considered a measure of management's ability.

annuitize

Refers to periodic payments of both principal and interest, resulting in a systematic liquidation of an annuity.

annuity

A contract where the buyer (annuitant) pays a sum of money (investment) to receive regular payments for life for a fixed period of time.

asked or offering price

This is the price at which a mutual fund's shares can be purchased. The asked or offering price means the current net asset value (NAV) per share plus any sales charge. For a no-load fund, the asked price is the same as the NAV.

asset allocation

A strategy of varying the asset mix of one's portfolio (stocks, bonds, cash, etc.) as conditions warrant. For our purposes, we use the Back of the Envelope Forecaster to signal such shifts.

asset allocation fund

This type of fund spreads its portfolio among a wide variety of investments, including domestic and foreign stocks and bonds, government securities, gold bullion, and real estate stocks. The asset allocation is meant to lower risk while providing favorable total returns. With some funds, the allocation of assets remains relatively constant, while other funds alter the mix as market conditions change.

asset value

Either total or per share. Total net assets of a fund are made up of market value of holdings plus any other fund resources such as cash, minus liabilities. Per share is determined by dividing the total by the number of shares outstanding.

automatic reinvestment

This service, offered by most mutual funds, lets you use your income dividends and capital gain distributions to automatically buy additional shares. As a result, you build up your holdings through the effects of compounding.

automatic withdrawal plan

An arrangement many open-end investment companies have that enables investors to receive fixed payments, usually monthly or quarterly. The actual payout is determined by the investor. Also called "check a month" plan.

back-end load

The fee (a contingent deferred sales charge) paid by the fund owner when withdrawing money from a fund.

balanced fund

A mutual fund that has an investment policy of "balancing" its portfolio, generally by including bonds, preferred stocks, and common stocks.

bands

The range of percentages that an investor may allocate to stocks, bonds, cash, or some other invest-ment class. For example, a moderate risk investor may be from 30% invested in stocks to as high as 70%. The balance would be in some combination of stocks and bonds.

basis point

A unit used to measure changes in interest rates and bond yields. One basis point equals .01% (or 1/100 of 1%). An increase from 8% to 10% would be a change of 200 basis points.

bear market

A market characterized by a downward trend in securities prices.

beta

Term used to describe the price volatility of securities. Standard & Poor's 500 Index is assigned a beta of one; anything with a beta above one is considered to be more volatile than the index, while anything below one has less volatility than the S&P index.

bid or redemption price

(as seen in some mutual fund newspaper listings): The price at which a mutual fund's shares are redeemed (bought back) by the fund. The bid or redemption price usually equals the current net asset value per share.

blue chip

The common stock of well-established companies with a stable record of earnings and dividends.

blue sky laws

Rules and regulations of the various states governing the securities business, including mutual funds, broker/dealers, and salespeople.

bond fund

A mutual fund whose portfolio consists primarily of fixed-income securities (corporate, municipal, or U.S. government bonds). The emphasis of such funds is normally on income rather than growth.

broker

A person in the business of effecting securities transactions for others, for a commission. There are two types of brokers: full-service brokers, who give advice, and discount brokers, who do not give advice (the investor must do his own research).

broker-dealer

A firm that buys and sells mutual fund shares and other securities from and to the public.

bull market

A market characterized by an upward trend in securities prices.

buy and hold strategy

A strategy using an "unmanaged" portfolio, with no effort to select undervalued securities or to forecast ("time") turns in market trends.

capital gains

The increase in the market value of securities held (net asset value of fund shares), which is the prime short- or long-term objective of many funds. A gain is called unrealized until a security is actually sold.

capital gains distributions

Payments to mutual fund shareholders of profits realized on the sale of securities in the fund's portfolio. These amounts usually are distributed to shareholders annually.

capital growth

This is the increase in value of a mutal fund's securities. Capital growth is measured by the change in a fund's net asset value per share. This is a specific long-term objective of many mutual funds.

cash (distribution) option

The fund shareholder elects to receive both dividend (income) and capital gains distributions in cash.

cash position

Cash plus cash equivalents (receivables, short-term bonds, and notes) minus current liabilities.

certificate of deposit (CD)

Generally, a short-term debt instrument certificate issued by commercial banks or savings and loan associations. (Euro CDs are issued by foreign branches of U.S. banks; Yankee CDs are issued by U.S. branches of foreign banks.)

charitable lead trust

A legal instrument designed to save federal estate taxes while at the same time providing an income over a period of years to one or more qualified charities. Once the trust is established, money is invested and the stream of income is paid to the charity for the term of the trust. The trust principal is then distributed to designated beneficiaries such as the children.

closed-end investment company

Unlike mutual funds (known as open-end funds), closed-end companies issue only a limited number of shares and do not redeem them (buy them back). Instead, closed-end shares are traded in the securities markets, with supply and demand determining the price. Also called *publicly traded* funds.

commercial paper (CP)

Unsecured promissory notes of corporations and various financial institutions, with maturities of up to 270 days. Used as a money market instrument.

commission

A fee paid to a broker or mutual fund salesman for the buying or selling of securities and so-called load mutual funds.

common stock

A security representing ownership in a corporation's assets.

common stock fund

A mutual fund whose portfolio consists primarily of common stocks. The emphasis of such funds is usually on growth.

compounding

The process that occurs through the reinvestment of interest, dividends, or profits. Growth thus occurs at the same rate that the investment itself earns, allowing the reinvestment money to multiply, rather than simply adding to the investment.

conservation of principal

Use of conservative securities to guard against a decline in the value of securities or a fund's portfolio.

consumer price index (CPI)

Index that analyzes the changes in prices for consumer goods and services over time. A general cost-of-living index (measure) based on a representative "market basket" of goods.

contingent deferred sales charge

A sales fee payable when the shareholder redeems shares, rather than when shares are purchased, frequently reduced each year that the shares are held. For example, if shares are redeemed less than one year after purchase, a fee of 5% of NAV might be charged; if redeemed in more than one but less than two years, 4%, etc. Also called a *contingent deferred sales load*.

contractual plan

A program for the accumulation of mutual fund shares in which the investor agrees to invest a fixed amount on a regular basis for a specified number of years. A substantial portion of the sales charge applicable to the total investment is usually deducted from early payments.

contrarian

An investor who does the opposite of what most investors are doing at a particular time. A contrarian fund generally invests in out-of-favor securities, whose price/earnings ratio is lower than the rest of the market or industry.

contrary indicators
Indicators that should be interpreted the opposite of how they might at first appear. Sentiment indicators are usually interpreted as contrary indicators, since if most investors are bullish, they are already invested; therefore, there are no more buyers and the market will soon go down.

convertible securities
A bond, debenture, or preferred stock that gives its owner the right to exchange that security for common stock or another type of security issued by the same company.

corporate bond
A marketable, long-term debt obligation of a corporation.

correction
Used in conjunction with a bull market. It is a sustained period of stock price declines in the midst of long-term rising stock prices. A correction is usually followed by another period of rising stock prices. A major correction refers to a decline of 10% or more in widely accepted stock market indexes. An extreme and long-term correction turns into a bear market.

cost basis
The original price of an asset, used in determining capital gains.

It is usually the purchase price, plus whatever distributions have already been paid (for mutual funds).

current income
Current dividend (income) distribution from a fund.

CUSIP
The Committee on Union Securities Identification Procedures, which assigns identifying numbers and codes to all securities. These CUSIP numbers are used when recording all buy and sell orders. Each mutual fund has a CUSIP number.

custodian
The organization (usually a bank) that keeps custody of securities and other assets of a mutual fund.

cycle
A pattern of swings in a trend that recurs on a regular time frame.

daily dividend fund
A fund that declares its income dividends daily. The fund usually reinvests or distributes them daily or monthly.

date of record
That date on which declared distributions are set aside (held separate, for payment to shareholders at a later date) and deducted from total net assets.

dealer
A person or firm who regularly buys and sells securities for others from his or her own account

of securities. In contrast, a broker acts as an agent for others. Frequently, broker and dealer functions are synonymous.

debenture

A bond secured by the general credit of the corporation, and usually not secured by any collateral.

debt instrument

Any instrument that signifies a loan between a borrower and a lender.

declaration of dividends

Announcement by issuer of bonds or equities of their decision to make a payment to their shareholders. Some companies do this on a regular basis, while others may declare a dividend only when company earnings have reached a certain predetermined level. Many money funds declare dividends daily but pay monthly.

default

Failure to pay principal and/or interest when due.

defined contribution plan

A Keogh or corporate retirement plan that permits employers to contribute the estimated amount needed to fund a predetermined annual employee retirement benefit.

deflation

A fall in the general price level of goods and services.

direct-purchase fund

A no-load or low-load fund whose shares can be bought directly, without going through a dealer, thus avoiding all or most of the sales commission. Also called *direct marketed fund*.

discount broker

A brokerage firm that charges a lower fee than a full-service broker to buy or sell securities. Typically, discount brokers offer fewer services as well, such as guidance or security recommendations. Recently, several of these firms have established a network to buy and sell funds from different families with just a phone call.

discretionary account

An account in which an investment advisor or broker has the full right to buy and sell securities without consultation or authorization of the investor.

disinflation

A slowdown in the rate of inflation without turning into deflation.

distribution fee

Under the 12b-1 plan, a fund or fund family that does not have its own sales force is allowed to take a percentage of the assets as a fee to pay independent brokers for selling its fund(s).

distributions

The payments of dividends or realized capital gains that a fund determines to pass along to shareholders, who can take them in cash or in additional shares, sometimes in fractions thereof.

distributor

The principal underwriter—either a person or a company—that purchases open-end investment company shares directly from the issuer for resale to others.

diversification

The policy of spreading your investments among a range of different securities to reduce the risks inherent in investing. Mutual funds automatically give you this diversification. Diversification is also important among various categories of investments.

diversified investment company

To be so classified, the Investment Company Act requires that 75% of a fund's assets be allocated so that not more than 5% of its total assets are invested in one company. In addition, it can hold no more than 10% of the outstanding voting securities of another company.

dividend

As distinct from a capital gains distribution, represents dividends from investment income.

dollar-cost averaging

Investing equal amounts of money at regular intervals regardless of whether the stock market is moving upward or downward. This reduces average share costs to the investor, who acquired more shares in periods of lower securities prices and fewer shares in periods of higher prices.

Dow-Jones Industrial Average (DJIA)

The most well-known measure of the performance of the overall stock market as represented by an index of 30 blue-chip stocks.

earnings

Profits generated by a company.

economics

The study of how people use limited resources—personal, commercial, national, or international—to achieve maximum well-being.

equity

In investments, an ownership interest by shareholders of a corporation. Stock is equity, as opposed to bonds, which are debt.

equity fund

A mutual fund that invests primarily in common stocks.

equity-income fund

A mutual fund whose objective is income as well as growth. Its portfolio typically consists of high-yielding common stocks, preferred and convertible issues, and bonds.

ERISA

Employee Retirement Income Security Act; the 1974 law governing the operation of most private pension and benefit plans.

exchange fund

An investment company that allows persons holding individual securities to exchange these securities for fund shares without paying a capital gains tax.

exchange privilege

The right to take all or some of the shares of one fund and put them into another fund within the same family of funds. This is considered a sale and new purchase for tax purposes (same as a switching privilege).

ex-dividend

For mutual funds (but not for securities listed on a stock exchange), that date on which declared distributions are deducted from fund total net assets. On the day a fund goes ex-dividend, its closing net asset value per share will fall by an amount equal to the dividend and/or capital gains distribution (although market movements may alter the fund's closing NAV somewhat as well).

expense ratio

Annual expenses paid by a fund (including management fees, custodial fees, transfer agency fees, legal fees, investment advisory fees, and distribution or 12b-1 fees) divided by the average shares outstanding of the period. The expense ratio does not include loads or commissions paid for the investor's purchasing, reinvesting, or selling the fund's shares.

face value

The value that appears on the face of a bond, usually $1,000. This is the amount the issuing company will pay at maturity, but it does not necessarily indicate market price.

family of funds

A group of mutual funds sponsored or managed by the same investment company. One company may manage several different funds, each with different objectives such as growth, income, or tax-exempt funds. Fund families frequently provide convenient telephone switching between funds.

Fed

Nickname for the U.S. Federal Reserve System.

Federal Funds Rate

Interest charged to banks that need overnight loans to meet reserve requirements. Since this rate is set every day by market forces, it is considered a sensitive indicator of the future direction of other interest rates.

fiduciary

An individual or corporation entrusted with certain assets for a specified purpose. Also known as trustee, executor, guardian.

fixed annuity

An annuity contract that provides for fixed payments at regular intervals.

fixed-income fund

A mutual fund whose portfolio consists primarily of fixed-income securities or bonds. The fund's objective is normally income rather than capital appreciation.

fixed income security

A debt security such as a bond and a preferred stock with a

stated return in percentage or dollars.

flexibly diversified

In contrast to a balanced fund whose portfolio at all times must be diversified among a generally stated minimum or maximum percentage of bonds and preferred/common stocks, flexible diversification means that management, at its discretion, may allot the percentage for each type of security.

front-end load

A sales charge paid by the purchaser for buying into a mutual fund. The sales charge typically can run as high as 4.0% for bond funds to 8.5% for stock funds.

full-service broker

A broker who offers investment advice and charges higher commissions than discount brokers.

fully invested

One hundred percent invested position. All money is considered to be earning dividends, capital gains, interest, or a mixture of any of these, in contrast to only a portion of the invested money having earnings capabilities.

fund

An abbreviation for mutual fund or open-end investment company.

fundamental analysis

Analysis of corporate management, products, markets, balance sheets, income statements, sales, earnings, and price-to-earnings ratios in order to forecast future stock price movements.

fund distributor

The organization responsible for selling fund shares to the public (no-load funds) or to securities dealers and others for resale to the public (load funds).

global asset allocation fund

A broadly diversified fund that typically invests across a number of markets to provide a hedge against declines in the U.S. market. Their holdings may include U.S. stocks, international stocks, U.S. bonds, often international government bonds, gold or gold mining shares, cash equivalents, and sometimes real estate securities. They try to obtain satisfactory performances in most all foreseeable economic climates—inflation, deflation, stability. *See also* asset allocation fund.

global fund

A fund that invests in the securities of the United States as well as those of foreign countries.

GNMA or "Ginnie Mae" fund

A fund investing in GNMA securities issued by the Government National Mortgage Association, a corporation that helps finance mortgages.

government securities

A general term that refers to any instruments of debt issued by the U.S. government or its agencies or instrumentalities.

gross domestic product (GDP)

Total value of all goods and services produced in the economy over a period of time. The rate of growth of the GDP is the primary indicator of the overall health of the economy. The numbers are released every quarter, expressed on an annualized basis, usually net of inflation (real GDP).

growth companies

Types of companies whose earnings (profits) grow steadily. In many cases their success is not tied directly to the overall health of the economy. Typical areas include food, consumer products, and health care. Because these stocks have growing earnings, investors are willing to pay more for them; consequently, they tend to be more volatile and have higher valuation measures.

growth fund

A mutual fund whose primary investment objective is long-term growth of capital. It invests principally in common stocks with growth potential.

growth-income fund

A mutual fund whose aim is to provide a degree of both income and long-term growth, usually through the purchase of common stocks paying high dividends.

hedge

To offset. To safeguard oneself from loss on a risk by making compensatory arrangements on the other side. For example, to hedge one's long positions with short sales, so that if the market declines then the loss on long positions will be offset by profit on the short positions.

hedge fund

A mutual fund whose policy is to hedge long position with short positions. Occasionally used to describe any aggressive fund.

high-yield bonds

High yielding, noninvestment quality, lower-rated bonds.

illiquid

An asset that is difficult to quickly convert into cash. According to SEC regulations, open-end investment companies (mutual funds) can invest no more than 15% of their capital in illiquid investments. This rule is aimed at assuring that the funds will be able to redeem their shares on demand. Real estate restricted issues, letter stock-securities requiring registration before they can be sold, are considered illiquid. *See also* liquid.

immediate annuity

An annuity contract that starts making payments to the annuitant almost immediately—within one year of the contract's purchase.

income dividends

Payments to mutual fund shareholders of dividends and/or interest earned on the fund's portfolio of securities after deducting operating expenses.

income-earned (distribution) option

The fund shareholder elects to receive dividend distributions in cash, and capital gains distributions are reinvested in additional shares.

income fund

This type of fund seeks current income rather than growth of capital. These funds tend to invest in stocks and bonds that normally pay high dividends and interest. *See also* equity-income fund.

index fund

This type of fund seeks to mirror general stock market performance by matching its portfolio to a broad-based index, such as the Standard & Poor's 500 Index.

indicators

Measurements that an analyst uses to help forecast a market's direction (stock market, bond market, etc.).

individual retirement account (IRA)

This is a personal, tax-deferred retirement account. Contributions can be tax-deductible for people who are not covered by a company retirement plan or, if covered, meet certain income limitations. Investment earnings on IRA money are tax-deferred, usually until retirement at age $59^1/_2$ or older. The tax deductibility of annual IRA contributions is limited to taxpayers who meet income guidelines defined in the Tax Reform Act of 1986.

individual retirement account (IRA) rollover

This is the action of moving your lump-sum pension or profit-sharing payments into an IRA. IRA funds can also be rolled over from one investment to another. A rollover involves the individual receiving the money and reinvesting it. Rollovers must be completed within 60 days and are allowed only once every twelve months.

individual retirement account (IRA) transfer

Movement of IRA funds from one trustee to another. The IRA investor does not receive the money; it goes directly to another trustee. For example, a common transfer is from a bank money market deposit account to a no-load mutual fund family. Both banks and mutual fund families are permitted to be IRA trustees.

inflation

The economic condition of rising prices for goods and services. It is characterized by an increasing volume of currency in circulation and a decline in the buying power of cash.

inflation rate

The rate of change in the prices of goods and services. Two popular measures of the inflation rate are the consumer price index (CPI) and the producer price index (PPI).

institutional investor

A large, professional manager of client and/or other portfolios (e.g., bank trust department or mutual fund portfolio).

institutions-only mutual funds

Mutual funds that allow only institutional clients, bank trust departments, corporations, stockbrokers, depository institutions, or pension funds to buy shares. Some funds that claim to be institutions-only will allow individuals to invest if they can meet the (usually high) minimum initial investment or invest through an institution.

international diversification

The use of domestic and international funds in the investor's portfolio to reduce overall portfolio risk for the level of return.

international fund

This type of fund invests in securities traded in markets outside the United States.

investment company

A corporation, trust, or partnership that invests pooled funds of shareholders in securities appropriate to the fund's objective. Among the benefits of investment companies are professional management and diversification. Mutual funds (open-end investment companies) are the most popular type of investment company.

investment objective

The specific goal, such as long-term capital growth or current income, that the investor or mutual fund pursues.

investment style

The particular method used by an investor such as emphasizing small cap stocks or value investing to meet their investment objective.

investor

A person seeking consistent, moderate securities profits (returns) over time.

investor sentiment

How positive or negative individual and/or professional investors feel about the prospects of a stock market (or bond market) rising in the near future.

irrevocable trust

A trust that cannot be changed. In an irrevocable trust, assets may be removed from an estate for estate tax planning purposes. For example, life insurance policies may be owned by an irrevocable life insurance trust. The proceeds of the estate are not subject to the federal estate tax because the policies are owned by the trust rather than the individual.

joint tenant account

An account with joint ownership in which the deceased's ownership share reverts to his or her estate.

joint tenants with right of survivorship account

An account with joint ownership in which full ownership of the account reverts to the surviving owner.

junk bonds
High-yielding, noninvestment quality, lower-rated bonds.

Keogh plan
This is a tax-deferred retirement account for those who are self-employed or are employees of unincorporated businesses. Keogh plans can use mutual funds as an investment option.

leverage
The use of borrowed money with invested funds to increase returns. The effect is to magnify profits or losses and increase the amount of risk.

liquid
May be easily converted into cash or exchanged for other assets.

liquid asset fund
A money market fund.

liquidate
To convert an asset into cash.

liquidity
The ability to convert a security to cash quickly and without a significant price concession from the previous trade.

load fund
Any fund that levies a sales charge up to 8.5%. A front-end load is the fee charged when buying into a fund; a back-end load is the fee charged when getting out of a fund.

long position
That part of a fund's portfolio which represents securities purchased for price appreciation in a rising market.

long-term funds
An industry designation for all funds other than short-term funds (money market and short-term municipal bond). The two broad categories of long-term funds are equity (stock) and bond and income funds.

long-term growth
A category of mutual funds that are concerned with long-term appreciation and not the generation of income. These funds tend to be average to above average in risk.

low-load mutual fund
A fund with a low front-end load of approximately 3% or less for the purchase of its shares.

management fee
The amount paid by a mutual fund to the investment advisor for its services. Industrywide, fees generally range from 0.5% to 1.0% a year of a fund's assets.

market extremes
A condition reached after a market has risen (or fallen) a considerable amount, especially if it occurs within a fairly short period of time.

market momentum
The inertia of a market to continue on its present course until there is some type of fundamental change.

market price

The last reported price at which a security has been sold.

market rate

A general term used to describe the current interest rate on a given instrument.

market timer

An investor who attempts to time the market (forecast) so that shares are sold before they decrease in value and bought when they are about to increase in value. Sometimes the strategy calls for frequent buy-and-sell decisions.

market timing

A strategy of moving from stocks to cash based on the readings of a forecaster. For our purposes, since we do not want to take the risks of being either 100% in or 100% out of stocks, we use the cycle forecaster to vary the style of stock fund, as well as the percentage of stock funds, bond funds, and money market funds.

maturity

The scheduled date for repayment of the principal amount of a debt instrument.

maximum capital gains fund

This type of fund seeks maximum capital appreciation through the use of a range of aggressive investment techniques. The fund may borrow money in order to provide leverage, engage in short-selling, and have a high portfolio turnover.

money market

The market for low-risk, highly liquid, short-term debt securities.

money market fund

Also called a liquid asset or cash fund, it is a mutual fund whose primary objective is safety of principal, liquidity, and current income. This is accomplished through the purchase of short-term money market instruments such as U.S. government securities, bank securities, bank certificates of deposit, and commercial paper.

money market instruments

Short-term debt instruments such as Treasury bills, repurchase agreements, bankers' acceptances, certificates of deposit, and commercial paper.

mortgage-backed securities

"Passthrough" securities created from pools of mortgages that are packaged together and sold as bonds. The monthly payments of interest and principal on the underlying mortgage debt are "passed through" to investors.

moving average

A mathematical method for determining trends in the stock market or stock market indicators. A moving average is calculated by adding a series of values for a certain time period and dividing the total by the number of values added. For the next figure, the earliest value is dropped and the current one is added. Example is a 200-day moving average of stock or market prices to forecast future price movements.

municipal bond fund

A mutual fund that invests in a broad range of tax-exempt bonds issued by states, cities, and other local governments. The interest obtained from these bonds is passed through to shareowners free of federal tax. The fund's primary objective is current tax-free income.

municipal securities

Debt obligations issued by states, countries, cities, towns, school districts, or other municipal agencies. The interest paid on these securities is generally exempt from federal income taxes and state and local taxes in the state of issuance.

mutual fund

An investment company that pools investors' money and is managed by a professional advisor. It ordinarily stands ready to buy back (redeem) its shares at their current net asset value; the value of the shares depends on the market value of the fund's portfolio securities at the time. Also, most mutual funds are open-ended, which means they continuously offer new shares to investors.

NASDAQ

An automated information network that provides brokers and dealers with price quotations on securities traded over-the-counter. NASDAQ is an acronym for the National Association of Securities Dealers Automated Quotations.

National Association of Securities Dealers, Inc. (NASD)

The trade association charged by federal law with policing the SEC regulations applying to mutual funds and over-the-counter securities, but not those traded on stock exchanges.

nest egg

Assets put aside to provide for a secure standard of living after one's retirement.

net assets

A fund's total assets less current liabilities such as taxes and other operating expenses.

net asset value per share

A fund's total assets after deduction of liabilities, divided by the number of shares outstanding. It is synonymous with the fund bid price, and, in the case of no-loads, also the offering or market price.

net investment income per share

Dividends and interest earned during an accounting period (such as a year) on a fund's portfolio, less operating expenses, divided by the number of shares outstanding.

net realized capital gains per share

The amount of capital gain realized on sale of a fund's portfolio holdings during an accounting period (such as a year), less losses realized on such transactions, divided by the number of shares outstanding.

no-load mutual fund

A fund that does not charge a sales fee for investment, reinvestment of dividends, and/or redemptions.

nondiversified investment company

A fund whose portfolio does not meet the requirements of the Investment Company Act of 1940 to qualify as a diversified investment company—for example, a fund that may invest up to 25% in the securities of one company.

offering price

The price at which shares are offered for sale. Same as asked price, which is net asset value per share plus any applicable sales commission.

open-end investment company

The more formal name for a mutual fund, indicating that it stands ready to redeem its shares (buy them back) on demand.

option income fund

A mutual fund that sells options on the shares in its portfolio to increase its income.

over-the-counter market

The market for securities transactions conducted through a communications network connecting dealers in stocks and bonds. The rules of such trading are written and enforced by the National Association of Securities Dealers,

Inc. (NASD), the same organization that provides self-policing of member firms in the distribution of mutual fund shares.

payment or payable date

The day on which a distribution is mailed to shareholders by a mutual fund. Usually, it is later than the declaration date, which is the day the distribution is announced by the board of directors, and also usually follows the date of record, which is the date the distribution goes ex-dividend.

payroll deduction plan

An arrangement some employers offer whereby employees may accumulate shares in a mutual fund. Employees authorize their employer to deduct a specified amount from their salary at stated times and transfer the proceeds to the fund.

performance

The percentage change in a fund's per share value over a specified period of time. As used in the mutual fund industry, it generally refers to total return, which includes the value of the income and capital gains dividends distributed during the specified period.

periodic payment plan

An arrangement that allows an investor to purchase mutual fund shares periodically, usually with provisions for the reinvestment of income dividends and the acceptance of capital gains distributions in additional shares.

portfolio

A group of securities or investment holdings managed collectively or owned by an investment company or an individual.

portfolio insurance

A strategy for limiting fund losses in falling markets while allowing participation in rising markets. Often options trading is employed as part of this strategy.

portfolio turnover

The extent to which a fund's portfolio securities are replaced in a one-year period. A fund with 100% portfolio turnover, on average, completely changed or sold all the investments in its portfolio in one year's time.

preferred stock

A class of stock that has prior claim on dividends before common stock shares. In the event of corporate liquidation, preferred stockholders have a prior claim on assets over common shareholders.

price moving average

Technical indicator that gauges the momentum of a security or index by comparing the price to an average price. Whenever the price is higher than the average price, momentum is positive; whenever the price falls below the average price, momentum becomes negative.

price-to-book value

The price of a stock divided by the per share value of the assets in the company. As with the P/E ratio, this ratio can help identify undervalued stocks.

price-to-earnings (P/E) ratio

The price of a stock divided by the per share profits generated by the company. The level of this ratio helps indicate if the stock is overvalued (high P/E) or undervalued (low P/E).

probate

The legal process in which a court transfers title to real and personal property and pays the debts, if any, of a decedent. Because of the costs, length of the process, and public nature of the records, many families are turning to the revocable living trust as an alternative method to transfer property at death.

program trading

A wide range of computer-assisted portfolio trading strategies involving the simultaneous purchase or sale of 15 or more stocks.

prospectus

The legal written document that describes a mutual fund, or any security, and offers it for sale. In the case of a fund, the prospectus contains information required by the Securities and Exchange Commission on investment objectives and policies, services, investment restrictions, officers and directors, procedure to buy and sell shares, and fees and financial statements.

proxy

Enables fund shareholders not attending an annual meeting to transfer their voting power to another person, usually fund management, to vote on fund business at the meeting.

prudent man rule

The rule that allows a trustee to use his own judgment in making investments as long as he acts prudently or conservatively. The rule comes from an 1830 court decision.

publicly trading investment company

A closed-end fund.

qualified dividend funds

Offered to corporations that want to take advantage of a provision in the tax code that allows U.S. corporations to exclude 70% of the dividends they receive from federal taxation. These funds invest in high-yielding common and preferred stock.

qualified retirement plan

A private retirement plan that meets the rules and regulations of the Internal Revenue Service. Contributions to a qualified retirement plan are, in most cases, tax-deductible, and earnings on such contributions are always tax-sheltered until retirement. Most company pension plans are qualified retirement plans.

rate of return (total return)

A fund's total return is calculated by taking the end-of-the-period NAV per share, adding back any per share dividend (income) and capital gains distributions, and computing the percentage change from the beginning-of-the-period NAV per share.

real estate investment trust (REIT)

An investment company that specializes in real estate holdings. Cannot be a mutual fund because investments are considered illiquid. *See also* illiquid.

record date

The date the fund selects as the cutoff date used to determine which shareholders will receive the fund's income dividend and/or net capital gains distribution. The record date is frequently the business day immediately prior to the ex-dividend date.

redeem

To buy back shares from the present owner. *See also* redemption price.

redemption fee

The charge levied by a few funds when shares are redeemed. Also referred to as a back-end load.

redemption price

The amount per share a mutual fund shareholder receives when he or she cashes in shares (also known as liquidating price or bid price). The value of the shares depends on the market value of the company's portfolio securities at the time.

red herring

A preliminary prospectus.

regional fund

Any mutual fund that concentrates its investments within a

specific geographic area. These funds are designed to take advantage of regional growth potential.

registered fund

A fund "registered" with the Securities and Exchange Commission (SEC) for the sale of shares in the United States.

registrar

The organization, usually a bank, that maintains a registry of the share owners of a mutual fund, and the number of shares that they hold.

regulated investment company

A fund that meets the income and diversification criteria required under law to avoid corporate income taxation.

reinvestment date

This is the date on which a share's dividend and/or capital gains will be reinvested (if requested) and used to purchase additional fund shares. Also called *payable date*.

reinvestment privilege

A service provided by most mutual funds for the automatic reinvestment of a shareholder's income dividends and capital gains distributions in additional shares.

repurchase agreement (repo)

A financial transaction in which one party "purchases" securities for cash while the seller simultaneously agrees to "buy" them back in the future at specified terms (usually the original price plus interest).

restricted security

One that requires registration with the SEC before it may be sold to the public. Because of this restriction, the security may not be considered a liquid asset and therefore may be priced at a substantial discount from market value.

return on investment

Percentage gain including reinvestment of capital gains and dividends, if any.

revocable living trust

A trust designed to transfer property at the death of the person(s) establishing the trust without probate. The living trust has become one of the most popular estate planning techniques in the last 25 years. By using a living trust rather than a will, families are able to avoid expenditures for court administration, settle the affairs of the estate more efficiently and without unnecessary delay, and maintain the privacy of the decedent's estate.

reward-to-risk ratio

A fund performance measure that relates the "excess" return (over the "risk-free" rate) to total or systematic risk of variability of the fund.

risk

The chance or possibility of loss associated with a particular investment.

risk-adjusted performance (return)

A measure of a fund's return performance adjusted for risk taken by the fund.

risk class

A category of securities or fund objectives with equal risk.

risk-free rate

The rate on a short-term, default-free security.

risk preference

The investor's feeling about risk, used to select a fund with a consistent objective.

risk tolerance

The level of comfort an investor has with the price movements of a security. Investors with low risk tolerance should invest in conservative funds, while those with a high risk tolerance can invest in more aggressive funds.

rollover

A term normally associated with IRAs and similar qualified retirement plans, it simply means substituting one legal trustee for another and transferring the assets to the new trustee. The IRS permits you to do this once every 12 months if you take possession of the assets for less than 60 days in the interim.

sales charge

An amount charged to purchase shares in many mutual funds sold by brokers or other members of a sales force. Typically the charge ranges from 4 to 8.5% of the initial investment. The charge is added to the net asset value per share when determining the offering price.

SEC (Securities and Exchange Commission)

An independent agency of the U.S. government that administers the various federal securities laws for the protection of the investor or the shareholder.

sector

A particular group of stocks, usually found in one industry.

sector fund

This type of fund invests only in a specialized industry or group of industries, such as health care or industrial equipment.

security analysis

Determination of the intrinsic value of a common stock or other investment to see if it is overvalued or undervalued relative to its current market price.

SEP

See simplified employee pensions.

series funds

A broad range of funds offered by a fund family. Each fund has its own investment philosophy, whereby it invests in only certain industries or investment types.

share (distribution) option

The fund shareholder elects to have both dividend (income) and capital gains distributions automatically reinvested in additional shares.

short-term bond fund

This type of fund invests in foreign and government securities with maturities usually not exceeding three years.

short-term municipal bond fund

This type of fund invests in municipal bonds with maturities not exceeding three years.

signature guarantee

A required signature by a fiduciary representative (banker or broker) to verify the signature and the identity of the shareholder.

simplified employee pensions (SEPs)

SEPs are employer-sponsored plans that may be viewed as an aggregation of separate IRAs. In an SEP, the employer contribution, limited to $30,000 or 15% of employee compensation, whichever is less, is made to an individual retirement account maintained for the employee.

single premium variable life (SPVL)

Investment Life. Similar to single premium whole life except that the premium is invested not in a separate account similar to a bank CD but in accounts similar to mutual funds. Some policies offer several choices of mutual fund-like investments, as do mutual fund families.

single premium whole life (SPWL)

Income Life. Under current law, the single premium is fully invested in a CD-like investment, the buildup of cash value is tax-free, and death benefits are exempt from federal income taxes. Annuities are an acceptable savings alternative for many investors.

social conscience fund

A fund that invests in the securities of companies that do not conflict with certain social priorities. Some social conscience funds do not invest in tobacco stocks, defense stocks, or South African stocks.

specialized mutual fund

A fund that focuses on a particular segment of the market and has a philosophy or stipulation the fund must follow or meet when investing. Examples are sector funds and gold funds.

speculative

Considered to have a high degree of risk.

speculator

An active securities trader who seeks profits from short-term price movements.

split funding

A program that combines the purchase of mutual fund shares with the purchase of life insurance contracts or other products.

stability

Relative volatility in a declining market. For example, a fund rated above-average for stability is one that declines relatively the least.

Standard & Poor's 500 Composite Index (S&P 500)

A measure of the performance of the overall stock market as represented by an index of 500 stocks.

subindex

The grouping of stocks comprising a part of a composite index. For example, the S&P 40 utilities, S&P 20 transportation companies, and S&P 40 financial institutions are classified as subindexes of the S&P 500 Index.

switch

Transfer of monies between funds in a fund family. *See also* exchange privilege.

systematic withdrawal plan

This type of plan is offered by many mutual fund families. You receive periodic payments drawn from your fund's dividend income and capital gain distributions and from your principal, as you specify.

target fund

A fixed-income fund whose portfolio matures within a given year. Generally structured as a series with each fund maturing in a different year.

taxable-equivalent yield

The yield on a tax-exempt security that is equivalent to the before-tax yield on a taxable security. The calculation for taxable-equivalent yield equals the yield on the tax-exempt security divided by one minus the investor's tax rate.

tax-deferred

Income or capital gains on which a tax is levied only when it is distributed to the taxpayer.

tax-exempt fund (tax-free fund)

A mutual fund whose portfolio consists of securities (usually municipal bonds or money market obligations) exempt from federal income tax.

tax-exempt money fund

A fund that invests in short-term, high-quality municipal securities.

tax-exempt securities

Usually refers to municipal bonds and other obligations that are exempt from federal taxes. Some municipal bonds, known as triple exempt bonds, are also exempt from state and local taxes, depending on the state laws where the bond was issued and where the buyer of the bond resides.

tax shelter

An investment used for deferring, eliminating, or reducing income taxes.

technical analysis

The analysis of past securities price and performance data as a means of predicting future price movements.

telephone switching

Process of selling one mutual fund and buying another at the same time by telephone. Switching is often between stock, bond, or money market funds within the same fund family and is a taxable event.

total return
A performance calculation that includes the fund's percentage change in net asset value plus the value of capital gains and dividends distributed and presumed reinvested over a given time period.

total return fund
A fund whose objective is to obtain the highest possible total return, i.e., a combination of ordinary income and capital gains. Funds usually invest in a combination of dividend-paying stocks and bonds. Similar to a balanced fund.

trade date
This is the actual date on which your shares were purchased or sold. Your transaction price is determined by the closing net asset value on that date.

trailing commissions
A small commission periodically paid to a broker or a financial planner to service an existing shareholder as long as money remains in the fund. A typical trail might be .25% per year. It is often paid out of the 12b-1 fee. Also called a *trail*.

transfer agent
The organization employed by a mutual fund to prepare and maintain records relating to the accounts of its shareholders.

Treasury bill (T-bill)
Short-term debt issued by the U.S. government at a discount from its face value. Maturities are three months, six months, and one year.

Treasury bond
Debt obligation issued by the U.S. government with a maturity ranging from ten to thirty years.

Treasury note
Debt obligation issued by the U.S. government with a maturity between one year and ten years.

triple tax-exempt fund
This type of municipal bond fund pays dividends and interest that are exempt from federal, state, and local income taxes to investors within a particular state.

trust account
A fiduciary account established and owned by the beneficiary's trustee.

trustee
The individual or institution that maintains administrative control over another's assets: a commercial bank, savings and loan association, mutual savings bank, trust company, or stock broker.

turnover ratio
The extent to which a fund's portfolio securities are replaced in a one-year period. A fund with a 100% portfolio turnover, on average, completely changed or sold all the investments in its portfolio in one year's time.

underwriter or principal underwriter

The organization that acts as the distributor of a mutual fund's shares to broker-dealers and the public.

unit investment trust (UIT)

An investment company that buys a fixed number of debt or fixed-income obligations and sells them to investors in units. The portfolio is not actively managed and is liquidated after a specified amount of time.

unmanaged portfolio

A market index portfolio. A portfolio that does not reflect the ability to select undervalued securities through fundamental analysis or forecast turns in the market trends or technical analysis.

valuation of the stock market

The potential of the stock market to rise or fall based on one or more indicators. An undervalued market has considerable potential to rise, whereas an overvalued market has less potential to rise, and has a greater potential to fall.

value companies

A type of company whose earnings (profits) have been depressed for a period of time but are now ready to rebound. They may also include companies in slow-growth industries. Usually, what differentiates value companies from plain old "bad" companies is some type of story of change or turnaround. Many cyclical companies fall into this classification. Because these stocks are already depressed, they tend to be less volatile and have lower valuation measures.

variable annuity

This tax-deferred retirement plan is an insurance product that allows you to specify and direct the investment choices. The annuity's value varies with the value of the underlying portfolio securities, which may include mutual fund shares.

variable life insurance

In contrast to straight life insurance policies, variable life lets you direct some or all of the cash value into the financial markets, most commonly through mutual funds.

volatility

The relative rate at which a fund share tends to move up or down in price relative to the market average or a mutual fund average. For example, a highly volatile fund is one that usually rises or declines far more than the average fund.

wash sale

For tax purposes, a wash sale occurs if securities (or options to buy them) are purchased within 30 days before or after the sale of substantially the same securities. The loss on the sale of the original securities may not be taken for tax purposes in such cases.

whipsawing

Losses that occur when a technical indicator gives a buy or sell signal and the market reverses course, eventually invalidating the original signal.

wire transfer

Use of a bank to send money to a fund or vice versa.

withdrawal plan

A mutual fund plan that allows a specified amount of money to be withdrawn at specified intervals. *See also* systematic withdrawal plan and automatic withdrawal plan.

yield

Income received from investments, usually expressed as a percentage of market price; also referred to as return. Usually computed on the basis of one year's income.

yield curve

The relationship between interest rates (or current yield of the security) to the maturity of a security.

zero-coupon bond

A bond that earns interest but does not pay it until maturity. A zero-coupon bond accumulates and compounds interest at the same rate that prevailed when the bond was bought. These are highly volatile fixed-income securities. A small change in interest rates can cause a dramatic movement in the market value of such a bond.

Index